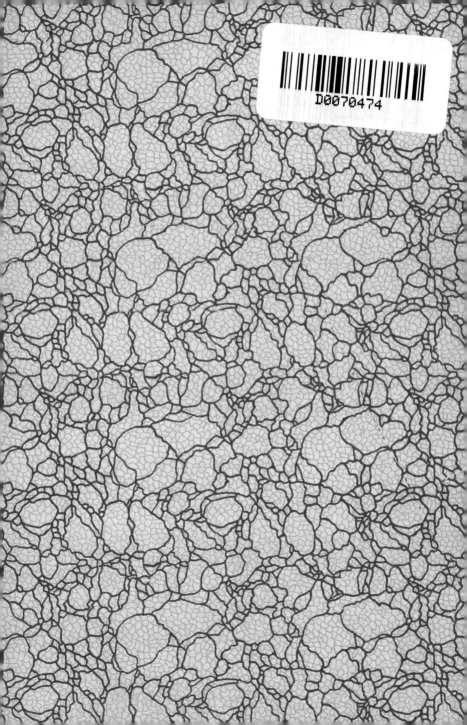

R. E. Golladay

SERMONS ON THE CATECHISM

VOL. I

THE TEN COMMANDMENTS

BY

ROBERT EMORY GOLLADAY, A. M.
Pastor of Grace Lutheran Church, Columbus, Ohio
Author of Lenten Outlines and Sermons

Published for the Au

THIRD THOUSAND

LUTHERAN BOOK CONCERN
1915

To the United American Lutheran Church of the Future; one in its Faith, one in the Confession of its Faith, one in its Evangelical Polity, this volume is Dedicated in Hope

INTRODUCTION

IT was twenty-five years ago or thereabouts, that the undersigned, now a parishioner of the author of this volume, first met him. Never will he forget the event, although, at that time, it appeared to him without significance. A farmer boy, stalking sturdily behind a plow — that was the first glimpse the writer of these lines received of the man now seen and heard by hundreds in a splendidly appointed city church, largely the result of the much loved pastor's labors.

On the occasion of the first meeting, I did not dream that the plowboy, already verging upon manhood, would rise to prominence in an intellectual sphere. His sphere, the cultivation of the soil in the highlands of the Valley of the Shenandoah, seemed fixed. But there was an intellectual strain in the lad that destined him to climb the highlands of thought. In that day there were not many books in the home of Robert Golladay, but such as there were had the quality of excellence. A few volumes of history and biography, the Bible, the Catechism, the Book of Concord, and an occasional magazine — but the very scantiness of the intellectual fare taught the lad concentration and the desire for more.

Not far from his home, upon a foothill of the Massanutten, stands a gray church where young Golladay heard the call for recruits for Christ's army. The two influences mentioned, intellectual and religious, revealed to the taciturn country boy his destiny and duty: to be a Gospel minister.

At that time, the Joint Synod of Ohio opened an Academy and Practical Seminary at Hickory, North Carolina, where this youth was enrolled as one of the first students. While that modest school never set itself the task of educating a learned ministry, it laid a foundation in a few aspiring minds upon which they succeeded in building a superstructure of pronounced success. Our friend and brother Golladay illustrates what opportunities our country contains for the man of grit and determination whose early conditions do not enable him to profit by the established educational order. In Germany, there is no access to the university as an accredited student save through a full college diploma; no access to the professions save through a diploma from the university. As Americans we rejoice in the fact that, with us, university opportunities are broader than university halls. Surrounding himself with books such as were calculated to amplify his limited early training — books on literature, language, history, philosophy, and theology; taking courses in these branches, as time and opportunity permitted, at Johns Hopkins and Ohio State Universities, the author of this book succeeded in securing an education not commonly found without the badge of thorough collegiate training. We mention this not to compliment the author, but to spur to action every youth in the church who feels within himself the power to rise. America and the American Lutheran Church hold opportunities for lofty service and success wherever ambition is accompanied by consecration.

Concerning the timeliness of this book little need be said. It is an exposition of the Law — God's Law. The message of the Law is needed in our congregations to-day as much as ever. Even where church attendance is gratifying, spiritual life is often on a rather low spiritual and moral plane. The preacher of these sermons strikes straight from the shoulder. Like Paul at Miletus, he can say: "I shrank not from declaring unto you the whole counsel of God." The range of topics treated in these sermons is virtually extensive with the spiritual needs and duties of our people. Subjects, the vigorous handling of which from the pulpit is likely to result in resentment upon the part of some of the hearers, are boldly dealt with from the standpoint of one who is accustomed to declaring: "Thus saith the Lord."

May the desire for the Word of the Lord which prompted Grace congregation, of Columbus, to hear these sermons in numbers of which even the heat of summer showed scarcely any diminution, characterize their reception everywhere, as, in their printed form, they are sent into homes and hearts; and may, also in this case, the Word of God accomplish that whereunto it has been sent.

C. B. GOHDES.

Capital University, September 22, 1915.

PREFACE

THE preparation of this volume, as well as the giving of it to a wider circle than that of my own congregation, came about by a process of natural development. About a year ago a large adult Bible class in our Sunday school expressed the desire that the fundamental subjects treated in our Catechism be again explained from the pulpit. This request was approved by the vestry and congregation, with the proviso that it should be at the chief or morning service. This accounts for the preparation of the volume now given the public.

Few of the sermons herein contained had been delivered when a goodly number of the members of the congregation asked whether they could not be supplied with copies of them. As no feasible plan for granting this request presented itself at the time, the idea was conceived of publication.

The attendance at our morning service is always good, and the attention usually all that could be desired. Never before, however, did it attain quite the standard reached during the delivery of these sermons. This helped to give some confidence that they might be helpful to others. In addition, it was the confirmation of a conviction long entertained that the average congregation, at least the average Lutheran congregation, wants something substantial in the sermons to which it listens; something which appeals to the mind and the heart and impels to action.

If the reading of these sermons gives to others a tithe of the pleasure and profit the author found in their preparation he will feel amply repaid. May they contribute, at least in some measure, to the upbuilding of God's Kingdom, and the glory of His precious name.

The author has given this book a general dedication, one which expresses one of the most sincere desires of his heart. In addition he wishes to dedicate this volume, in a special sense, to the members of Grace congregation, Columbus; a congregation that has faithfully received the preached Word, and responded to the appeal for every good work.

He wishes also in this public way to acknowledge the brotherly interest, and the many helpful suggestions of his esteemed parishioner and friend, Prof. C. B. Gohdes; also the assistance of another friend and ministerial associate, Rev. H. J. Melcher, who kindly assisted in the work of proof correction.

Columbus, Ohio, October 1, 1915.

TABLE OF CONTENTS

CONCLUSION

OUR LUTHERAN CATECHISM

"Sanctify the Lord God in your hearts; and be ready always to give an answer to every man that asketh you a reason of the hope that is in you with meekness and fear." — 1 PET. 3, 15.

BEGINNING to-day a new Church Year, we take up for consideration our Lutheran Catechism. This is not something new in the Church. It is often done in the German Fatherland, where there are provinces that require, by churchly statute, a periodic series of sermons on the Catechism; at least this was formerly the case. In our Church of this country the several chief parts of the Catechism are often given systematic treatment from the pulpit. In both lands, however, this is usually done at a secondary, or evening, service. Surely, this handbook of our Christian faith deserves treatment at a time when the largest possible number of our people will be benefited thereby.

Preaching on the Catechism! Some people, not familiar with the facts in the case, may exclaim, as we have heard them exclaim: "See how those Lutherans exalt a man made book! They leave the Bible and preach on a Catechism." And not a few Lutherans, who have not yet learned to appreciate their great heritage, are much impressed by such criticism. Those who know Luther's Catechism never speak thus, for when we go to this book we are not leaving the Bible. On the contrary, in this way we are learning to know, in the best possible way, the Bible itself.

If I were to take a leaf from this Bible and give it to you to read, would it be any the less God's Word than if it were still bound together with the other leaves in God's Book? Luther's Catechism is more than a leaf taken from the Bible. It is a selection and an arrangement of the leading truths of God's Holy Word, presenting, in a way easily understood, the fundamental truths of the Way of Salvation. All that is human about this book is the arrangement and a brief explanation, itself often given in the language of the Bible. Luther himself declared the Catechism to be simply a compend of the Holy Scriptures.

We need not expect that, because we have, in a way, known the Catechism since childhood, a series of sermons on it must necessarily deal only with commonplace truths, easily uttered, and easily understood. There are truths in the Catechism which the angels have not yet exhausted. This means that the one who undertakes to expound these truths has on his hands a large task. Preaching God's Word is always delightful, as well as blessed work. But preaching sermons worth hearing, on any subject, especially two or three a week, is not an easy task for even the most fertile and experienced man. To make this series profitable to myself and to you, will take work; and the worker will need God's blessing. To this end I implore your prayers.

Some of you, who have a special liking for those portions of Scripture which give history and biography and are thus full of action, may incline to tire of the discourses that deal largely with the mere statement of truths. But I ask you to remember that the purpose of all truth is that it be wrought into our lives and then reproduced in our living. Thus shall we be qualified to help God make the right kind of history. This thought ought to sustain us in the consideration of the most serious truths, even though our natural inclination would lead us into other, and less difficult, fields.

Only by prayer and fellowship with God can sermons be properly prepared; and only thus can they be profitably heard or read. May none of us ever be found lacking in this kind of preparation, and none of us shall ever be found without a blessing from Him from whom all blessings flow.

To-day we ask your further attention while we present some introductory thoughts on:

Our Lutheran Catechism

We will speak of ITS ORIGIN, ITS PURPOSE, and ITS CHARACTER.

I. The Origin of our Lutheran Catechism is a subject which ought to be interesting to every lover of history, and of absorbing interest to every one who bears the Lutheran name.

As its name indicates, the little text-book that we use as the medium for instructing all those who wish to become communicant members of our Church and with which every such member ought to be familiar, was prepared by Dr. Martin Luther. This was the first as it is, admittedly, the greatest modern book of its kind. But Luther did not originate the idea of instructing young and old in Bible truth. That came from God and is as old as the Bible itself. Early in Israel's history, God said to those people, with respect to the very commandments which form the first part of our Catechism: "These words, which I command thee this day, shall be in thine heart. And thou shalt teach them diligently unto thy children, and shalt talk of them when thou sittest in thine house, and when thou walkest by the way" (Deut. 6, 6, 7). In the New Testament, parents are charged to bring up their children in the nurture and admonition of the Lord (Eph. 6, 4). And older people are admonished, not only to continue in the things which they have learned in earlier life (2 Tim. 3, 14), but to grow in their knowledge of God and Divine things, and develop in the Christian life (Eph. 4, 13ff.).

We will now recount the circumstances which led Luther to prepare the Catechism. In 1527, ten years after the beginning of the Reformation, he began a visitation of the churches in Saxony. Luther, with several assistants, visited one part of the country; Melanchthon, with similar associates, the other part. They spent two years in this work. Wherever they went they examined the people with respect to their knowledge of God's Word. Not the children only; but the older people as well, even grayhaired fathers and mothers, pastors as well as laymen, were thus examined. The condition revealed by this visitation was appalling. Out of multitudes of people, even of those known as educated, only one or two would be found who knew so much as the Commandments, the Apostles' Creed, or the Lord's Prayer, the pastors often knowing but little more than the people. On his return, after this experience, Luther prepared his Catechism, using materials he had previously collected. Indeed, there are two Catechisms. Of the Larger Catechism, prepared especially for pastors and teachers, most of our people, unfortunately, know but little. It consists of a series of addresses on the various parts of Christian doctrine. The Smaller Catechism, the Enchiridion, as it is called, was intended especially for the home, to be used by parents for their own profit and as a text-book for the instruction of their children. The explanations of the five chief parts, forming the second part of the Catechism commonly in use, do not form the Larger Catechism and was not prepared by Luther; this was a later addition. It is the Smaller Catechism, the Catechism of the people, which we Lutherans have generally in mind when we speak of our Catechism.

Let us not think that we are alone or peculiar in having and appreciating a confessional Catechism. All the great historic Churches have them. And some of the denominations that formerly said some very uncomplimentary things about our adherence to our Catechism and our thorough instruction in its truths, have themselves prepared such handbooks. The Methodist Church is one of the most recent to prepare a Catechism. In form it is modeled closely after ours. And in many other quarters, where, judging from history, we should have least reason to expect it, men are lifting up their voices and loudly proclaiming that, if the Church is to retain her hold on the people and prosper, she must return to the practice of more thorough instruction of young and old in the fundamental truths of God's Word.

II. The Purpose our Catechism is to serve is another point well worth our earnest consideration.

We have seen the condition which prevailed before Luther wrote his Catechisms. It was to help correct this condition that they were written. They were to help the people to realize in their lives the teaching of our text. They called themselves Christians, but they scarcely knew what it meant to be a Christian. They had no assured foundation on which to rest their hopes. They did not know what God had done for them, they did not know what God required of them. They were Christians in little more than name. If they had a vague hope that, in some way, God would take care of them, they certainly were not able to give a reason for their hope. Being so sadly deficient in their knowledge of God, and lacking all enlightened affection for Him, their lives were coarse and their actions often reprehensible. Assuredly God was not sanctified in their hearts. To give these people what they so greatly needed, Luther wrote for them this little Catechism. His object was to reveal God to them in all the majesty of His sovereign power and holiness, and in the wealth of His condescending love, and, at the same time, to put in their hands a glass wherein they could see themselves as they really were — poor lost sinners, who could be saved alone by faith in Christ. In this way they could find God's Word a firm foundation on which to rest their soul's salvation. At the same time there would be opened to them a never failing fountain for their cleansing, and a constant source of strength for the beautifying of their lives.

We are living in better times than those immediately following the Reformation. Our people are much better educated in every way. They know a great deal more about God's precious Word. And yet there is room for the old Catechism in our day; indeed, great need of it. There are still too many who are not able to give a good reason for the hopes which, in a way, they entertain. There is too much eagerness on the part of both parents and young people, to get through with the little book as soon as possible; all too quickly it is laid aside and, only too often, forgotten. There is everywhere among Christians too much eagerness for the glittering, but ofttimes shallow, generalities of religion, but not enough love for the enduring, fundamental truths by which men live.

It is unquestionably true that the character of our whole Christian life depends on the thoroughness with which these simple fundamental truths are wrought into our soul-life. The architect, noted for the symmetry of his designs and the classic beauty of his work, is much concerned about the hidden foundation on which the edifice he plans is to be erected. The splendid spires, the massive columns, the entablatures, the gracefully vaulted ceiling, the overspreading roof, all these depend for their serviceability and lasting beauty on the substantial character of the foundation on which they stand. The temple of Christian character also has a foundation. It is God's pure, powerful Word; of this the Catechism is a simple presentation.

There is another reason why we, in our day, need especially to emphasize the teaching of the Catechism. We have been passing through one of the periodic seasons of outcry against doctrine. The battle-cry of those thus minded has been, Give us more religion, more Christianity, and less doctrine. There is some evidence that this wave of suicidal madness is subsiding, though it is by no means past and will not entirely pass. The Universalists, judging from their theological position and history, would be about the last to speak for more doctrine. But a recent issue of one of their leading religious papers had this to say on the subject: "There is a wide-spread disposition to minimize the value of theology. And the statement that the world needs religion more than it does theology is exceedingly popular. And yet a religion without a theology is just as efficient as a boneless man. Much of the religion of the day is flabby because it is hung on a flabby theology." To all of which we say a hearty — amen. Only, the theology must be that of God's Word, and not the product of human reason.

The Lutheran Church has always stood for doctrine, the whole doctrine of God's Holy Word — the doctrine which is fraught with the life of God, to be wrought into the life of man. Luther's little Catechism is the heart of this Word. And he who knows it, has at his command the best simple, but fundamental, system of theology in existence; and he will never be at a loss when asked to give a reason for the hope he entertains.

For still another reason, there has never been a time when Christian people were more in need of being well grounded in the fundamental truths of God's Word, as set forth in the Catechism. This is an age of extensive, but ofttimes superficial and unbiblical thinking and writing on religious subjects. Many of the novelists and playwrights of the day feel called on to deal with religious and moral questions. Their object is plain. By dealing with these fundamental problems of human life, they multiply manifold their chances of gain. Most of these people, however, are not properly qualified to treat these subjects; many of them, by training and life, are absolutely disqualified for the task. As a result of the way in which these subjects are often treated, many of our people are much at sea in their religious and moral thinking. We need, on this account, to have a few simple, fixed principles as standards by which to judge of these things. We must have in our souls a few things, at least, of which we can say: These are fundamental truths; that which does not agree with these principles is false. And if we know the truths of God's Word, as set forth in the Catechism, we shall have just such a standard; and to abide by its verdict will save us much perplexity and many heartaches.

Let us not forget the special purpose Luther had in view in writing the Catechism. He intended it to be used in the school and the Church. But, above all, he meant it to be a home book. At the head of each one of the five chief parts of the Catechism stand these words: "As the head of the family should teach it in all simplicity to his household." Fathers and mothers! how have you lived up to this suggestion of the great Reformer? — a suggestion backed up in a thousand-fold manner by all the teaching of God's Holy Word. School books, many of them permeated with the poison of misbelief and unbelief; novels, many of them so flagrantly misrepresenting life that they are the worst kind of breeders of discontent, many others so full of lecherous suggestions that the souls which absorb them are likely never again to become free from their filth — these books cover many parlor and study tables, finding their way there in spite of watchfulness, because their poison is often adroitly disguised, and the grinning skeleton hidden behind the captivating beauty of classical language: but the poison is there, and our young people imbibe it. But where is the family Bible? Where is the well-thumbed Catechism? Where is the evening devotion? Where is the drill in the fundamental simplicities of our precious faith? Oh, parents! remember that if you have not done your duty in this respect also, one of your highest and holiest duties, then only a miracle of grace can keep you from reaping in bitter tears what you have sown in carelessness.

III. Let us now give a few thoughts to the Character of Luther's Catechism, and the esteem in which it is held.

Whether this little book may properly be called a system of theology is a question much discussed.

Whatever one's view may be on this point, there is unquestionably an orderly historic development in the truths it presents. This is what Luther himself says about it:

"First, the Ten Commandments of God, the doctrine of doctrines by which the will of God is known, what God would have us do, what is wanting in us.

"Secondly, the Apostles' Creed, the history of histories, or the highest history, wherein are delivered to us the wonderful works of God from the beginning, how we and all creatures are created by God, how all are redeemed by the Son of God, how we are also received and sanctified by the Holy Ghost and collected together to be a people of God, and have the remission of sins and everlasting salvation.

"Thirdly, the Lord's Prayer, the prayer of prayers, the highest prayer which the highest Master taught, wherein are included all temporal and spiritual blessings and the strongest comforts in all temptations and troubles, and in the hour of death.

"Fourthly, the blessed Sacraments, the ceremonies of ceremonies, which God Himself has instituted and ordained, and therein assured us of His grace."

How small a book is this Enchiridion! Only a few pages; and the words of explanation, how simple! We probably felt that we knew it all before we were a dozen years old. And, no doubt, one reason why so many lay aside their Catechism at the time when they lay aside their school books, if not before, is the impression, so widely prevalent, that it is only a child's book. It is a child's book, indeed, the best of its kind in existence. But it is also a man's book, a woman's book, as well. Have we exhausted the idea of God? of the moral law? of the redemption in Christ? of the establishment, development, and influence of the Kingdom of God? of the privilege and blessing of prayer? of the nature and efficacy of the Sacraments? Till we can answer these and kindred questions in the affirmative, let us not feel ourselves above the use of this little book. Doubtless, if we knew more about what many of the brightest minds, not only in the Lutheran Church, but in all the leading historic Protestant Churches, have said of the Catechism, we would appreciate it more ourselves. Historians and teachers have joined with theologians in singing its praise, and in telling of its influence.

We think the Catechism so simple, and, as to its words and arrangement, it is so; but a noted theologian, Doctor Lyserius by name, declared that if pastors spent their whole lives in explaining the hidden wisdom of God contained in these simple words, they would not exhaust it. Doctor Jonas said: "The Catechism may be bought for six-pence, but six thousand worlds could not pay for it." The celebrated Loehe pronounced it the only Catechism which could be prayed — splendid praise, indeed. Prof. Bugenhagen, a profound theologian, always carried a copy of the Catechism with him, and chided his students when they failed to give it the study he felt it deserved.

Leopold von Ranke, the noted German historian, thus characterizes this little manual: "It is as childlike as it is profound, as comprehensible as it is unfathomable, simple and sublime. Happy he whose soul was fed by it, who clings to it. He possesses an imperishable comfort in every moment, and, under a thin shell, a kernel of truth sufficient for the wisdom of the wise."

Doctor Martin Luther gathered the precious truths contained in the Catechism from the Bible, with which he was so familiar, and gave them this arrangement. If ever a man knew its content he assuredly was the one. Here is what he says of it: "There is this shameful vice and secret infection of security and satiety; namely, that many regard the Catechism as a plain, unimportant statement of doctrine which they can read over once, and then throw into a corner, and be ashamed to read it again. But this I say for myself: I also am a doctor and a preacher, yea, as learned and experienced as all who have such presumption and security. Yet I do as a child who is being taught the Catechism. Every morning, and whenever I have time, I read and say, word for word, the Ten Commandments, the Creed, the Lord's Prayer, the Psalms, and the like. And I must still read and study daily, and yet I cannot master it as I wish, but must remain, and that right gladly, a child and pupil of the Catechism."

We cannot neglect the Catechism without revealing one of two things: ignorance of its value, or indifference to its saving truths. I appeal to you, young people, who wish to grow up respected and useful men and women, walking in the path of truth and righteousness; I appeal to you, fathers and mothers, who have an interest in your own souls, and love your children and desire their highest good; I appeal to you, all of you, who love the Church of God, its work of missions, who pray, "Thy Kingdom come"; I appeal to you, pastors, shepherds of the flock purchased with the blood of God's own Son, you who are to lead this flock into the green pastures and by the still waters, — let all of us give more attention to the old simple truths of the Catechism: here the enduring foundation of Christian life is laid, here the mainspring of right action is put into human souls.

If we Lutherans are wise, if we exert our energy in building, if we profit by our mistakes of the past, if we go in and take possession of what is rightfully ours, our dear old Church is destined at no distant day to be the first Protestant Church of our land. We should not only desire this but pray for it and work for it; not because of the prestige it will give us, but because of the opportunity of doing good it will afford us. If we are true to ourselves, true to our heritage, true to our standards and the God who gave them, we shall have much to do with moulding the moral and spiritual forces of our great land, and thus in deciding its destiny. The way we honor and use these fundamental Catechism truths will decide whether this influence will be for lasting good.

"O God, may we e'er pure retain
The Catechismal doctrine plain,
As Luther taught the heavenly truth
In simple style to tender youth."

OUR CHRISTIAN FOUNDATION

Christ's Answer to Man's Question

"What is truth?"— ST. JOHN 18, 38.
"Sanctify them through Thy truth;
Thy word is truth." — ST. JOHN 17, 17.

THE first question of the second, or explanatory, part of our Catechism is: "What is your faith?" To this question the answer is given: "I am a Christian." Yes, we call ourselves Christians. And blessed are we if our claim is true. All the gold and gems in the universe would not pay for the treasures that we now have, and the others to which we have become heirs, if we are truly Christians — God's dear children.

To be a Christian, however, means something very definite. To be a Christian signifies much more than to be religious. The Confucian and the Buddhist, worshippers of heathen gods, are religious; but they are not Christians. He alone is a Christian who believes in the triune God and is baptized into this name. More particularly still, he alone is a Christian who believes in Jesus Christ and trusts for his salvation only in His gracious work of redemption.

But, pray you, where do we learn of all these things? Is there any authoritative record from which these truths may be learned? It is written with authority: "The heavens declared the glory of God, and the firmament sheweth His handiwork"

(Ps. 19, 1). The heavens, the earth and all things therein, are written all over with messages traced by the finger of God, all telling of His wisdom, power and goodness.

If our vision were keen enough, if our understanding were complete enough, we could perchance read the whole story of God's power and goodness in and through the things He has made. But our vision has been shortened and darkened and our power of understanding very much curtailed, even perverted. We see the evidences of this in the vulgar, foolish notions concerning God and His works generally held by those who have no guide but nature for their teacher. These mistakes are not in nature, but in man's misinterpretation of nature.

The world to-day can know God aright only through the revelation which He has given of Himself in His Word, the Bible. "How shall they believe in Him of whom they have not heard" (Rom. 10, 14). To be a Christian in truth, one must believe what is said in the Scriptures concerning the triune God, concerning Jesus Christ and His work of redemption. "Search the Scriptures; for in them ye think ye have eternal life; and they are they which testify of me" (John 5, 39). Here we have the only authoritative, infallible record of these and other Divine things.

Christianity is the religion resulting from the knowledge and acceptance of God's Word, or Revelation, as over against the religion resulting from the study of nature. Protestantism is that form of Christianity which stands for an open Bible and its authority, in distinction from churchly tradition. Lutheranism is that form of Protestantism which stands for the absolute authority of God's written Word in opposition to those who would weaken it by virtually giving reason authority over it.

Are we Christians? Protestant Christians? Lutheran Christians? Then we have a clearly defined, an absolutely safe, indestructible foundation on which to stand. It is the impregnable Rock of Ages, the Bible, God's revealed Word.

This question of the Church's attitude toward the Word of God is one of the greatest importance. It is one on which all our future discussions rest. It should, therefore, receive the most careful, prayerful consideration. Indeed, it demands this. Let us, accordingly, consider:

Our Christian Foundation; Christ's Answer to Man's Question — What is Truth?

I. The question is: "What is Truth?" This was the question of a particular man; but, in a sense, it is the question of humanity.

Many of you recognize this question as the one put to Christ by Pilate, the same man who is held up to the scorn of the Christian world every time the Apostles' Creed is repeated.

Let us recall the circumstances. It was at the time of Christ's trial. He was standing before the Roman governor, to be tried for His life. He stood there a captive already condemned to death by the Jewish Church. Jesus had no human title to any earthly possessions, no, not even to so much as a humble place where to lay His oft weary head. Nevertheless, undaunted and with unshaken confidence in the outcome of His finished work, Jesus still spoke of a Kingdom that was His. Pilate was quick to note this and turned to Him sharply with the question: "Art thou a king then?" And Jesus made reply: "To this end was I born, and for this cause came I into the world, that I should bear witness unto the truth."

A King of Truth! A Kingdom of the truth! Here is a vision presented which has not yet been universally realized on the earth. Albeit, there is a King of Truth who rules also on earth and a Kingdom here, the ruling principles of which are truth. This King is Jesus Christ. This Kingdom is His Church, bought with His blood, created by His Spirit, ruled by His Word.

"To this end was I born, and for this cause came I into the world, that I should bear witness unto the truth" (St. John 18, 37). What a sublime ideal! The noblest souls of all the ages have been enamored of truth, they have been truth seekers. But Christ's declaration made little impression on Pilate. He felt and declared, at no little trouble and danger to himself, that Jesus was a harmless person not deserving punishment. He doubtless regarded Jesus as a harmless enthusiast, a dreamer of impossible dreams, a mild fanatic. So all the reply Pilate made to Jesus' statement, and that probably with a sneer and a contemptuous toss of the head, was: "What is truth?"

Alas! the question which probably meant so little to Pilate, means equally little to multitudes to-day. Especially is this true where the question is presented in its religious significance. Instead of asking with all earnestness, What is truth? men are asking, What is expedient? They are seeking for short cuts to some selfish goal, even though in seeking it every principle of truth and honor has to be sacrificed.

Men have become proud of their intellectual achievements. Human learning vaunts itself. The slogan is: "Let us investigate and accept only the truths so revealed." As a result we have confusion everywhere. Very many of the learned of all ranks and degrees, while professedly devoted to truth, have forsaken the greatest standard and anchor of truth — God's Word. As a result, there is no certainty at any point. And many, like Pilate, are asking in mockery: "What is truth?"

Would to God there were more honest, serious asking of the question — "What is truth?" Comparatively few there are who are gripped by the thought of the beauty and importance of truth. There is so much shallow thinking and so much lack of thinking on this subject. And nowhere is this more in evidence than in the field of religion. How frequently the expression is heard: "Oh, it does not matter what a man believes, just so he lives right." This is as much as to say that there is no truth to be believed or that it is a matter of little importance whether one knows it or not. If there is no such truth, then there is no standard of right conduct.

In the everyday world of human effort it is insisted that men must know how to do things, and do them according to established principles. Suppose a manufacturer wanted an engineer and so advertised. If a man applied, who, in answer to questions, had to admit that he knew nothing about an engine, that he had never, in all his life, tried to run one; but declared that he was an honest man and his intentions were good, do you think he would get the job? Would you take a pair of old shoes to a man to be mended if he did not know his business? But in the greatest business in the world, in the business of saving one's soul, in the business of correct living so as to attain a desired goal, this false motto, that it does not matter what one believes is accepted, whereby the principle is set up that man needs no instruction, no guidance; but should be allowed to stumble blindly along. According to the words of Christ, we shall be judged not only as to what we have done or left undone; but as to our motives, why we have done things or left them undone. The rule of judgment of human life and conduct is the truth — God's Word. "The Word that I have spoken, the same shall judge him in that day" (St. John 12, 48).

When a wise man becomes sick he does not call in a quack doctor. He wants a man who knows his business; a man who knows how to diagnose his case and what remedies will operate against given ailments. That all the world is morally and spiritually ill, few men deny. But some say, and many more seem to act on the principle, that it is a matter of indifference as to what is to be done about it; that there is no remedy for the ailment, and that, if there should happen to be one, it makes but little difference whether we take it or not.

Brethren, let us not be so foolish! Let us not act like the ostrich, which, when it scents coming danger, is reported to do no more than stick its head in the sand, seemingly thinking that it has thereby escaped the danger. There are ills all around us, in all of us. They do not grow better of themselves. Their tendency is constantly to grow worse. They thrive by feeding on themselves. And their end, if not cured, is destruction, present and eternal. Can they be cured? Is there a remedy for them? Yes, there is a remedy, an unfailing remedy. It is the truth: God's truth!

Truth! Precious gift of God to man! The ointment for blinded eyes! The one remedy for human ills! The one agency for the redemption of a lost world!

Truth! How men should love it. From our mother's knee we ought to be taught to prize truth above all other possessions. Men have given their lives for the truth, and all ought to be willing to do so. Only by so surrendering our life do we find it and realize its true end. By error, by falsehood, we lose our way and perish. Only by the truth do we live and thrive. Like the infant child let us feed at the breasts of truth. As strong men and women let us love it and fight for it. And as the radiant star led the wise men from the East to the object of their search and gave them the joy of finding their hearts' desire, so shall truth lead us safely through the mists and bogs of a sin-accursed earth into the joy and peace and blessedness of the perfect life.

II. "Father, * * * thy Word is truth." This is the answer Christ gives to the great question: "What is truth?"

In the foregoing general discussion of the question, "what is truth?" my aim has been to awaken at least an intellectual interest in truth; to show the need of truth in every sphere of human activity and especially in the sphere of religion. Incidentally I have also indicated the source of all spiritually enlightening, soul-saving truth; namely, the Word of God. This is the point which we shall now seek to give special emphasis, and, at the same time, point out the confessional position of our Lutheran Church toward the Word of God.

When Pilate so lightly asked one of the greatest questions ever formulated by man or angel, Jesus did not answer it. For Him to have done so, would have been like casting pearls before swine. The words that I have used as Christ's answer to Pilate's question were not spoken as such. These words, "Father, * * * Thy Word is truth," are a part of Christ's highpriestly prayer, the prayer offered on the way to Gethsemane on the night of His betrayal. They were accordingly spoken on the evening of the day preceding that on which Pilate asked his question. While, therefore, not a direct answer to Pilate's question; it is the best answer to that question ever given. God's Word is the truth — the only truth we have to show us the way to heaven and give us the strength to follow it.

In speaking thus far of truth, I have not attempted to define it. Though we should constantly seek to get a clearer vision and a firmer grasp of truth, it would probably be just as well if no one attempted to give a comprehensive definition of it. Truth is infinite; finite mind cannot compass it, consequently never fully define it. The philosophers of the various schools have dealt much with the problem of truth; but, as was to have been expected, they have not found in human philosophy a basis of agreement; nor will they ever succeed.

No human mind can range through the whole domain of truth. It is as immeasurable as God, its author — the One in whom all truth centers. Truth is one of the essential attributes of God Himself. Truth is, so to speak, the very substance of Deity. It is the foundation of the perfections of the Godhead. Without truth, God cannot be conceived as existing. If it were not that God is what He says He is, that what He says is strictly in conformity with facts, that He will fulfill all His promises, we should be wholly at sea in our views and thoughts about Him. These fundamental principles give us certitude in those limited spheres where we are capable of examining God's nature and works. As there is no God but the true God, so, without truth, there could be no God.

In the physical universe the so-called laws of nature are but a form of God's truth. Their unchangeableness is but the immutability of truth. Upon these laws, as upon the promises of God, men rely; by them, they regulate much of their conduct. If these laws were capricious, if the same results did not always follow the same causes, all life would be in jeopardy. But these are truly laws of God. He has implanted them in His creatures; He has written them with His own finger on all His work; and He alone can suspend or change them.

The connecting link between the truth directly and specifically Divine and the truth which is of man and the universe is Jesus Christ. He is the embodiment of all truth. In Him and through Him, man receives a new birth into the truth. Truth, then, in its deepest meaning, is not a mere abstraction, but a living, moral, spiritual substance and power. It is something that a man may not only study and measure; it is something that he can appropriate and, more and more, become. Truth is something which transforms the man who comes into harmony with it and sets him free. The truth as such, the objective truth, becomes a living element that moulds its lover into its own likeness.

Where shall we find this truth? Truth, some measure of it, may be found in many directions and by divers methods; but the truth which makes men children of God and keeps them as such, is found in only one place — the Bible, the Word of God. This is what Jesus tells us in our text. "Father, * * * thy Word is truth." By this Word Jesus unquestionably means not only the words He Himself had spoken, the burden of the Gospel record; but what God had revealed to mankind through the prophets, and what was yet to be revealed through the inspired apostles.

We now stand face to face with the point which, above all others, it is our aim at this time to emphasize; the position of our Church with respect to the Word of God. In its entirety we accept it as God's Word, revealed by Him through inspired men. We are not unacquainted with what, in all ages, men have said against this position. They have made the law of evolution to embrace even the Bible. To them the Bible is only a book full of man's thoughts about God and Divine things, a record of human discoveries along the line of religious things, religious experiences. To us the Bible is what it claims to be and what the best experience of all the ages has proven it to be — the revelation of the mind of God, of so much of the mind of God as man is capable of receiving and needs for his guidance here below to the blessedness of the life that is to be. "All Scripture is given by inspiration of God, and is profitable for doctrine, for reproof, for correction, for instruction in righteousness; that the man of God may be perfect, thoroughly furnished unto all good works" (2 Timothy 3, 16, 17).

True, men wrote the Bible; but they wrote God's thoughts. "We know the things that are freely given to us of God. Which things also we speak, not in the words which man's wisdom teacheth, but which the Holy Ghost teacheth" (1 Cor. 2, 12, 13). I do not concern myself about whether these amanuenses of God always understood in its completeness the truths they proclaimed. But this we are obliged to hold and this the Lutheran Church maintains against all gainsayers, these men wrote God's truth as He revealed it to them. "Holy men of God spoke as they were moved by the Holy Ghost" (2 Peter 1, 21). We are bound by everything written in this Word of God. We refuse to be bound by anything not written in this Word or clearly involved in its teaching. This is the confessional basis of our Lutheran Church. And there is not a recognized theologian or minister of our church in America but stands firmly on this foundation.

We are chided as narrow and lacking in scholarship because of our stand, but we are unmoved by it. Those who are so disposed to criticize us are privileged to make their own Bible, to eliminate or incorporate as they see fit. We choose to walk in the old paths. We know that for thousands of years the wits of the world have unlimbered their batteries and fired their salvos, volley after volley, at God's Word. "Nevertheless the foundation of God standeth sure." Without any spirit of boasting or taking any credit for superior penetration, we feel that we can apply to ourselves, with respect to spiritual truth, the words of the Psalmist: "I have more understanding than all my teachers: for thy testimonies are my meditation" (Psalm 119, 99). And we may recall, for the encouragement of those who are inclined to tremble at the formidable array of intellectual lights opposed to the doctrine of plenary inspiration, that multitudes of men in every walk and calling of life, men the unquestioned equals in native ability and learning of any of the opponents of a fully inspired Bible, have maintained the inspired character and absolute trustworthiness of the Scriptures as God's revealed Word.

On this Word of God we build. The truth of this Word is the content of our faith. The heart of this book is the heart of our doctrinal system: Jesus Christ the God-man, the Redeemer of the world, through faith in whose name we are forgiven, justified, sanctified and saved. By this Word of God our lives must be controlled. Far from us be the thought that this precious Word was given us only as a pabulum for hungry intellects or as material with which to perform mental gymnastics. The truths of the Bible come out of the life of God, to be wrought into the life of man. And the human life which actually recognizes and accepts the truth of God thereby surrenders itself to God to be wrought anew into His image. Divine truth, in its last analysis, is but the revelation of Jesus Christ. He is the incarnation of truth, of God. He came that men might have life. And it is impossible for Jesus Christ, who is the truth and the life, even to begin to live in a human life and leave that life as it was before. In the verse, part of which forms our text, Jesus says: "Sanctify them through thy truth; thy Word is truth." The Word of God is a power: a power for enlightening the understanding, for bringing us into new relations, for transforming our affections, for directing our activities into new channels; the result of which is to make us Christ-like and fit us for heaven. The process may be slow, the results unsatisfactory to ourselves; but the process must be there, and some of the results must show themselves.

And now what does all this imply as to our relation to this Word of God? What are we to do with our Bibles? That this Word occupy the central position in our doctrinal system is necessary, that we make much of it in our Confessions is proper, that this Book of books be in evidence on our study tables is becoming. But is this all? No, this is not enough. We must use the Bible. It should be our book of daily counsel. It is not only to be talked about, it is to be the daily food and drink of our souls. The Psalmist's words concerning the judgment of God ought to be true of each of us with respect to all of God's words. "More to be desired are they than gold, yea, than much fine gold: sweeter also than honey and the honeycomb" (19, 10). When this Word has passed into the sphere of human experience, when through the medium of this Word God actually speaks to us, and Jesus Christ comes to live with us and in us, then it is our source of strength in every godly work, our unfailing comfort in every trouble, our assured hope in death.

"Then said Jesus to those disciples which believed on Him, * * * if ye continue in my Word, then are ye my disciples indeed, and ye shall know the truth, and the truth shall make you free" (St. John 8, 31, 32).

GOD THE LAWGIVER

"I am the Lord thy God." — EXODUS 20, 2.

OUR Catechism is appropriately called the Layman's Bible, which means that the fundamental truths of God's Word are there made easily accessible for our people. One of the introductory questions of the catechism is: "What is in general the right use and benefit of all these chief parts?" The answer is: "That we may learn to know who we are, and how we stand in the sight of the Lord our God; who God is, and how we may become reconciled and united with Him." With the central thought here presented we now stand face to face. In this introduction to the commandments, which applies to all the ten as well as to the first, God stands before us as the speaker. He has an epoch-making revelation to give to the children of men.

God! What a thought! In this little word the greatest problem that can ever engage the mind of man or angel is presented. God! In this little word all true philosophy, all true science, is compassed.

Man, of all earthly creatures, is distinguished by this, that he not only beholds and uses the things about him, but wants to know the causes operating back of them and through them. The animals, as their nature dictates, eat and drink, sleep and wake; when the Queen of the East arises to drive the shades of night before her, they return to their lairs or start forth to browse; they eat what they find to suit their appetites; they blink at the silent torch-bearers of the night and the resplendent mistress of the day; they receive the falling rain, endure the cold of winter and the heat of summer: but, so far as we know, there is no reflection on the how or the wherefore of all this. With man it is not so. He contemplates the changing seasons. He gathers the fruits of the earth. He passes his days amid the objects and events of this ever-changing and yet never-changing order. By the very constitution of his being and judging from all that experience and investigation have taught him, he is certain there is something back of all these phenomena of nature. He is sure there is a workman back of all this variety of splendid handiwork, a giver of all these bountiful gifts, who, in wisdom and power, must be in keeping with the results He produces. Who is He? What is He? Whatever the particular ideas with respect to Him may be, whatever the local or national name ascribed to Him, all the world has united in calling Him God — the Author, the Final Cause, the Sustainer of all things. Christian people are glad for any true light that philosophy or science may throw on the subject of the person and nature of God, but our source of knowledge is God's Word — His own revelation of Himself.

We are now engaged in studying the problem of God's person and nature with special reference to its relation to the Law, the holy Ten Commandments, therefore we ask your devout, prayerful attention for the study of this all-important subject,

God The Lawgiver

I. Let us consider, first of all, the Nature and Attributes of God. What does God say about Himself in His Word? What do we find in that other volume of His revelation, the book of nature, to illustrate or corroborate this?

Is it worth while spending any time on this subject? There are some who say God is unknown because unknowable. There are comparatively few atheists in the world, men who positively deny the existence of God; but there are a good many agnostics, those who deny that we can know anything definite about God: whether He is or is not, what He is or what He is not.

We readily grant that there is a sense in which God is not known, and cannot be known to us. We can never with these limited, sin-weakened minds of ours grasp all that God is or has done or can do. There are things of which men can say, I have analyzed this; I have resolved it into its parts, I know its constituent elements, the principles of its construction, the laws of its operation. In this sense we can never speak of knowing God. That would be to make God as small as the compass of our circumscribed human minds.

Let me give you a little illustration of the impossibility of the human mind fully to comprehend God. Most of us feel that this earth is a rather large place, and, in a way, it is. In reality, however, and by comparison, it is only a little speck of dust in this great universe. If this earth were snuffed out of existence, it would not mean nearly so much, so far as the material universe is concerned, as if one of the many, many millions of stars which twinkle in the heavens on a starry night were removed. We think this earth, with its twenty-five thousand miles circumference, rather large. And when they speak of the sun being more than ninety million miles distant it begins to stagger us. But they tell us that the nearest of those fixed stars that look down on us from the heavens is twenty billions of miles away. Light travels at the almost inconceivable velocity of one hundred and eighty-six thousand miles in one second. In the time it takes me to raise my hand it would encircle this globe more than seven times. But, though light travels at the rate of eleven million one hundred and sixty thousand miles in one minute, astronomers tell us that the average distance of those fixed stars that we see in the sky with the naked eye, is so far away that it would take a ray of light from one of them a hundred and twenty years to reach the earth. They further tell us that powerful instruments have discovered stars so far distant that it would take from the time of Abraham, four thousand years ago, to the present day for their light to reach the earth. And there are other magnitudes of which men have caught glimpses that are still more wonderful.

I am not giving you these statements as a lesson in astronomy, but to emphasize the statement that no human mind is capable of fully appreciating many of the fairly well established facts concerning this material universe. They can be stated in words. They can be set down in figures. They can be demonstrated by the fixed rules of geometry. But the human mind is incapable of grasping their full meaning. We can follow them a certain distance, but after that the mind wanders off into a vague dream in which there are no clearly defined ideas. And now, remember that back of all this incomprehensible immensity and grandeur, is the author of it all, the ruler of it all — God. He it is, as the prophet Isaiah says, "who hath measured the waters in the hollow of His hand, and meted out the heavens with the span, and comprehended the dust of the earth in a measure, and weighed the mountains in scales, and the hills in a balance" (40, 12). Is it strange that we cannot fully comprehend Him? The Psalmist was not speaking from the low level of human ignorance, but from the height of wisdom when he said concerning God and His ways: "Such knowledge is too wonderful for me; it is high, I cannot attain unto it" (139, 6). And Isaiah was but voicing the thought of God after Him when he declared: "As the heavens are higher than the earth, so are my ways higher than your ways, and my thoughts than your thoughts" (55, 9).

There is a sense, then, in which God is unknowable; but also a sense in which He is knowable. We cannot weigh, measure, or analyze Him. But we do know that He exists and much of what He has done and is doing. No man, as yet, has been able to define magnetism, gravitation, light, electricity, or life; but we know that they exist and a good many things about their uses. So it is with

God. We cannot take into our minds all that God is or has done, but we can take in all that is necessary for our needs. This wonderful God, in the person of His dear Son Jesus, deigns to come and dwell in our hearts and, by sweet heart-fellowship to make up the deficiency of our minds. The character of our knowledge of God and our experience of God determines the character of our religion and our life.

In our study of God we Christians do not begin with nature. The heathen do so, and St. Paul tells us that this revelation of His eternal power and Godhead is so clear that they are without excuse for their godlessness (Romans 1, 20). But we have a much clearer light. We come to our knowledge of God from the quiet and sublime height of God's own revelation of Himself in His Word.

And now, what kind of God is He who has here revealed Himself? One of the first and most important points is that God makes Himself known to us as a personal being. He is not a mere force. He is not a mere life-principle pervading all things. He is not a mere abstract intelligence or universal mind. Personality is not easy to define. But you have a fair idea of what is meant when we speak of a human being as a person. You have a conception of what is meant when we speak of the person of Jesus Christ. Now we must not lose sight of this when we think or speak of God. He is a being, the original one, who can say "I — I am the Lord thy God." He is possessed of self-consciousness and a will. He knows Himself to be God; all His actions are self-directed; He is a God who is one and undivided, but, mystery of mysteries! existing in three persons.

Here now are some of the attributes, or qualities, that the Scriptures clearly reveal as inherent in the person of God. He is an eternal Spirit, the original, uncreated, unchangeable, self-existent being. All else besides Him are creatures. He is the Creator. All creatures depend on Him, He depends on nothing. God is all-powerful; there is nothing impossible to Him except to do wrong, the very perfection of His being precludes this. He is everywhere present. He is here with each one of us in a personal relation; and ten thousand times farther away than any man-made telescope has ever penetrated or any dream of man has ever reached, there God is, — not with a part of His being, but with His whole Divine personality. God knows all things: our inmost thoughts, the falling of a hair, the death of a sparrow. He knows every part, as well as the entire working of this sublimely great and intricate universe, the very smallest part of which only has perhaps come within the scope of human understanding. All this is part of the everyday knowledge of God. He is holiness itself, and no unrighteousness is possible with Him. He is truthful, perfectly so. Indeed, when the converging lines of truth which thread this great universe are followed to their point of radiation, they are all found to center in God. And, more wonderful still, this great Being, only the outline of whose transcendent character we are capable of bringing within the purview of our understanding, is infinitely condescending, tender and merciful to us, the frail, sinful children of men. These are but scattered sign-posts along the way to the knowledge of God, into which knowledge the very angels seek to penetrate.

No wonder that the Psalmist, meditating on the immeasurable greatness of God and His works and the littleness of man, exclaimed: "When I consider thy heavens, the work of thy fingers, the moon and the stars, which thou hast ordained, what is man, that thou art mindful of him? and the son of man that thou visitest him?" (8, 3, 4).

What study is comparable to that which has as its subject God and His works? What subject ought so to hold the mind and soul of man in thrall? It is said of the pantheistic Jewish philosopher Spinoza that he was a God-intoxicated man. In a higher, nobler sense this ought to be true of every Christian. We are told in Scripture that the very angels in heaven, as they surround the everlasting throne on high, cover their faces and fall down in adoration before God. Is this God our God? Do we prostrate ourselves in adoration before Him? Is meditation upon His person and His works a delight to us? Do we trust Him implicity, love Him and serve Him?

II. The Sovereignty of God is at all times a subject of absorbing interest to those who contemplate the person and works of God. In a special sense does it press for consideration in a study of the Ten Commandments, God's holy Law.

By the sovereignty of God we mean His absolute dominion over all things. Among men, in the affairs of nations, there is a recognized sense of authority. Whether it center in one man, as in an absolute monarchy, or whether it be vested in a sovereign people, there is a recognized source of authority. The person or the persons in whom this authority is centered may not be able, often, indeed, are not able to exercise to the full the authority with which, theoretically, they are clothed. All things human have their decided limitations. But with God there are no such limitations. He is, in the highest, fullest sense of the word, an absolute monarch. There is nothing that He cannot rule, nothing that He does not rule. There is not a human being on the earth, not a sphere in the farthest stretch of space to which God does not give His Law.

This sovereignty of God is not a quality or attribute of the nature or essence of God in addition to those previously enumerated, but a right of His, arising from the perfection of His being and His relation to the universe as its author. If God is the great, unchangeable Spirit, infinite in wisdom and power, possessing truth and righteousness as inherent attributes of His being, absolute in all His perfections, the Creator and Preserver of the universe, then He is, of right, its Lord, its absolute Ruler. All things are His by right of possession. "The earth is the Lord's and the fulness thereof; the world, and they that dwell therein" (Psalm 24, 1). All things are His by right of His perfect ability to control them and bring them to the end He desires. "He doeth according to His will in the army of heaven, and among the inhabitants of the earth: and none can stay His hand, or say unto Him, what doest thou" (Dan. 4, 35). This is a truth established not only by the nature of things, but frequently proclaimed and insisted on in God's revealed Word. "Our God is in the heavens, He hath done whatsoever He hath pleased" (Psalm 115, 3). "Of Him, and through Him, and to Him, are all things" (Romans 11, 36).

The fact of God's sovereignty is indisputably established. Nature hints at it and Revelation confirms it. But like the person and nature of God there are mysteries connected with this problem of God's sovereignty which man can never dwarf to the diminutive size of his own intellect. There are, however, some things we can know because they are revealed to us, and it is well for us to keep them well in mind. For one thing, God can never be deposed from His lordship. It can neither be ignored nor rejected. It binds all human beings as inexorably as the laws of nature, which is but God's sovereignty in another sphere, bind the material universe. It is true, men may temporarily refuse to own God's sovereignty and trample God's laws under their feet. But in the very act of so doing they are drawing the network of God's laws about them for their own punishment. It is here just as it is when men outrage the laws of health: for the time being they seem to do it with impunity, but the inevitable day of reckoning comes. Heaven and earth shall pass away, but not one jot of God's decrees shall fail of complete fulfillment.

Another point to be remembered about God's sovereignty is that it is always exercised in perfect accordance with His infinite holiness and love. The idea of sovereignty vested in men, unless sufficiently safeguarded, is looked upon with suspicion, because so frequently abused. God's sovereignty, although properly absolute, is the sovereignty of a Father, perfect in sympathy and love. There are many experiences in the lives of men and nations which are strange and perplexing, and some that, to our imperfect understanding, seem even to contradict the supremacy of a sovereign whose ruling principles are justice and love. But let us remember that we see only as through a veil, darkly. We must believe the Father's Word. We must accept the assurance that He who holds the reins of the supreme government, ruling and overruling all things, is guided not only by infinite wisdom, but by infinite love as well; a love which seeks not only the present temporal good of his children, but above all their spiritual and eternal good.

This is the God in whose presence we are to stand as we study His Word. Until we have an adequate idea of Him, His Law will not mean much to us. On the foundation of the person, nature and work of God Himself we must build the whole structure of our religion. Without this first step our Christianity will be a structure hanging in midair, without a support. And this doctrine of the sovereignty of God plays a very important part in the structure of this foundation. It gives us peace and repose. It makes us confident. It assures us that our lives are not the sport of circumstances, and that they are not ruled by an impersonal, unfeeling fate. So long as our hand is in God's hand, no circumstance, no folly of man, no malice of Satan can in reality injure us. We are in the care and keeping of Him who is infinite in His wisdom, power and love.

This is the God who stands before us and says: "I am the Lord thy God." He is the one who gives us the Ten Commandments, the sum of the moral law. As we study these commandments, let us remember that through them God is saying to us: This is what I forbid, this is what I require of you.

Is this God your God? Is this the God to whom you have surrendered yourself? Have you enlisted in His service? Remember that it is written: "This is eternal life to know thee, the only true God, and Jesus Christ whom thou hast sent" (St. John 17, 3).

THE ORIGIN AND NATURE OF LAW

"I am the Lord thy God. . . . Thou shalt, . . .
Thou shalt not." — EXODUS 20, 2, 3, 4.

WHEREVER we go in God's universe, into whatever sphere we direct investigation, we cannot proceed far without becoming conscious of the operation of unseen, intangible forces. In other words, everywhere we find Law. There is not an atom of dust floating through space; there is not a flower which blooms, not a leaf which fades and falls; there is not a stream which, ever broadening, flows from its tiny fountain, onward to the sea; there is not a star in the vast canopy of heaven, traveling its path through the millions of sister spheres; there is not a thing anywhere but is governed by Law.

Man, little man, playing his little part in his little corner of this immeasurable universe, is given to boasting of his freedom, of his independence of all forces not set in motion by himself. In doing so he only shows his ignorance. He cannot raise a hand, he cannot take a breath, without being subject to forces other than those set in motion by himself. Constantly there are forces pressing him whither he would not go, bringing results which he regrets, but cannot escape. Wise men, as far back as authentic history takes us, observed these things. It is true of the Hebrew prophet, it is equally true of heathen sage. The constitution of human nature, the law of mind, impelled men to seek the cause producing these results. Inspired men were taught to name it — God. Uninspired men often gave it a name which means God; generally, however, they gave to these forces working in things a name which means birth, that which gives to things their nature.

Man has what, perhaps for want of a better name, is often called freedom. He can place himself in opposition to Law. He can refuse obedience to Law. He can do what is forbidden by Law. But if the laws he opposes are those which inhere in the nature of things, when he steps out of the circle of the influence of one law he steps into the circle of another. He subjects himself to the inevitable penalty of the law he has sought to outrage. So far as the more vital laws are concerned, this shows itself in his own physical life. When he obstructs or defies Law through license, instead of meeting its requirements in obedience, the results tell on his physical being. If it is a matter of moral wrong, there is an inner voice which chides him and makes him ill at ease. And even where this voice, which we call conscience, has, by mistreatment, become so paralyzed that it does not actually chide, there is still a kind of animal instinct which causes the offender to flee in fear, even when no one pursues; or turn to defend himself like a hunted animal at bay. What is the explanation of all this but the presence of a dim, half-conscious recognition of that which wise men call Law?

Any man who takes the step we took last Sunday must take the step we propose today. Any man who says God must say Law. Any man who recognizes and accepts the existence of God, with the attributes which Revelation ascribes to Him, must recognize the existence and operation of Law.

Let us take up for further consideration the very difficult, but absorbingly interesting subject of Law. We will take as our theme:

The Origin and Nature of Law

I. Human law is a subject worthy of the earnest thought of all Christian people. We have to do with it, in one way or another, every day we live. Christian people often do not take the part they ought to take, and, by spirit and training, are qualified to take, in the making of our laws. But the true Christian everywhere gives the finest example of reverence for law and of obedience to it.

Possibly you are waiting for me to tell you, before we proceed further, what Law is. Ever since men have lived together in social or business relations, there have been laws. Centuries before the Christian era there were laws and systems of laws. Every country with any degree of civilization has a mass of laws. In view of this it may surprise you to hear that there is not a single definition of Law, even human law, which is generally accepted among legal men. This ought to have the effect of keeping the wise men of the world a little more humble. But inability to give at least a fairly satisfactory definition of law is due, in our judgment, to the fact that so many of the intellectual lights of this world leave God out of their calculations. Law is but the operation of those principles which God, the Creator of all things, has implanted in His creatures, each according to its nature and its purpose. Those principles which operate in mere physical things we call natural laws. Those principles operating in man and leading to the formulation and adoption of rules for human conduct, were, in former ages, also called laws of nature; but are now generally called simply human laws. Those laws for the regulation of human life which are revealed in the Bible, and of which the Ten Commandments are the sum, we, in a specific sense, call the Law of God.

Interesting as it might be, helpful as it ought to be, we shall not now discuss, at any length, present human laws. One observation, however, we feel impelled to make. Seldom has the world been in more need of reverence for the majesty of Law than now. The tendency is toward the rejection of all authority. Everyone wants to be a law unto himself. One great reason for this condition is that God has been so largely ruled out of His universe. People do not see Him, as they should, back of all Law. Another factor contributing largely to this condition is the needless multiplication of laws. Our governmental bodies have come to be largely grist-mills for grinding out laws. Part of them are wholly useless; part of them are made for the classes as over against the masses; and another part of them seem to have the purpose of invalidating existing laws so as to make their administration difficult. We need not more but fewer laws. We need fewer laws, but more Law. We need a return from the maze of entanglements called laws to the fundamental, inalienable, and indestructible principles of human righteousness and justice, wisely and firmly administered. We want things to come to such a state that the poor man, when he stands before the law, will get justice; and that the rich man, with his millions, cannot defeat justice. When this time comes there will be more reverence for Law. But it will not come till those who make laws and administer laws, recognize and are influenced by a higher Law than that which comes from human mind.

The one point in which we are especially interested in this part of our discussion, is this — how did there come to be such things as human laws? They exist not only in Christian lands, but everywhere. And they cover almost every conceivable human relationship and activity. So universal are certain fundamental ideas concerning human relations that it is conceded that they are the result of a disposition, or tendency, essential to man's nature.

After the eclipse of the knowledge of God, and of His will and ways, which came with sin, certain portions of the race gradually fell deeper and deeper into ignorance and sin. And again certain portions would rise to a greater or less degree of culture. We need not be surprised or disconcerted by this evidence of development among men. God is still the God of this world. He did not give it over altogether to the prince of disorder. God is still King beyond the Kingdom of Grace. And He has used many people not spiritually His children for the purpose of bringing certain blessings through them to humanity. The development of human law is one of these blessings.

Everywhere men had a certain consciousness of right and wrong in human relations. And to some extent they would practice them. These customs and usages of mankind are the early forms of what afterwards came to be enacted into law. The foundation of the whole fabric of American and English law can be traced back to Rome and Greece. And with these people they were not altogether inventions, but a harvest gathered elsewhere and subjected to the law of growth under the stimulation of their genius. Many of the better laws of the older nations were echoes of Sinai.

In this connection, only one more point is to be settled. How did man, the natural man, come to have this knowledge of law as a basic element of his being? How did he come to have a certain indwelling consciousness of right and wrong in human relations? Many of the greatest men of the world have said: "It must have come from the great Power which made man and rules him." The Bible is very definite, and says Law came from Him who created man and who says to all the children of men: "I am the Lord thy God, Thou shalt, * * * Thou shalt not."

The process of the development of human laws which we have described is exactly that which St. Paul describes to the Romans when he says: "When the Gentiles, which have not the law (the written law), do by nature the things contained in the law, these, having not the law, are a law unto themselves, which shew the work of the law written in their hearts, their consciences also bearing witness, and their thoughts the meanwhile accusing or else excusing one another" (2, 14, 15). In other words, while there has been a development in human laws, God planted the elements of Law itself in man's heart. And we would not be claiming one whit too much in saying that all human law worthy of the name, is in reality a fragment of Divine Law.

II. The Divine Law, in the sense of God's Law as revealed and summarized in the Ten Commandments, is the point we shall next consider.

Everywhere, as we have seen, there are principles, or laws, at work. The object of their operation is that the creatures in which they operate may serve the purpose, or attain the end, for which they were created. And back of all these laws stands God. He is their author. From Him they derive their energy. By Him they are still controlled. They can never alter, never cease, till He wills it.

In man also God originally implanted an operative principle similar to the law of nature. As naturally as water flows down hill, as certain birds fly south in autumn and north in spring, as naturally as the buds begin to grow when the spring showers begin to fall and the warm winds to blow, so natural was it once for man to do the will of God. Sin has changed all this. It did not, however, entirely eradicate this law. Man still retained a certain consciousness of God and of obligation to Him. But it soon became very, very dim and sadly perverted. To the natural man's mind God soon became a distorted, ugly monster. And what he conceived to be the will of God was equally distorted. Men felt the need of being religious, but they broke the highest and holiest laws of the true God in the worship of their distorted ideas of God. In the place of the true God, they bowed down to images, animals, and creeping things. God had put holy desires and feelings in man's heart. These were to find expression in the worship of God and in the service of man. But now men committed murder, adultery, and every other kind of abomination, in the holy name of religion and as a worship rendered to God. This is the effect of sinful nature upon the conduct of man.

The time finally came when God determined to give a new revelation of His Holy Will to mankind. It was, in substance at least, the old Law. But it was given in a new, a written, form. Given for all men, it was temporarily entrusted to the special guardianship of the particular people whom He had chosen for the purpose of keeping alive His name among men, and through whom He was going to work out and perfect the plan for the redemption of humanity — the Jewish people.

After long years of debasing servitude on their part, God, by the might of His outstretched arm, set this people free. He led them through the Red Sea. At length, in the third month, they encamped by Sinai. Here God commanded them to sanctify themselves. While darkness covered the mountain and the thunders pealed, while the lightnings flashed and the mountain trembled to its foundation, God came down to deliver His holy Law. Great laws have been given to the world under impressive circumstances, but never before or since in the annals of the race, have such laws been given, by such a law-giver, under such sublime, awe-inspiring circumstances.

These are the laws to which we are to give special attention. We have known their words since our early childhood. But we have never exhausted their meaning and never shall. Nor let us forget that in these words the Almighty God Himself is speaking to us. He is not setting up a system of morality merely for our admiration. He does not say: "Here is something which it will be very nice or very profitable for you to do." No, they are laws. With respect to them the Eternal God says: "Thou shalt * * * Thou shalt not." And remember the absoluteness of His authority: the heavens shall be removed and this solid earth destroyed, but not one word of this Law shall fail. These obligations must be met or their penalties endured. If a man puts his hand in the fire, he will be burned. If he falls into the water and cannot get out, he will drown. If he falls from a precipice, he will be crushed. These are the inevitable results of the laws of Nature. And God's moral laws have to be obeyed or the penalties endured; that is all there is to the matter. Because we have not met these obligations we are now suffering the penalties in disordered lives. And unless we do meet them, and meet them perfectly, or find some one qualified and duly authorized who can meet them for us, we shall forever suffer the penalties of disordered lives. Thank God, such an One has been found. It is Jesus Christ.

There are other Divine laws, in the sense in

which we here speak of Divine laws, besides those contained in the Commandments. There were certain temporary laws which God gave to the Jewish people. They had to do with personal conduct, family and social life; with fasts and kindred external observances. When God said that such things should be done, the doing of them became obligatory, and the failure to do them incurred guilt. These temporary, or ceremonial, laws have been set aside. But the laws summarized in the Ten Commandments are moral laws. They have to do with things which are in themselves right or wrong. They apply to us just as much as they did to the Jews. Indeed, they apply to all people, in all times and everywhere. The customs and habits of men change, the Moral Law can never change. It inheres in the nature of God's creation. Righteousness is not right simply because God requires it. He requires it because it is right. Sin is not sinful simply because God prohibits it. God forbids it because it is sin. With such fundamental matters does this Law treat.

Law exists in the very nature of God. It rests, when traced to its source, on the sovereignty of God. Moral Law, we may say, is but the expression of the eternal and unchangeable principles of right inherent in the very nature of God. But Moral Law, as we know it, came into being only after sin became a reality in God's creation.

Brethren, in order adequately to appreciate the nature and dignity of Law, especially the Moral Law, we must bear with us an adequate conception of the nature and dignity of God the Giver of the Law.

It will help us also to know in advance the purpose of God's Law. It is to be a rule of life, it is true. But before it can be this, it must serve another purpose—convince us of sin. The very form of the Law is such that it emphasizes this truth. All the commandments but two are negative, they say: "Thou shalt not." Through their very form God would tell us of our natural tendency toward evil. "The heart is deceitful above all things, and desperately wicked" (Jer. 17, 9). Before it stands God — God, saying, with all His sovereign power and majesty: "Thou shalt not."

On the other hand, even in the awe-inspiring declarations of the Law, God brings Himself and each one of us into a very close personal relation. He says: "I" and "thou." "I am — thy God; Thou shalt not." The groundwork of our national law is the principle that the liberty and well-being of the individual is paramount. That is the principle of God's Law. "I" and "thou;" God and the individual. In this way He seeks to remind men that, though they are morally bankrupt and ever prone to err, they are still in a sense his children. The object is to inspire them with the desire to again be restored to His image. Yes, even God's voice from Sinai is a voice of love that would win us to the path of life. "The law was our schoolmaster to bring us unto Christ, that we might be justified by faith" (Gal. 3, 24).

THE PROHIBITION OF IDOLATRY

"I am the Lord thy God. * * * Thou shalt have no other gods before Me. Thou shalt not make unto thee any graven image, or any likeness of anything that is in heaven above, or that is in the water under the earth: thou shalt not bow down thyself to them, nor serve them." — EXODUS 20, 2-5.

UNIVERSALLY men have felt the need of a God. Man is a created being, he is dependent, he cannot live by himself. It is in God that we live, and move and have our being (Acts 17, 28). Man feels this; hence, because of the very constitution of his being, his soul cries out for God. We have been told how our own American Indian, with a far-away look in his eyes, and an unsatisfied hunger gnawing at his heart, would wander away from his fellows, out on the plain, up to the mountain-top, and there stretch forth his hands and imploringly lift up his voice to the Great Spirit for His presence and His help. So, to a greater or less degree, it has been always and everywhere among men. Jehovah declares that only the fool thinks he can live without God (Psalm 14, 1).

The result of this implanted imperishable craving, a craving in the natural man like unto that of the plant for air and sunshine and water, leads those who do not know the true God to make gods for themselves. If sin had not made man perverse, if his senses were not dulled and blinded by "the god of this world," this craving for God would lead men to a reasonable knowledge of the true God, at least to the knowledge of "His eternal power and Godhead" (Romans 1, 20). But because of this blindness and aversion to the absolute truth, man's unaided search for God usually leads him only farther and ever farther from the true God.

The history of the nations is in no small part a history of religious strivings; a history of man's gods and the service rendered them. In so far as it is the history of false religions, it is a dark picture — a picture of ignorance, of cruelty, of lust. This is the final and inevitable course of humanity when it forsakes the true God and follows the gods of its own devising. Thus St. Paul describes the course of those who turn away from the living God: "As they did not like to retain God in their knowledge, God gave them over to a reprobate mind, to do those things which are not convenient, being filled with all unrighteousness, fornication, wickedness, covetousness, maliciousness; full of envy, murder, debate, deceit, malignity; whisperers, backbiters, haters of God, despiteful, proud, boasters, inventors of evil things, disobedient to parents, without understanding, covenant breakers, without natural affection, implacable, unmerciful" (Romans 1, 28-32). This is God's own description of the course of those who turn their backs on Him.

With meekness, with a mind open to the truth, with a desire to profit, let us give prayerful attention to God's teaching in the First Commandment. We shall take as our subject, the Prohibition of Idolatry.

Idolatry

The words idol and idolatry are very common in the speech of men, but the origin and the depths of all human woe are contained in them. As all life, all religion, all true progress, all lasting happiness, all glory, all blessedness is contained, in embryo, in the word — God; so all death, all delusions, all misery, all hopelessness, all the darkness of endless despair, is summed up in the word — idolatry. The idolater dethrones God, not from His seat of authority in the heavens, — that cannot be done; but from His throne in the idolater's heart, and in place of God he sets up some kind of delusion of his own invention; or, if the false god is not altogether a delusion of a diseased imagination, it is one of those dark, malignant spirits which first defying the sovereign authority of God, were cast down from heaven into outer darkness.

Idolatry, according to the Old Testament teaching, is the acknowledgment and worship of any other god than the One who revealed Himself to Israel as the Creator of all things, the loving and compassionate Father of his people who promised them a Redeemer to undo the ills they had brought on themselves, and who was constantly sending His Spirit to work in their hearts and bring them back into fellowship with Himself and keep them in His loving service.

In the New Testament, idolatry is still more clearly defined as the denial of the triune God, Father, Son and Holy Ghost, and the refusal to worship this God alone. When God is thus dethroned, chaos reigns in man's soul. The universe becomes an unexplainable riddle. Life becomes a sad, sad nightmare. Unknown remain both its origin and destiny. Idolatry lost Paradise to the race. It opened the fountain for that swollen and still swelling torrent of tears that shall know no diminution or assuaging till the last human pulse has ceased to beat and the last eye has grown dim in death.

God would not be the God He is if He did not do all Divine wisdom and love can do to reclaim His blinded, wandering, dying children. He has been doing this always and in many ways. Only once did He do it more effectively than when, from Sinai, he thundered His denunciation against idolatry; namely, when He spoke from Calvary.

Our text for today presents to us again the great God of whom we have heard in former addresses. His name is Jehovah, the One who ever was, and is, and ever shall be, the changeless One. The heavens, that incomprehensible expanse, peopled with millions of worlds, is His throne. The earth is His footstool. He produced it all by His Word of power. His will is its Law. This God, the embodiment of all conceivable virtues, infinite in all the qualities which make up His being, the absolute Sovereign of all things, He in whose honor the morning stars sang together, and before whose throne the Cherubim and Seraphim fall in adoration — this God came down to stand before the children of men and claim their undivided allegiance. "I am the Lord thy God. * * * Thou shalt have no other gods before Me." God has rights in this world. One of these rights, in many respects the first, is the recognition of His Kingship and the reverent and filial service of his subjects. Nor shall God give up this right: He is a jealous God.

These words prohibiting idolatry came down through the thunderings and lightnings of Sinai to Israel, but the message was for the world and is for all time. Though four thousand remarkable years have passed since that time, though races and civilizations have come and gone, the words still stand: "I am the Lord thy God. * * * Thou shalt have no other gods before me." The world has found no other true God. Jehovah, the God of the Bible, is still God. We know Him better than ancient Israel knew Him, for we have looked into His mind and heart through that last great revelation of Himself in His Son Jesus Christ, but He is the same God. And when that long expected day shall break, the day on which the assembled nations shall surround His throne of judgment, the God of Sinai, the God of Calvary, will still be God. "He is our God forever and forever."

The Prohibition of Idolatry

The prohibition of every kind of idolatry is contained in the First Commandment. "Thou shalt have no other gods before Me," includes everything in the nature of false worship; but the prohibition was unquestionably first directed against the gross forms of idolatry so generally prevalent at that time. And this gross kind of idolatry is the phase of the subject to which we shall chiefly confine ourselves today.

The Jewish people were established as a protest against idolatry. Abraham was called from the midst of an idolatrous nation to establish this people. Terah, the father of Abraham, was an idolater and probably a carver of idols. The patriarchs, under the tutelage of the Holy Spirit, doubtless made much progress in their knowledge of the true God. But at the time the Law was given, the chosen people had just emerged from a galling servitude of almost four hundred years in the midst of a powerful nation — the Egyptians. The Egyptians, two thousand years before Christ, had an extensive literature and wrought wonders by their skill. But they were worshippers of fourfooted beasts and creeping things. This practice unquestionably had its influence on the Hebrews. After their deliverance, they were surrounded by warring tribes of fierce habits and rude ideas, all of whom were idolaters. Some worshipped the heavenly bodies, others bowed down to various animals, while others wrought their conceptions of Deity into wood and stone, "graven by art and man's device." Israel, as her history proves, had a decided tendency toward appropriating the false gods of her idolatrous neighbors. It was against this gross form of idolatry that the First Commandment was first of all specifically directed. This, we think, is borne out by the words which accompany the commandment: "Thou shalt not make unto thee any graven image, or any likeness of anything that is in heaven above, or that is in the earth beneath, or that is in the water under the earth." These words seem to indicate the form of idolatry that God had first of all in mind. Some people go so far as to interpret these words about graven images as an injunction never, under any and all circumstances, to make a symbol, or representation, of anything heavenly; yea, forbidding the making of a likeness of any earthly creature. The all-sufficient answer to this argument is that not very long after the giving of this commandment God Himself required those who were preparing the Divinely appointed house of worship to make many representations of things on earth and in heaven. We will mention only the carved figures of the two angels who were to guard the mercy-seat in the Holy of Holies (Deut. 25, 17f.).

Neither the First Commandment nor its explanation forbids the making of works of art or their proper use in worship. Pictures of Christ, of scenes from His life, of angels and the like, are works of the imagination, guided in some instances by meager description. There are no likenesses of them from life. But these pictures of sacred persons and places in our churches, schools and homes often have a salutary effect. They have helped to lead many a wandering thought, many a slumbering affection, back to God and sacred things. But they must not be worshipped. "Thou shalt not bow down thyself to them, nor serve them." They must not be allowed to stand between the worshipper and God, the only true object of worship. Much less should we seek to worship God through them. This is idolatry. Israel often did this, and was severely rebuked and punished for it by God.

Israel, in spite of its tendency toward idolatry,

in spite of many failures, sometimes on the part of only a portion of its people, sometimes on the part of the nation almost as a whole — in spite of all this, Israel for thousands of years, held to its Sinaitic covenant; it worshipped Jehovah, the one true, living God, the Creator and Ruler of all things. But it did this only as the result of God's continual pleading, His repeated warnings and frequent chastisements. Finally, at a time when Israel was holding fast most tenaciously to its God-given forms of worship, and when the smoke of its many sacrifices ascended daily toward heaven, God declared that it was all an abomination to Him; for, while still holding largely to the form of sound words and practice, it had lost God Himself and its hold upon Him. And when the highest of all revelations of God was given to Israel in the person of Jesus Christ, it knew Him not and rejected Him. This was the culmination of Jewish idolatry. And God took away its light; Israel lost its national life, as it had lost its place in the kingdom of God.

Idolatry always presages decay and ruin. The Greeks and Romans came into the flower of their national life almost two thousand years after Israel began to flourish in Palestine. In some things, these people, after the lapse of nearly two thousand years, are still teachers of the world. Their genius for the beautiful in literature and art will not be forgotten while the world stands. But in the height of their glory they carved images, built magnificent temples in which to place their idols, and then fell down before them and performed unmentionable deeds in their service. And they fell as the nations before them fell, and as nations since then have fallen. Why did they all fall? Because they knew not the true God, because they enthroned and worshipped idols. And so it has been with many other powerful nations.

You may say, These things happened so long ago that it is a matter of only antiquarian interest to us. Not so fast, my friends! Idolatry of this gross kind still flourishes. Millions of our fellow-men still fall down before reptiles and fourfooted beasts; millions still stretch out their hands toward the heavenly bodies, but know not the true God who reigns above them; millions of them worship the spirit of dead ancestors; many of them even fall down in fear and supplication before the prince of darkness, the devil himself. Does this mean nothing to us? Does this not impose some obligation on us? Even in lands like our own, multitudes are idolaters, worshipping all kinds of gods, from self and pelf to imaginary beings of every sort, bred in the conceits of their own brains. For all these there is but one end. "Know ye not that the unrighteous shall not inherit the kingdom of God? Be not deceived: neither fornicators, nor idolaters * * * shall inherit the kingdom of God" (1 Cor. 6, 9, 10).

The Duty Imposed

The First Commandment is not a simple negation. God is never satisfied when men merely break their idols or even, in some measure, disabuse their minds of erroneous ideas concerning Deity. God's perfections call for recognition and allegiance; His blessings invite man's praise; His Fatherly love and care calls for love and service. Luther, therefore, was perfectly correct when he explained this commandment to mean that men should fear, love and trust in God above all things.

The fear of God! that is something we have been taught in these modern decades to cast away as a remnant of a less cultured age. But the world needs again to learn to have a right, a holy, fear of God. He is not an ogre or a tyrant; but He has an undying wrath against all ungodliness. Nowhere else can such awe-inspiring, such terrible denunciations of sin be found as are found in God's Word. He says, speaking of the very sin of idolatry: "The Lord is the true God, He is the living God, and an everlasting King. At His wrath the earth shall tremble, and the nations shall not be able to abide His indignation" (Jer. 10, 10). To those who have tasted and found how good the Lord is, this fear becomes a childlike, reverent awe; a feeling in keeping with the truest love and the most perfect confidence.

This God, the absolute Sovereign, the compassionate Father, who can endure no rival, in whose favor alone is life and blessedness, is He our God? If so, then our obligations have only begun. It is impossible rightly to know God, to be a true child of His, and not desire that He should reign supreme in every human being's heart. We owe it to every one still sitting in the darkness of idolatry to seek to set him free from his bonds. Our ancestors were once idolaters of this gross sort. They bowed down to images and offered human sacrifices to the imaginary gods of the stream and the forest. To what do we owe our emancipation? On what has been built the towering structure of western civilization? On what foundation rests our modern conception of law, of liberty? What has been the hidden fountain from which has flowed the modern idea of popular education? What has been the true sustaining force behind every true bill of human rights? We owe it all to the overthrow of idolatry and to the dignity and sacredness which came into human life when man recognized himself a child of the true, the living God.

And how did we come into possession of this truth? Almost two thousand years ago there lived in Palestine a Jew, dwarfed and deformed in body; but in whose mind there glowed the fire of genius and in whose heart there burned the Divinely lighted flame of faith in God and of love for God and man. To this man was given the significant vision that God "hath made of one blood all nations of men;" that he had sent His Son to redeem all men, that there was one heaven for all that, through Christ, would come back to the allegiance which the First Commandment requires. This vision broke down the limits of national pride in St. Paul's soul. He went forth to bring the world back to the old allegiance, through the New Evangel. And westward the course of Christian Empire has made its way till it has reached and embraced us. And we must now do our part to speed the movement on its way.

Even this does not exhaust our obligation. Indeed, it presupposes the recognition of another obligation, one which we must constantly seek to discharge with increasing faithfulness. If we have taken Jehovah to be our God, we must be His loyal subjects in life as well as in word. God is not truly enthroned in a man's heart till that man desires to conform his life, his daily conduct, to the standard God has set for him in His Word. God says to all his children: "Ye shall be holy; for I the Lord your God am holy" (Lev. 19, 2; 1 Peter 1, 16). All Christians are to remember that they are members of a chosen generation, a royal priesthood, an holy nation, a peculiar people; that they should show forth the praises of Him who hath called them of darkness into His marvelous light (1 Peter 2, 9). Are we showing in this way that we have given up idolatry?

"I am the Lord thy God. * * * Thou shalt have no other gods before me." "Thy God" — these words are spoken to you, to me and to all men. He is the God of all men. And He wants to be acknowledged as God by all men and served by all. "We should fear, love and trust Him above all things." This "we" also includes you and me and all men. And to love and trust is but another way of spelling service.

Are we doing our part in writing the history of the kingdom of God? Are we doing our part in helping to destroy the idols of the world? Are we responsive to the operations of the Holy Spirit, who would give God His true place in our lives, and who would lead us and help us to do our part in bringing it to pass that God, the living God, may come into His own in the lives of all mankind?

"From all that dwell below the skies,
Let the Creator's praise arise:
Let the Redeemer's name be sung
Through every land, by every tongue."

MODERN AMERICAN IDOLS

"Thou shalt worship the Lord, thy God; and Him only shalt thou serve." — MATT. 4, 10.

IN our recent address we spoke of idols and idol-worship, but confined ourselves closely to the grosser forms of this great sin. Though we pointed out that idolatry of this kind still largely prevails and that the simple fact of its existence entails on all the children of God the solemn duty of making the true God known, a duty we cannot shirk without guilt, still it is possible that a good many have felt that the sin of which we spoke was a thing far removed from our life, something altogether of another world, if not of the long ago.

It is true, we are living in times far removed from much of that of which we spoke; and we are living under conditions quite different from those in which carved images and similar things are generally worshipped. We are living in a century which was to give us a decided foretaste of the millennium. We are living under a so-called Christian government. Most of us never saw a graven image which people have worshipped, unless it was in a museum or in the possession of a returned missionary. Still, there are plenty of idols and idol-worshippers all around us. I doubt not that there are as many idols in New York, Chicago, and Columbus as there were in ancient Babylon, Athens, or Ephesus.

I ask you to give serious, prayerful attention to a subject considered by some unnecessary, but in truth a sober, awful reality. My subject is:

Modern American Idols

I wish it to be understood that the idols of which I shall speak are neither exclusively modern nor exclusively American. Some of them are doubtless as old as history, as old as perverted human thought. And they are found and worshipped in other lands called Christian besides our own. All that I want to emphasize is that they are idols of today and idols of America, idols which we have to face and with respect to which we have individually to make decision.

These idols are of two general classes — those of the mind and those of the heart.

I. The idols of the mind are those ideas and systems devised by the human intellect that rob God of His authority because they are permitted to control the heart and life.

The very first of these idols, and the parent of them all, is perverted reason, which has always been one of the ruling gods of humanity. But I doubt whether in the course of history, reason, this power of the mind, has ever been worshipped as it is today.

During the mad carnival of violence and lust known as the French Revolution, which was nothing but the ripe and inevitable fruit of unbelief, France sought to put reason on the throne of God. Under the leadership of a band of rabid atheists, the people blasphemously shouted: "The King of heaven must be dethroned just as the kings of earth." The Bishop of Paris, with his priests, denounced Christianity. A great petition was brought to the Convention asking that Christianity be formally abolished. The Cathedral of Notre Dame was renamed "The Temple of Reason." A woman of ill repute, fantastically adorned, having been drawn in a carriage through the streets amid shouting throngs, was led to this newly named "Temple of Reason" and seated on the high altar. Then those devotees of unbelief and blood, with the bawdy element of the city, danced around her, blasphemously paying her divine honours. In thousands of apostate churches throughout the land this ungodly ceremony was soon repeated. While this excess of madness soon wore itself out, France paid the price of an apostasy from which, we believe, she has not yet wholly recovered.

I do not mention this event simply as an historic instance of the deification of human reason, but as one of the leading sources through which there has come down to our time a widespread tendency to put human reason in the place of God. Not only much of the philosophy and science of today, but much of our learning in every department, is permeated with a "heady, highminded" spirit, which unhesitatingly exalts human mind above the authority of God in His Word. Materialistic evolution, which rules God out of His universe and makes all things, including man, the result of chance; the sciences, whenever their representatives recognize nothing but the so-called laws, or forces, of Nature as the cause and sustaining principle of all things; the prevailing Pantheism, which makes a grain of wheat, a rose, and the human being merely diverse stages of the only deity known to it, the life principle in nature: these and other kindred theories are of the same piece with that French deification of Reason. It puts the human mind in place of God, dethroning the God of the Bible.

Why do we mention these things? Are they of practical concern to plain Christian people? They are; for they are gods virtually set up for our worship today. They come into our homes through very many of the books, magazines, and newspapers of the day. They are gods which are set up before the immature minds of our young people in many of the books forced upon them in the schools which we have to support. Especially are they flaunted in the faces of our young men and women in many of the advanced schools. These things are held up as the necessary marks of modern education. The attempt is often made to make out those who will not accept these dicta as lacking the very elements of a liberal education; and such modern idolaters would even make it appear that those who will not bow to this fetish of modern philosophy and science are troubled by mental deficiency.

Are we going to bow down before this modern idol or not? Never! The God of Heaven, who has revealed Himself in His Word, is our God. His Word is the truth. There is not an iota of contradiction between the truth of this Word and any other truth in all the universe. If there is a contradiction between this Word and any other supposed truth, God's Word is right and that supposed truth is an untruth. This is the only position in keeping with the First Commandment: "I am the Lord thy God. Thou shalt have no other gods before Me."

This exaltation of human reason operates in still another direction, namely, in the sphere of faith. It is not unknown to you that the idea largely prevails that it does not matter much what a man believes about the person and nature of God, just so he sincerely believes there is some kind of supreme being. This idea is widely heralded in all kinds of modern literature; not infrequently it is loudly proclaimed even from Christian pulpits. This is the spirit of modern liberalism. Baal, Buddha, and Brahma, the Allah of the Mohammedan and the great father of the modern Jew, are put on a level with Jehovah, the eternal God of the Bible, who spoke the last word of the revelation of Himself when He sent His beloved Son down from heaven to be the world's Redeemer. What does it mean when men say that the opinion of these people is as good as that of the Christian but this, that every one is to be allowed to be the maker of his own god? This is nothing but old heathenism revamped. If the subject of God was a matter of opinion merely, we should agree. One man has as much right to his own opinion as another. But God is not a creation of man's mind. He has never been conceived correctly by unaided human mind. God has revealed Himself in the Bible. We have no right to despise or persecute those who are determined to hold to these opinions. But we are untrue to God, ourselves, and these deluded people if we grant that their position is as good as ours. Admitting, as our self-styled religious progressives do, that the religions of Mohammed, of Buddha, of the Mormons, are also revelations of God, differing from ours only in degree, but not in character, they virtually dispense with Jesus Christ. The Christian religion is the revelation of God through His Son, while all other religions merely set forth the abortive efforts of man's reason to discover God.

The ancient Greeks believed in a god. They even held that the man who did not believe in a supreme being was essentially immoral, a danger to the peace and security of the State, and sometimes subject to banishment. Theirs were strong convictions, but they did not result in the knowledge of the true God; nor did they satisfy God, who says: "I am the Lord thy God. * * * Thou shalt have no other Gods before me." I do not hesitate to say that I believe that wherever in the world there is an earnest person honestly seeking God, whose soul cries out for the true, the living God, God will find a way of bringing that man to a knowledge of Himself. But if the man is to be helped and saved, he must come to know God, God in Christ Jesus, not some caricature of God. God is a jealous God. He says: "I am the Lord, that is my name; and my glory will I not give to another" (Isa. 42, 8).

Nor are the Hebrews free from the blight of idolatry. For two thousand years they were God's chosen people. It was to them that He revealed

Himself at Sinai in the giving of the Law. It was to them that He spoke, first of all, through the prophets. It was through them that He gave the world His Son. And He came, first of all, to them. After Christ came, down to this day, they have called God by the names through which He had revealed Himself to them. They still have the old Scriptures which God gave to them through the prophets. They have their temples, where they meet and devoutly worship. But they have not the true God. They are idolaters. They are worshipping a god of their own creation. That sounds rather severe, and some say it is bigotry. But if anyone has a quarrel with this statement, let him remember that he has his quarrel, not with me or any other man, but with God Almighty and His Word.

We must bear in mind in this connection that God has revealed Himself as a triune God — a God who is one as to essence, but three as to person: Father, Son and Holy Ghost. This truth is contained in the Old Testament, but clearly revealed in the New. The God thus revealed is the only true God, and he who has not this God of Scripture has no God. For a man to say that he has God, because he has set up an idea of his own as his god, does not give him the true God, any more than a man has a million dollars because he says he has them.

This position is borne out by God's Word. Jesus says to the Jews: "He that honoreth not the Son honoreth not the Father which hath sent Him" (St. John 5, 23). Again He says: "It is my Father that honoreth me, of whom ye say that He is your God; but ye have not known Him." "Ye neither know me, nor my Father. If ye had known me ye should have known my Father also" (St. John 8, 54, 19). Once more God says: "Whosoever denieth the Son, the same hath not the Father" (1 John 2, 23). All that I ask you to remember is that these are not my words, but statements of God's Word.

And now, while these words of God are still fresh in our minds, we come to another subject along the same line. It is a delicate subject, because a burning one. But I should be faithless as a steward of God's Word and false in my love to you, my hearers, if I failed to speak of it. Many of the secret societies of the day stand charged with idolatry. Most of them require a mere belief in a supreme being, and this satisfies most people. But I ask you, What are the names given to this supreme being? Do they mean by these names the triune God of the Bible? If so, why do they not say so. The simple truth of the matter is that many of those who expound these systems from the inside say plainly that they do not mean the triune God of the Bible. Indeed, many of those French atheists and English deists, who wanted to dethrone the "King of Heaven" and put reason on God's throne, had much to do with giving their modern form to the systems of the older leading organizations.

I know they say to-day that each one may put his own interpretation on these terms. The Jew may think of his god — a god without Christ; the

Mohammedan of his god; the Christian of the triune God, and so on to the end of the long list. But think of standing up beside a man, using the same form of worship, using the same name he uses in calling on God, when you know that he would spit on the name of the Christian God. More than this, you know that some of these organizations expressly prohibit the use of the name of Christ in their services. Remember that you have just heard the Word of God say that he that hath not Christ hath not God. And again, Christ says: "Whosoever shall deny Me before men, him will I also deny before my Father which is in heaven" (St. Matth. 10, 3). And God says: "Whosoever * * * shall be ashamed of Me and of My words in this adulterous and sinful generation, of him also shall the Son of Man be ashamed, when He cometh in the glory of His Father with the holy angels" (St. Mark 8, 38).

I know there are splendid men in these orders, men of exceptional intelligence and fine moral character, who do much for each other. Nor do we deny that there are true Christians, God-fearing men, there. But they are there because they have not seen the inconsistency in which they are involved. If God's Word is true, then the system, as such, is false. The god there worshipped is not the true God, and men endanger their souls when they take part in its worship. If men want organizations for social or business reasons, why do not Christian men insist that they shall be free from those things which contradict God's Word? Then we would not only not oppose them, but probably join them. As it is now, as I understand the matter, I would not thus endanger my soul; no, not for all the fertile acres lying between the Chesapeake Bay and the Golden Gate, between the Great Lakes and the Gulf of Mexico. I say these things not in the spirit of ill will, for I have some dear friends, whose noble qualities I much esteem and whom I love with all of a brother's love, who are members of some of these orders; but in the spirit of obedience to Him whose plan of salvation and solemn warnings I can abridge only to the hurt of my soul and at the risk of my own salvation.

There are so many of these modern idols in the sphere of the human intellect that lack of time forbids our attempting to enumerate them. But there is one, a comprehensive one, which we must at least mention. It is the exaltation, the deification, of human achievement. Human inventions, human progress, world-commerce, the amassing of swollen fortunes, great armies bristling with bayonets, navies with frowning guns, death-dealing airships, and submarines which mingle with the monsters of the deep — these are the gods before which multitudes fall in awed admiration and to which they burn the incense of devoted service. Even peace advocates build their plans chiefly on the uncertain foundation of mere human culture and in the interest of mere worldly projects. God Almighty, who says: "I am the Lord thy God. * * * Thou shalt have no other gods before Me," "Be ye holy, for I the Lord thy God am holy;" Jesus Christ, who sets before us a new and ideal Kingdom of truth, of purity, of peace, of fellowship with God; the Holy Ghost, who calls men to repentance and faith and brotherhood and loving service — this triune God and the enduring blessings of His revelation receive no attention on the part of many, little attention on the part of many others, and they call forth an interest altogether too feeble and inadequate on the part of the best. Indeed, the world has great need of drawing near again to Sinai and listening to the voice thundering down from its cloud-capped summit: "I am the Lord thy God. Thou shalt have no other gods besides Me."

II. The idols of the heart are the creature possessions, the comforts and pleasures of life, on which men set their affections; the things which absorb men's thoughts and energies.

In classifying certain objects as idols of the heart, we do not mean to signify that the intellect plays no part in the process; nor do we wish to imply that the intellectual creations of which we have spoken are not at all enshrined in the heart. The point of emphasis here is that the class of objects of which we shall now speak have the affections as the chief seat of their enthronement. These are the things for which men quite generally long, of them they think, for them they are willing to slave. In other words, to these creature blessings they give the attention which should be given solely to God.

"Thou shalt love the Lord thy God with all thine heart, and with all thy soul, and with all thy mind, and with all thy strength." This is what Jesus says we all owe to God. But how often home, or store, or farm, or bank account looms so large in people's vision and occupies so large a place in their affections that God is crowded out and forgotten. These things are worth while; they are all gifts of God, who wants us properly to appreciate and use them. Laziness in embracing opportunities to acquire a portion of these gifts of God is to be condemned. Carelessness in taking care of what we have of these things and improving them is equally unworthy a child of God. But none of these things must be allowed to usurp God's place in our hearts. "Ye cannot serve God and mammon," says Christ.

These things have been given by a kind heavenly Father as means to help us on our heavenward way. As such they are good, are to be carefully guarded and used with gratitude. But even good things may become impediments. Clothing, food, and accoutrements are necessary to the success of an army. But when a strategic point is to be taken by a forced march, every ounce of burden not necessary at the moment may have to be discarded for the time being. So the material gifts of God are blessings, but when they begin to loom so large that they hide the Giver, they become impediments, and must either be surrendered or relegated to their rightful place.

Another god that is occupying the hearts of a great many people is pleasure. Many people are pleasure-mad. They live only for pleasure. They toil, some of them even restricting their use of nourishing food and good books to the end that they may have wherewith to gratify their desire for amusement, entertainment, excitement. The theatre, the picture show, the dance hall, and other places of diversion have as devotees not only worldlings; even many professing Christians worship more at these shrines than they do in the church.

Entertainment, pleasure, as an innocent diversion from the serious business of life, has a legitimate place in life. We advocate no gloomy view of life. The Puritan, who replied to his nephew, descanting, as they walked to church on a lovely spring morning, on the beauties of nature, "Aye, aye, sir, but this is not the day to speak of such things," did not have the right conception. God is the centre of all beauty, as He is the centre of all goodness. But the heart must not rest in the creature. It must be led by the beauty of the creature to the greater loveliness of the Creator. And the mad chaser after pleasure, much of it of very low type if not actually vulgar and demoralizing, gradually loses his appreciation of the higher beauties of the world and the nobler pleasures of life.

Many people enshrine other persons in that place in their hearts which God of right should occupy. Human beings ought all to love one another with a love much greater than usually exists. Even in the usual family circle there is room for improvement in this respect. However, not infrequently men go to the other extreme: we find parents or children, husbands or wives whose whole wealth of affection is centered in some person, who thus takes God's place. And how often we have heard these persons complain with bitterness of God's treatment when disease or death laid its hand on the object of affection. This is idolatry. And of such Jesus says: "He that loveth father or mother more than me is not worthy of me: and he that loveth son or daughter more than me, is not worthy of me" (St. Matth. 10, 37).

Sometimes it is not love but fear that leads one person to render to another the deference that God only should receive. Peter was guilty of such idolatry when he denied Christ. In his heart at that moment not Christ was God but Caiaphas. Any person who fawns before another and lies or otherwise sins in order to win his favor, virtually makes the person thus feared and served his god.

The adulation of the rich and the aping of their ofttimes silly manner, expressed by the unseemly conduct to which men will stoop in order to win their notice, is another species of idolatry of which many are guilty.

Perhaps the most frequent idol put in the place of God is the little god, self. How many are trusting solely to their own wisdom, shrewdness, strength! Their own advantage and honor are the only things of which they think. God is never thought of save, perhaps, as a far-off shadow. If these people ever think of a future life, they rely on their own merit to ensure their safety. But when they come with their wonted confidence to God's judgment seat, they shall hear the disappointing words, "Depart from me, I never knew you."

These are but a few of a long list of idols which men everywhere are serving. As Luther says, "That upon which you set your heart, and in which you trust is properly your god." But, remember, it is with these idols as it is with the images made as professed objects of worship: God will not share the throne of man's heart with any of these things. God says we cannot serve two masters. And He is not going to be one of two or more deities that men try to serve.

God's claims are very high. It is nothing less than this that we fear, love, and trust in Him above all things. He asks to be first in our thoughts, first in our affections, to subordinate to Him all else. In this we have all failed to a greater or less degree. How shall the failure be made good? In only one way. Jesus Christ fulfilled this supreme commandment. When He becomes our Savior, His fulfillment of the Law becomes our fulfillment.

"Thou shalt worship the Lord, thy God; and Him only shalt thou serve." "Little children keep yourselves from idols" (1 John 5, 21).

THE USE OF GOD'S HOLY NAME

"Thou shalt not take the name of the Lord thy God in vain; for the Lord will not hold him guiltless that taketh His name in vain." — EXODUS 20, 7.

WE take up for study to-day the Second Commandment. A glance should suffice to show its close relation to the first. God has been standing before us in the awe-inspiring grandeur of His person. "I am the Lord thy God." He demands that we banish all false ideas of Himself and all worship of false, imaginary gods, which would steal away the honour due Himself, the true, the living God. "Thou shalt have no other gods before Me." But who is this God who speaks with such authority? What is His nature and His disposition? This we learn from His names and His works, as they are given us in His Word. When this commandment, therefore, requires us to honour God's name, it is the same as requiring us to honour God Himself; for we cannot separate God's name from His Person, as in the case of human beings.

Men everywhere recognize the propriety of honouring the names of those who have distinguished themselves in working for human progress. Those who have wrought thus unselfishly for the public good are gratefully remembered. Their names are inscribed on the pages of history and cherished by those who have profited by their labours. Monuments of various kinds are erected, often at public expense, to perpetuate the memory of their deeds and kindle the spirit of emulation. The names of Washington and Lincoln will be thus cherished while this great nation exists. In the sphere of religious effort, the names of men like Luther, Livingston, and others, will be kept alive while the Church of God continues to preach the Gospel of a crucified Christ and to win men from darkness to light. These men have long since been gathered to their fathers, but their names still live and are capable of inspiring those who follow them with a higher courage, a steadier purpose, and a more fervent zeal.

How much more universally ought the holy name of God be remembered. In a much greater degree it ought to inspire us all to everything that is holiest and best. There are some on whom it has this effect. No one, however, reverences God's name so fully as he ought. Many forget and neglect it. And many use this holy name only to dishonor it. Before all such stands Jehovah the God of Sinai, saying: "I am the Lord thy God; thou shalt not take the name of the Lord thy God in vain."

In the study of this Second Commandment, let us keep in mind this leading thought — the Use of God's Holy Name.

There are three points of emphasis upon which we shall dwell: God's holy name; the abuse, and the reverent use of God's holy name.

God's Holy Name

How small, how insignificant, do those who know most of God, His works, and ways, feel when they draw near the Divine Presence. The great Gospel prophet was once given a vision of heavenly things. In that vision, he saw the princely angels, with covered faces, round about the throne, shouting back and forth: "Holy, holy, holy is the Lord of hosts: the whole earth is full of His glory" (Isa. 6, 3). The natural feeling of all purified hearts is that of holy awe, which inclines to adoring silence in the Great Presence or speaks with greatest circumspection.

God dwells in a light to which no man can approach. When it shone forth in the incarnate Son on the Mount of Transfiguration, it blinded the beholders. It is by the avenue of His names that we approach, as near as possible for man, to the presence and knowledge of God. Each work of God, each expression of His will, serves the purpose of helping to reveal some feature of His manifold nature. He is El, the mighty One; Eloah, the One to be feared; El Shaddai, the omnipotent One; Adonai, the owner, the ruler, the Lord. He is the tender Shepherd, the watchful guardian and keeper of his people. The attributive words just, holy, merciful, gracious, loving, truthful, and many others too numerous to mention, are revelations of the nature of God. They are not mere titles, but descriptive names. No one name, nor yet the combined names of God, can ever exhaust the riches of His Being. As no space can confine God, so no name comprehensive to man is capable of containing Him. The heaven of heavens cannot contain God, how much less a word, however expressive. But from the sum of God's names as He has revealed them in His Word, we gain all needed knowledge of His person and nature.

There is one name of God on which we desire especially to dwell. It is the name not unknown to God's people of the Old Testament, but which received its true significance for humanity only as it fell from the lips of Jesus Christ, who is both God's Son and our brother. It is the name — Father, "Our Father who art in heaven." The ancient nations gave high-sounding names to their gods. But from high heaven alone was given to the prodigal, homesick sons and daughters of men this name of God so full, so sweet, so satisfying — the precious name, Father. We may be fatherless and motherless, but we need not be without One who will be more than father and mother to his children. And His embrace will be all the more tender and satisfying because of our forlornness. This name, Father, does not repel, but attracts. Before our Father-God we still stand in awe and prostrate ourselves in adoration; but we may still draw very near to Him, pour out our wants into His ear, put our hands confidingly in His and feel the breath of His benediction on our fevered brows.

There is only one name of God which comes to the ears of mortals with, if possible, a shade of sweeter meaning than even that of Father. It is the Father's name for His other self, the name of His Son — Jesus, Saviour. Over two hundred names and titles are given to the Son of God in Scripture. Each adds something toward filling in the outline of that sublime figure which, for two thousand years, has been the dominant force in the world's history. But of all the pictures presented, the one which appeals most to the weary, way-faring children of men is that in which the Mighty Son of God stands, with outstretched hands, and pleading voice, entreating them to come unto Him for healing and rest; for He is Jesus — Saviour.

Such is the very brief outline of what is meant by the name of God in the Second Commandment. Of this name He says: "Thou shalt not take the name of the Lord thy God in vain." In spite of all warnings against it, there are many who misuse God's name. Let us, therefore, also consider:

The Vain Use of God's Holy Name

In the explanation of the Second Commandment, Luther says: "We should fear and love God that we may not curse, swear, use witchcraft, lie or deceive by His name."

With respect to cursing, or profanity, it ought not to be necessary to speak in any decent, cultured community. Profanity is not only a great sin, but an unmistakable evidence of ignorance and innate coarseness of character as well. Good manners ought to keep people from cursing even if they have no religion. There was a time when bluster and profanity were thought to be distinguishing marks of a gentleman. Fortunately, that type has somewhat decreased. To-day, only boys with immature bodies, who would be considered men; and men with immature minds, are given to profanity. Not only is profanity heard in the foolish form of brag and bluster; but many men, in passion, still call on the holy name of the loving God, asking Him to damn their fellowmen. If a Christian, in weakness, should so far forget himself, his manners, as well as his religion, as blasphemously to use the name of God, there is but one right thing for him to do, and that is, like Peter, to go out into solitude and repent with shame and bitter tears. With respect to this very sin the Lord says to us, through the Apostle James: "With the tongue bless we God, even the Father; and therewith curse we men, which are made after the similitude of God. Out of the same mouth proceedeth blessing and cursing. My brethren, these things ought not so to be" (James 3, 9, 10). Even under the greatest provocation the true child of God seeks to live on a higher plane. Christ places before us an ideal which makes profanity impossible even under the most trying circumstances. "Love your enemies, bless them that curse you, do good to them that hate you, and pray for them that despitefully use you, and persecute you, that ye may be the children of your Father which is in heaven" (St. Matth. 5, 44, 45). As for those who have made no Christian profession and own no allegiance to God, we wish that every time they thus dishonor God's name there might be some one standing near with the courage to repeat God's threat against such blasphemy: "The Lord will not hold him guiltless that taketh His name in vain." In olden times those who blasphemed God's holy name were stoned to death. This form of punishment has been removed, but the same guilt remains; and God will see that it does not remain unpunished.

The improper use of the oath is another way in which God's name is frequently taken in vain. Taking the oath, or swearing, is calling God to witness that we speak the truth. This is permissible, as the Word of God plainly shows, under justifiable circumstances; for instance, if the glory of God or our neighbor's welfare is thereby enhanced, or if the civil authority or the duties of office require it.

Under all circumstances, the taking of an oath is a serious matter. In the most solemn way, Almighty God, the holy and true, is called upon to be a witness and a party to a transaction. By all that is holiest in heaven, men pledge their good name, their honor, in taking the oath. And it is recognized everywhere that he who will not be held to the path of truth and honesty by such considerations, is utterly devoid of all sense of obligation or honor. And yet perjury, or false swearing, is not uncommon. Men dare thus to outrage God's Holy name and risk a sentence in the penitentiary at the same time. One of the causes contributing to this condition, we are convinced, is the frequency with which the oath is used. The government requires the oath with entirely too much frequency and for purposes for which a simple affirmation should suffice. All kinds of human organizations pledge their members by the most horrible kinds of oaths to do things and refrain from things, of which they know absolutely nothing when the oath is taken. In a business transaction, where only a few dollars, or it may be only a few pennies, are at stake, men use the holy name of God in appealing to the truth of their assertion or the honesty of their dealing. In this way, men have made the oath a common thing; and, as with most other things made common, men think but little of its sacredness.

Not till God, in His greatness, His holiness, His unswerving justice, becomes once more a living reality to men; not till men learn to tremble, as they ought, when God speaks; not till men stand humble and devout before God's throne, not till then will men refrain from swearing to their souls' hurt. But let those who will not be restrained know that God says: "Ye shall not swear by my name falsely, neither shalt thou profane the name of thy God" (Lev. 19, 12). And Jesus speaks so decisively against all useless, foolish swearing that some have understood Him to be prohibiting all swearing. Listen to Him, and tremble as you think of His judgment, ye who have sworn falsely or foolishly: "I say unto you, swear not at all: neither by heaven, for it is God's throne; nor by the earth, for it is His footstool; neither by Jerusalem, for it is the city of the great King. Neither shalt thou swear by thy head, because thou canst not make one hair white or black. But let your communication be: Yea, yea; nay, nay; for whatsoever is more than these cometh of evil" (St. Matth. 5, 34-37).

A useless or foolish oath, taken thoughtlessly or in a moment of weakness, ought not to be kept. To do so, is to heap sin upon sin, as did Herod, who, under the influence of a foolish oath, supplemented it with murder—beheading John the Baptist.

The time when they burned witches is long since past; but the subject of witchcraft, of which the Catechism speaks, in explaining the Second Commandment, is not, on that account, antiquated. If we do not have witchcraft in the old form, the principle still lives. The devil is too wise, and too active, to allow anything which will harm the souls of men to fall by the way. He always finds a substitute for the old evils or brings them out in a new guise to catch the unwary.

Spiritism is one of the modern forms of witchcraft. It professes to do wonders, and to do it in the name of God. Much of it has been proven a humbug. But it may not all be so. In Bible times there were men and women who did wonderful things through the power of the devil. And there is no Biblical reason for denying that they can do so now. But whatever temporary advantage might accrue through the use of such an agency or any other like it, the true child of God recoils in horror from the thought; for witchcraft is not only an employment of Satanic power, but it is frequently performed in the name of the holy God. All this is strictly forbidden. "There shall not be found among you anyone that * * * useth divination, or an observer of times, or an enchanter, or a witch, or a charmer, or a consulter of familiar spirits, or a wizard, or a necromancer. For all that do these things are an abomination unto the Lord" (Deut. 18, 10-12).

And even though some such dark power be directed against us, we need have no fear; it can go no farther than God permits, and He never allows anything to come upon his children that He can not work into a blessing for them (Rom. 8, 28). Let us but learn to know God well and to walk in fellowship with Him through Christ, and we shall neither want the help of any other power, nor fear the worst it can do. "He that dwelleth in the secret place of the Most High shall abide under the shadow of the Almighty. I will say of the Lord, He is my refuge and my fortress; my God, in Him will I trust" (Ps. 91, 1, 2).

The lying and deceiving of which this commandment speaks as a vain use of God's name is not the lying of which the Eighth Commandment tells us. This falsification is that in which God's name and honor are specially involved. It is such lying as that of which Jacob was guilty when he deceived his blind father, and assured him that the Lord had helped him to do what he was doing (Gen. 27, 20). It is such deception as that of which men are guilty when they lie and say: "The Lord knows I am speaking the truth." It is the kind of lying and deception of which men and women are guilty when they say, We are God's children, and go to church on Sunday, but live as the devil's children all the week. It is the kind of deception of which men are guilty, when they profess to be teachers of God's Holy Word and guides for men on the way of life, but so twist and emasculate this Word that God Himself could scarcely recognize it. Dowieism,

Eddyism and Russellism are but recent striking examples of this perversion of God's truth. This perversion of God's truth is the very thing of which God speaks when He says: "Behold I am against the prophets, saith the Lord, that use their tongues, and say: He saith. Behold I am against them that prophesy false dreams, saith the Lord, and do tell them, and cause my people to err by their lies, and by their lightness; yet I sent them not, nor commanded them: therefore they shall not profit this people at all, saith the Lord" (Jer. 23, 31, 32).

The Reverent Use of God's Holy Name

If men rightly knew God and were rightly disposed toward Him, there could be no other than a reverential use of His name. This is the point, then, that ought to be of special interest to us Christian people. God is not satisfied if we keep from using His name in vain; that is, thoughtlessly, flippantly, or with malice. God wants us to use His name, but to use it as his dear children — reverently, lovingly.

When God appeared to Moses on Horeb in the burning bush, and Moses started to draw near, God stayed him and said: "Put off thy shoes from off thy feet, for the place whereon thou standest is holy ground." Speech also is to have its holy ground — and the holy of holies for the tongue is when the name of God is used. In the spirit of awe we should use God's holy name. It is a sacred, a blessed name. The Jews, in former times at least, would not step on a piece of paper lying on the street, for fear the name of God might be written on it. Would to God there was more of this reverence for His name among men today!

Not to use God's name at all is a violation of this prohibition: "Not take * * * in vain." The person who never reads God's Word, never joins in singing His praise, never prays, is constantly breaking this Second Commandment of the Law. The Jews, in the olden time, because of a misunderstanding of Leviticus 24, 16, which speaks of blaspheming God's name, refused to repeat at all the name of Jehovah, known as the "Revealed Name" of God. And they used various substitutes for this name. Such a mechanical expedient is not what God wants, but it showed care to avoid misuse of God's holy name; a care all men should exercise in the right manner. It was Jesus Christ, the King of heaven, the Prince of the sons of men, who taught men to bow their heads and say, in words which should breathe the deepest purpose: "Hallowed be Thy name."

We should call on God in trouble. Men may be sympathetic and helpful. But help is needed which God alone can give. "Call upon Me in the day of trouble. I will deliver thee, and thou shalt glorify Me" (Ps. 50, 15). When trouble threatens, of whom do we think first? Too often God is the last person of whom we think. And we should intercede with God not only for ourselves, but for others as well. "I exhort, therefore, that, first of all, supplications, prayers, intercessions, and giving of thanks, be made for all men" (1 Tim. 2, 1).

In days of health and prosperity; indeed, at

all times, for all days are good days for the child of God, we should use God's name in praise and thanksgiving. "Bless the Lord, O my soul; and all that is within me bless His holy name. Bless the Lord, O my soul, and forget not all His benefits" (Ps. 103, 1, 2). This was the song of the Psalmist, and it is the song of every true child of God.

With respect to all violations of this Second Commandment, whether by using God's name wrongfully, or not using it at all, God says: "Thou shalt not take the name of the Lord thy God in vain." This is a word with which men may not trifle. Assuredly, if God is going to sit in judgment on every idle word men speak, as Christ says (St. Matthew 12, 36), He cannot overlook or fail to punish the vain use of His name. He says: "The Lord will not hold him guiltless that taketh His name in vain." "Not guiltless," that means literally, not clean. The man who does not live up to God's requirements is morally unclean. We often speak of the man who is honest in his business relations, who is true to his wife, who is guarded in his language, as a man of good moral character. But he is only relatively or humanly so. In its final analysis, the test of moral cleanness is man's relationship to God and His laws. Until a man's heart is right toward God he is not truly a moral man. He has cut himself off from the very fountain head of morality, or true, full life. And guilt, whatever its nature or degree, means penalty.

On the other hand, no use of God's name which is only of the lips is a reverent use. In form it may be perfectly correct, but unless it comes from the lips of those who actually acknowledge God's kingship over their hearts and lives, it is not a reverent use. Jesus tells us of those who shall say: "Lord, Lord, have we not prophesied in thy name? and in thy name have cast out devils? and in thy name done many wonderful works? And then will I profess unto them, I never knew you, depart from me, ye that work iniquity" (St. Matt. 7, 22, 23). Only those who have faith in God and love for Him can use His name with reverence.

Not one of us, no man living, has met to the full the requirements of this commandment. What is to be done about it? In the sixth chapter of Isaiah, the prophet tells us of a vision of heavenly things. After seeing it, he cried out: "Woe is me! for I am undone; because I am a man of unclean lips, and I dwell in the midst of a people of unclean lips." Then an angel of heaven came, having a live coal, which he placed on the prophet's mouth, and said: "Lo, this hath touched thy lips, and thine iniquity is taken away, and thy sin purged." Jesus Christ is the living coal of God's giving. When He touches our hearts, our iniquities of speech and every other kind are taken away, our sin purged. With Him in our hearts, we are the temples of God, and the godly words that come from our lips rise as incense to the glory of God.

GOD'S HOLY DAY

"Remember the sabbath day, to keep it holy. Six days shalt thou labor, and do all thy work: but the seventh day is the sabbath of the Lord thy God: in it thou shalt not do any work, thou, nor thy son, nor thy daughter, thy manservant, nor thy maidservant, nor thy cattle, nor thy stranger that is within thy gates: for in six days the Lord made heaven and earth, the sea, and all that in them is, and rested the seventh day: wherefore the Lord blessed the sabbath day, and hallowed it." — Exod. 20, 8-11.

MOST of you, I trust, remember the lessons of the catechetical class. Indeed, you should have advanced much in your knowledge of God's Word since then. However, if you remember but so much as you then learned you will recall that the commandments are divided into two tables. The first three commandments form the First Table. These treat of man's direct, personal relation to God Himself.

In all the commandments it is God who is speaking to us. But in these three He tells us how we are to treat Him personally. We are to have no other gods. He, our Creator, the author of all our blessings, claims our adoration. He demands the highest thoughts of our minds, the deepest love of our hearts, our truest service. We are not to profane His holy name. We may use it: indeed, we are to use it, but not abuse it. In the Third Commandment this direct personal relationship is still maintained. We are here reminded of the necessity of a day wherein to contemplate in a direct and undisturbed way, the exalted person and works of God. The Second and Third Commandments are but a continuation, or development, of the First; giving occasion for the elaboration and application of the truths therein contained.

As the subject of our study this morning, let us consider:

God's Holy Day

There are three points we will discuss as briefly as clearness will permit: they are, the Primitive and Mosaic Sabbaths, and the Lord's Day.

I. THE PRIMITIVE SABBATH. At the close of the account of creation, Gen. 2, 2, 3, the inspired writer says: "And on the seventh day God ended His work which He had made; and He rested on the seventh day from all His work which He had made. And God blessed the seventh day, and sanctified it; because that in it He had rested from all His works which He had made." This was the establishment of the Primitive Sabbath, called also the Paradasaic, and the Pre-Mosaic Sabbath.

There are those who question whether there ever was a Sabbath before Sinai. Their chief arguments are, first, that it is not expressly stated, in the account in Genesis, that it was a day for man's observance; in the second place, that there is no further mention of the day until the giving of the Sinaitic covenant; and, finally, that the institution of the Sabbath at Sinai is sufficient proof that no such day was observed before. We submit that there is some weight in these arguments, but not sufficient to counter-balance the arguments against them.

The words in Genesis about God resting on the seventh day, and blessing it, and sanctifying it, can have no meaning comprehensible to us, aside from this that it was to be an example for man's imitation. God did not need a day of rest for Himself. "The everlasting God fainteth not, neither is weary" (Isa. 40, 28). He set apart the day and blessed it for man's use, as a day of rest and worship. This is the view of many of the greatest theologians. It is Luther's view. He says: "These words (namely in Gen. 2) were written alone for us. When God worked six days and rested the seventh, He had it recorded for our sakes, that we should do as He had done." Again Luther says: "This day was ordained for Adam before he fell into sin; are we to understand, then, that it was to apply to him after he fell into sin? There is no doubt about it. Adam was to work in the Garden of Eden before the fall, as well as he had to work afterwards. The only difference being that in the one instance the work was a pleasure, a delight; in the other it was attended with so much weariness that it became a thorn in the flesh. In like manner was Adam to observe the Sabbath before and after the fall. The only difference being that in his fallen condition he needed the day for bodily rest more than he did before."

It seems that this is unmistakably substantiated by the words of the Mosaic law contained in our text. The ground here given for setting apart the seventh day as the Jewish Sabbath is the identical one contained in the creation record. If the Jewish people needed a special day of rest and worship, the children of God in the earlier days needed it: and there were children of God in those earlier days. Further, if an appeal to the Hebrews to observe the Sabbath on the ground of God's cessation of active creative work on that day, and His act of sanctifying it, would have a salutary effect two thousand years after the event, would it not have the same, or a greater force soon after the creation? The Sabbath was to be kept by the Hebrews in remembrance of God's creative work and after the example of His rest. This injunction and the reasons assigned would apply to the earlier people as well as to Israel.

It is true, that between the statement in Genesis about God's resting on the seventh day and sanctifying it, and the giving of the Law at Sinai, with its Third Commandment, there is no express mention of the Sabbath. There is, however, much evidence showing that there was a constantly recurring seventh day observed by at least some of the people. And it is best accounted for by the supposition that the people retained some knowledge of the Sabbath ordained by God (Gen. 7, 4; 8, 10-12; 29, 27; 50, 10).

The claim that the institution of the Mosaic Sabbath is sufficient evidence that no such day existed previously, is answered by the remainder that all the commandments given at Sinai had been given before; they had been written in man's heart. They were natural laws. There is no valid reason why the Sabbath should be an exception. It was a law of man's nature, reinforced by God's precept and example, that he rest and worship on the seventh day. But sin, as in all other things pertaining to God and Divine things, largely obliterated in the course of time the knowledge of the Sabbath and its observance. At Sinai the Law was repeated and emphasized. This, it appears, is contained in the word of the commandment itself — remember — "remember the Sabbath day."

Another proof confirming the existence of the pre-Mosaic Sabbath we find in the traces of the Sabbath existing among nearly all the ancient nations, such as the Persians, Assyrians and others. A tablet was recently found on the site of ancient Ninevah that is supposed to be as old as the founding of Israel in the time of Abraham. This takes us back more than five hundred years before the giving of the Law at Sinai. This old tablet speaks of the Sabbath, and gives the word in practically its Biblical form. How do we account for this save on the ground that all the ancient peoples knew, by tradition, and at least faintly, of God's original Sabbath established in Paradise.

If we turn to Exodus 16, we find that the children of Israel observed the Sabbath a month, probably many months, before they came to Sinai. It was doubtless the old creation Sabbath they were observing, which was soon to be so strikingly reestablished as a part of the written law of Israel.

Jesus said to the Jews of His day: "The Sabbath was made for man, and not man for the Sabbath" (St. Mark 2, 27). The Sabbath was to serve man. In its observance man was to achieve his highest physical and spiritual good. Was God careless of the good of man till the Jewish people came on the scene? Assuredly not. The Sabbath was not alone for the Jews, it was for humanity, so far as its essential nature and purpose is concerned.

It may be said that this question of a primitive Sabbath is one of little importance. I am not ready to grant that it is so. It is associated with a problem of great importance. I am convinced, by Bible teaching and the history of nations, that a seventh day for rest and worship is part of God's plan for the world and has been so from the beginning; that the Third Commandment is but an expression of that which is needed by the very constitution of man, and that he, consequently, can reach his highest physical and spiritual good only when this law of rest and worship is observed. And when we think that in Paradise God's first children, in their state of sinlessness, observed this day to their advantage, it helps to emphasize all the more our need, the world's need, of a day of rest and undisturbed communion with God.

II. THE MOSAIC SABBATH is the name given to the day of rest and worship reestablished at Sinai and observed by the Jewish people.

For twenty-five hundred years the children of men had experienced the vicissitudes of a sin-cursed life. God's chosen people had spent four hundred years in bondage. At the time of the giving of the Law they had been liberated, and were to be established in a land of their own, where they were to become a great nation. One of the first things

God did for them was to reestablish the Sabbath. Let us not forget that one of the ten laws, written by the finger of God Himself, was this Third Commandment reestablishing for the Jewish people, as a national institution, the day of rest and worship.

The Sabbath was to be to the Jewish people, as our text clearly shows, a constant memorial of God's creative power and goodness. At all times, but especially on the day when man is enabled to escape from the absorbing and exhausting round of daily toil, his thoughts should be led to contemplate the greatness and the goodness of God. The diversified wonders and beauties of the earth; the towering mountain peaks, the fertile valleys, the broad spreading plains, the dazzling wonders of the starry heavens — all these things should lead man's thoughts to the great Workman whose handiwork they are.

In addition to being a constant reminder of God's creative work, and of His resting therefrom, the Sabbath was to be to the Jews a reminder of God's faithfulness in delivering them from their bondage. In Deuteronomy five, where the commandments are again recorded, it says: "Remember that thou wast a servant in the land of Egypt, and the Lord thy God brought thee out thence through a mighty hand and an outstretched arm; therefore the Lord thy God commanded thee to keep the Sabbath." There is no contradiction in the two accounts of the giving of the Law, or in the two things of which the Sabbath was to be a memorial. To all men it was to be a memorial of the creative power and goodness of God. To the Jews, in addition, it was to be a memorial of their deliverance from Egypt; of the wonders God wrought to soften Pharaoh's heart, the passage of the Red Sea, the pillars of fire and cloud, of the food miraculously given, and the like, all of which was to call forth their joyous praise and their most heartfelt thanksgiving.

The Sabbath was to the Jews a constantly recurring reminder of the covenant God had made with them. He had promised them an earthly, national inheritance. Through them also the Redeemer was to be given to the world. Through faith in this Redeemer they were to find grace, pardon and salvation. Of these and other related promises the Sabbath was to be a perpetual reminder: "My Sabbaths ye shall keep; for it is a sign between me and you throughout your generations, that ye may know that I am the Lord that doth sanctify you" (Exod. 31, 13).

We should not forget that the Jewish Sabbath was also largely a day of rest, a rest in which servants and even beasts of burden participated. The general activities of life ceased. So strictly were the Sabbatic regulations enforced that, at times at least, gross violations were punished with death. But after all, the Sabbath was a day of rest that it might be above all a day of worship. Just what form this worship took in the early days we do not know. But essentially no doubt it was much like the worship of God's children in all other ages; for, fundamentally, man's needs are always the same. The general description of the worship of God's people as given in Deuteronomy thirty-one would apply to our worship in this modern day. "When all Israel is come to appear before the Lord thy God in the place which He shall choose, thou shalt read this law before all Israel in their hearing. Gather the people together, men and women, and children, and the stranger that is within thy gates, that they may hear, and that they may learn, and fear the Lord your God, and observe to do all the words of this law."

III. THE LORD'S DAY. The Jewish Sabbath, so far as a particular day was concerned, and many of the observances therewith connected, was of a ceremonial or temporary character. When they had fulfilled their purpose they came to an end. St. Paul tells us these things were shadows of better things to come. When Christ, who was the One foreshadowed, came the shadow passed away (Gal. 4, 5; Col. 2, 16, 17). But while the ceremonial elements passed away, the moral element, the obligation to worship God, remained. There is to be a day, a seventh day, devoted to rest and the special worship of Almighty God.

In the New Testament there is no trace of a particular ordinance changing the Jewish Sabbath into the Lord's day. Neither did Christ say when He instituted Baptism and the Lord's Supper, that these institutions were to take the place of Circumcision and the Passover. He simply instituted the New Testament sacraments, and the old gradually fell away. So it was with the Lord's day. He simply informally consecrated a new day, and the old gradually fell into disuse.

On the cross Christ said: "It is finished." All types and prophecies were then fulfilled. Redemption was an accomplished fact. A new era was ready to dawn. Jesus rested in the grave after His great work; rested till after the Sabbath was past. Then He came forth on the first day of the week, the author of a new, a spiritual creation. The shadows had passed away, for the Sun of righteousness had arisen. The sorrow which had filled the hearts of the disciples gave way to a boundless joy. They now began to understand the Savious and His mission. This understanding was completed on Pentecost, and the power to apply it was given at the same time. A holy, burning love filled their hearts; a love which could lead only to worship and to service. This desire to worship naturally brought the disciples together. And in their minds there was but one appropriate time for this united service, a time which Providence had been indicating from the very first — the day of Christ's resurrection, the first day of the week. Was it not on this day that He arose and first appeared to them? Did He not appear a week later to drive away the doubts of which one of the apostles was not able to rid himself? Was it not on the same weekly anniversary of the day of the resurrection that the miraculous gift of the Holy Spirit was bestowed? Were not all their joys and their hopes centered in the facts which this day commemorated?

Some say it was the Church which selected the Lord's day as the special day of worship. In a sense, yes; but in a higher, truer sense it was God Himself. God's providence, which regulates or overrules the minute affairs of our every-day life, was not absent in this important step in the Church's history. God gave us our Lord's day, not by an act of special institution, but by His special providence in guiding his disciples. And we would not be justified in changing the day save by another providential guidance equally clear. This is supported by Scripture evidence lacking, to my mind, very little of the strength of a direct institution. In addition to the reiterated Gospel statements about Christ's rising on the first day of the week, appearing to the apostles once and again on that day, and sending the special enduement of the Holy Spirit on that day, there are many statements in later books of the Bible indicating that the Lord's day was observed as a special day of worship during the lives of the apostles. In Acts twenty, St. Paul tells us that the Christian congregation at Troas assembled on the Lord's day to celebrate the Lord's Supper. In his first Epistle to the Corinthians (16, 1, 2) the same apostle, speaking of the collection for the poor at Jerusalem, gives this direction, which he says he had previously given to the church in Galatia: "Upon the first day of the week let every one of you lay by him in store as the Lord hath prospered him." Again, in Rev. 1, 10, St. John says: "I was in the spirit on the Lord's day." These passages, while not discussing the question of the institution or particular observance of the Lord's day, clearly indicate its general observance.

It is interesting also to hear what the earliest church fathers have to say on this subject. Ignatius, the disciple of St. John, tells us that those who had arrived at a newness of hope, no longer observed the Sabbath, "but lived according to the Lord's life." Justin Martyr, who lived about the middle of the second century, says: "On the day called Sunday, there is an assembly of all who live either in the city or in the rural districts, and memoirs of the apostles and the writings of the prophets are read." Dyonisius, bishop of Rome, who lived near the close of the second century, says, in a letter addressed to the congregation at Rome: "Today we kept the Lord's holy day, in which we read your letters." The record of Iranæus, bishop of Lyons, writing about the same time, says: "The mystery of the Lord's resurrection may not be celebrated on any other than the Lord's day, and on this day alone should we observe the breaking of the sacred bread." In the second year of the third century Tertullian wrote: "Sunday we give to holy joy; we have nothing to do with Sabbaths or other Jewish festivals." And in the early part of the fourth century Constantine, by imperial edict, made Sunday the day of rest and worship for the Roman Empire.

Thus we see that the day we observe, our Lord's day, can be traced back, step by step, to the day of Christ's resurrection. It came into general observance in the Church, not by the decrees of synods, or imperial edicts; but by the leading of God's Spirit. Every day, to the child of God, is a Lord's day, a day for worship; still there is a special day of rest and worship, and of it we may truly sing:

"This is the day the Lord hath made,
He calls the hours His own;
Let heaven rejoice, let earth be glad,
And praise surround the throne.

"Today He rose and left the dead,
And Satan's empire fell;
Today the saints His triumph spread,
And all His wonders tell."

THE PROPER OBSERVANCE OF THE LORD'S DAY

"Remember the Sabbath day to keep it holy." — EXOD. 20, 8.

"The Sabbath was made for man, and not man for the Sabbath." — ST. MARK 2, 27.

"And let us consider one another to provoke unto love and to good works: not forsaking the assembling of ourselves together, as the manner of some is; but exhorting one another: and so much the more, as ye see the day approaching." — HEB. 10, 24, 25.

THE day of rest and worship, as it has been observed from the creation to the present time, we have already considered. This subject, considered from the viewpoint chiefly of the day itself, is one of no slight importance. The very fact that for all these thousands of years there has been a day so observed gives great weight to every plea for its proper continuance and observance. But after all it is not the day in itself which is the matter of chief importance. It is to serve a purpose, and that purpose is the chief concern. Christ says: "The Sabbath is for man, and not man for the Sabbath." This means that the Sabbath was not a day set apart to be observed for the sake of the day. If there were no people to be served there would be no Sabbath. This day was given to promote man's good. The same applies to the Lord's day. It is a measure of time just as any other day, a day consecrated by many sacred memories; but its object is to bring these things to man's attention, that he may be blessed through their acceptance. The Proper Observance of the Lord's Day is the important subject to which we shall give our attention at this time.

The Lord's Day as a Day of Rest.

That the Sabbath, in both its pre-Mosaic and Mosaic forms, was in part a day of rest, we remember. This means that it was to be preceded by days of toil and burden-bearing. In the true sense of the word there can be no rest till men have borne the burden and heat of the day. That this is contained in the Third Commandment many do not seem to remember. The commandment as given to the Jews says: "Six days shalt thou labour, and do all thy work."

Many people look upon work as a curse, and one of their ideals of life is a state of freedom from toil. This is a perverted conception of life. God's plan for man is that he shall be a worker, even as He the everlasting God is Himself a worker. Sin has put the sting into toil and made it burdensome, but man's original state of innocency was one of blessed activity.

In the New Testament God's law respecting work is re-enacted. I speak of it as God's law because the expression of His will is law for his children. To certain people who, because of erroneous opinion, had become idle, the Lord through his apostle says: "We beseech you * * * work with your own hands, as we commanded you; that ye may walk honestly toward them that are without, and that ye may have lack of nothing" (1 Thess. 4, 10-12). Again the Lord says to these same people: "When we were with you, this we commanded you, that if any would not work, neither should he eat" (2 Thess. 3, 10).

These and similar truths need to be brought forcibly home to a considerable portion of humanity. The dream of many is of a modern Arcadia where the cornucopia shall pour into the lap of idleness all the blessing of bountiful nature. Such people would have life to be one grand frolic. No condition would sooner bring ruin to the children of men. Work is necessary to man's well-being. This is so irrespective of the fact that this is his usual means of supporting his physical life. Work helps to impress the truth that life is real, life is earnest. Work helps to develop character; it is a blessing, not a curse. Work reminds the thinking workman of the fact that he is privileged to co-operate with the Master Workman in carrying out His plans for the general good of humanity. And if things were among men as they should be, no one, though he could command thousands of dollars, would be permitted to partake of God's bounty till he had first rendered some adequate service for that which he receives.

There is, however, a danger on the other side. Those who would have without working are many. But those in whom the spirit of greed is abnormally developed are also many. Urged on by the hope of gain, these people work every day if possible, and just as many hours each day as possible. And where possible, if they employ help, they require the same of them. To prevent us from bringing about our own undoing, God ordained a day of rest. The particular day made obligatory upon the Jews is not binding upon us; but God has led his people in the choice of a day, and it is still a seventh day.

Our physical welfare demands this regularly recurring day of the cessation of toil. The most practical and painstaking investigation has proven beyond a shadow of doubt that a man can accomplish more work in a given time, say a month or three months, and do it better, if he rests one day out of seven than if he works continuously. God wants us to work, but at the proper time He wants us to rest. He does not want us to become drudges, mere working machines. The person who works seven days a week instead of six will sooner or later have to pay the penalty in the form of physical ills. God knew what He was doing when He provided a day of rest for man. It was to meet a law of man's nature. And His motive was love for man, a desire to promote his well-being.

The labour problem is a burning one in our day. It is often asserted that the labouring class has turned against the Church. Perhaps no larger proportion of this class has turned against the Church than of any other. If the working man, as well as all other men, knows what is best for him, if he wants to keep his heritage of robust manhood, and manhood's vision of better things, let him not forget or despise God's ordinances, especially this pertaining to the Lord's day.

Those who make of the Lord's day a day of pleasure, in the pursuit of which they probably put more energy than they do in a day of toil, are not keeping it to their physical welfare.

On the other hand, when we speak of the Lord's day as a day of rest we do not mean a day of sleepy inactivity. People often make of the Lord's day an occasion for eating and drinking to excess. The result is that they do themselves much harm, far overbalancing the benefit derived from their rest. This helps to account for the well known fact that there are twice as many accidents happen in places of business on Monday as on any other day. For the Lord's day to be a day of rest it must not be a day of indulgence; and it need not be, indeed, it ought not be, a day of torpid inactivity.

Considered merely from the point of view of a day of rest, the Lord's day should be a time for looking at ourselves and the world from another angle than that of the daily round of toil. It is a time for special contemplation of what is back of all this phenomena of life, for the study of our deeper selves, of our whence and our whither, of our place in the sun. To do this in a reasonable way will not interfere with the proper observance of the day as a day of rest.

The Lord's Day as a Day of Worship

As a day of rest the Lord's day is worthy of our careful study. As such a gift of God it should inspire men to gratitude and thanksgiving. But where the chief emphasis is to be placed in the consideration of this commandment Luther well shows in his explanation of it. He says that it means that "we should fear and love God, that we may not despise preaching and His Word; but hold it sacred and gladly hear and learn it." In this explanation, as in so many others, Luther showed his masterly, I unhesitatingly say, his God-given wisdom. He knew that unless men truly loved God, honoured His Word, and from such motives kept His holy day, rules and regulations imposed from without would be in vain.

Israel in her days of worst hypocrisy and formalism had more stringent regulations for Sabbath observance than ever before. But there was always a way of getting around them when they wished so to do. And even when they outwardly kept the day God declared that He was not thereby honoured. The day was not rightly kept because the right motive was lacking.

The Lord's day may not be rightly kept though a man refrain from every form of activity. Many a person remains at home all day Sunday and imagines that he has properly kept the day. Inactivity and silence do not meet the requirements of this commandment. The Lord's day is not rightly kept till God is rightly honoured. This does not mean that the other six days may be so completely secularized that God need never be thought of during them. God is to be honoured every day. He is to be honoured in all things. In the daily toil of life. performed faithfully by a child of God, to the end that thereby His name may be glorified, and His plans furthered, God is truly honoured. The true child of God can not live through six busy, trying days without being impelled to find times, though they be but brief moments, in which to speak to his all-wise and all-loving Father. His own needs will drive him to this, also his sense of gratitude. But this is not all that our good requires, that God asks, and His honour demands. God is a universal sovereign. The honour of His name, the good of His cause among men, requires that He be publicly acknowledged, and publicly worshipped by his loyal, loving subjects. This is the side of obligation. But true worship is not wholly a matter of outer necessity. It is on the part of true worshippers equally a matter of inner compulsion. Our sense of need nowhere else to be supplied, our consciousness of dependance on the arm of the Almighty, the soul-craving which can be met only by fellowship with the Author of our being, these things impel to worship from within. And those of kindred spirit are drawn by the invisible bond of fellowship with God to unite in their supplication and adoration.

All this of which we have been speaking centres in the public worship on the Lord's day, though it is not confined to it. God has given us His holy Word, through which He speaks to us, through which we learn rightly to know Him. God has ordained that this Word, which is not only a Word giving instruction, but a Word bearing power to quicken dead souls, be publicly proclaimed. And that along with the reception of this truth, with its light and life giving power, there should be joined our sacrificial offerings of prayer, praise and adoration. And no one who habitually absents himself, without necessity, from the public services of God's house is keeping this Third Commandment which says: "Remember the Sabbath day to keep it holy." Such an one does not honour God because he does not honour God's Word.

There are instances in rural districts, in cases of sickness, and occasionally from other cause, where men are prevented from regularly participating in these public services. This need not keep one from meeting God's requirement as set forth in the Third Commandment. If one cannot meet with a congregation of the same faith, let him meet with the church in his own house. This is the way the Christians often did in the early days. Where but two or three are assembled in the name of God He is with them as truly as if they were assembled with a great congregation. And though a man be a stranger in a strange land, he need not be deprived of his spiritual privileges and blessings. God and one devout soul, in a closet or on a desert waste, meet all the requirements of the highest and most blessed service.

We need the Lord's day and its holy ministries aside from the direct spiritual blessings we receive at the time. We need it in order to be kept mindful of our relationships, in heaven and on earth. We need it to keep from becoming too much absorbed in the things of this world. It furnishes us equipment for the struggles of the week. We need patience, courage, vision, strength; these hours of communion with God, and contemplation of heavenly things, supply these much needed qualities. The light which the Lord's day throws upon the great problems of life serves as a perpetual reminder of the true meaning of the other six days of the week, and keeps us in preparation for the eternal Sabbath that awaits all the redeemed and purified children of God.

Pastors are often asked whether there are any rules by which the Christian may direct his general conduct on the Lord's day. There are no specific regulations beyond those we have already given. For the body it is to be a day of rest and recuperation. For the soul it is to be a day of instruction in the truths of God's Word, a day of worship, of holy meditation. Beyond this we have no specific directions. However, this is a safe general rule; the conduct of life on this day should not belie the profession we make with our lips. If one is truly spiritually minded, well instructed in the Word of God, living in fellowship with Christ, truly desirous of honouring God and of enjoying His blessings, it can be safely left to such a person's conscience as to the specific manner in which that portion of the Lord's day shall be spent which is not devoted to worship.

Those who are closely confined during the week, after having devoutly taken part in the services of God's house, need have no scruples as to the propriety of taking a quiet walk in the country, thus to enjoy the beauties of God's handiwork. With equal propriety a Christian may call on his friends or spend the time in reading useful books. If we have in our hearts the law of the indwelling Christ, the law of faith and the love begotten by faith; if we seek the rule of right living in God's Word, we will not go far amiss in our observance of the

Lord's day, or any other day. One thing is certain, people so influenced will not make of the Lord's day a day for idly gadding about, nor spend it in the mad chase after pleasure, nor make of it, if it can possibly be avoided, a day of toil. The tendency to make of the Lord's day a mere holiday is not in keeping with the teaching or spirit of God's holy Word.

It has always been observed that there is a close relationship between the manner of observing the Lord's day and the state of the Christian Church. Where God's holy day is sanctified; where it is observed as a day of prayer and praise, where the object of men is to get a better knowledge of God through the study of His holy Word, and God is honoured as the sovereign of men's hearts, there the Church will be found to be in a flourishing condition. But where the Lord's day becomes a Continental or Mexican holiday, a day of riotous pleasure, of fun and frivolity, there the Church loses its power. Indeed, it was observed by St. Augustine, almost fifteen hundred years ago, that when the Lord's day is not kept as a Lord's day it soon degenerates into a devil's day. There is usually more wickedness perpetrated on this day than on any other one of the seven. This is accounted for in part by the fact that more people are at leisure then than at any other time, and when not controlled by the Spirit of God soon fall into evil ways.

Parents, where and how do you spend the Lord's day? Are you, by word and example, showing how the Lord's day should be kept? Are you making it a day of brightness, one of the brightest of all the week? Are you leading the way to the house of God and to the family altar? Are you making it a day which sheds its benediction over all the other days of the week?

Parents, tell me where your boys and girls are on Sunday, and what they are doing, and we will be able to tell you with much accuracy the kind of characters they are cultivating, and the kind of men and women they will likely come to be. Those who have no reverence for the Lord's day, no love for the services of God's house, have no reverence for God Himself, no respect for His laws. And it is not difficult to tell to what end they will come, unless a change is made; for such people will have little regard for any human institutions or laws further than they can be made to serve their own selfish interests.

Human institutions have come and gone. The forms of even not a few Divine ordinances have changed. This is true, as to some of its non-essentials, of the day of rest and worship. But as to its essence and fundamental purpose the Sabbath has survived all changes. Men and nations with set purpose have sought to destroy it, but it has survived all onslaughts. It is not everywhere observed as it should be, but everywhere this day of days, this day of rest and worship, this day which God gave us for the rehabilitation of tired bodies and tried souls, speaks forth its benediction to the children of men; pointing them to the skies, and keeping them mindful of the fact that there remaineth a rest for the people of God — an eternal

Lord's day of uninterrupted and unmediated fellowship with the Lord of life and glory.

"Thine earthly Sabbaths, Lord, we love,
But there's a nobler rest above;
To that our longing souls aspire,
With ardent love and strong desire."

THE SUPREME DUTY OF MAN

"And one of the scribes came, and having heard them reasoning together, and perceiving that He had answered them well, asked Him, which is the first commandment of all? And Jesus answered him, the first of all the commandments is, Hear, O Israel; the Lord our God is one Lord: and thou shalt love the Lord thy God with all thy heart, and with all thy soul, and with all thy mind, and with all thy strength: this is the first commandment." — St. Mark 12, 28-30.

THE giving of the Ten Commandments leads us back into the dim, distant days of Old Testament history. They were given just about as long before the birth of Christ as it is since that central event of all history.

A question very much discussed in certain quarters, is the conception of the law of God, as embodied in the Ten Commandments, which the Israelites had at the time it was given them. How much did they see in the commandments? They probably did not see all that the world has been taught to see in them since that day. But there is a more profitable question for our consideration. It is this, what did God intend to convey through the commandments He gave? What did He expect men to come to see in His Law? Where shall we find the best answer to these questions? In the answer of the prince of teachers, Jesus Christ.

It is generally conceded that the Sermon on the Mount is, at least largely, an interpretation of the Moral Law. There Jesus shows us what the

Law means when it stands before us in the simple majesty of its God-given nature, stripped of all human embellishments, all mere externalities. And there we see more clearly than elsewhere that the Law itself deals with the inner life.

In our text Jesus gives us, in answer to a direct question, His interpretation of the First Table of the Law which we have just concluded. His is always the last word on any mooted question. As we have considered the Old Testament commandments, we will now consider the New Testament interpretation of the first three. It sets before us The Supreme Duty of Man: to love God supremely; to speak His name reverently; to worship Him becomingly.

Loving God Supremely

Two of the three commandments of the First Table are negative: "Thou shalt have no other gods before me." "Thou shalt not take the name of the Lord thy God in vain." Only the third is positive in nature: "Remember the Sabbath day to keep it holy." But Christ's interpretation of these commandments shows that man's supreme duty is not discharged when he has refrained from setting up for worship some false god, or when he has kept his lips from blasphemy. The supreme duty of man is to love God supremely.

"Master, which is the great commandment in the law?" This was a question warmly disputed by the Jewish theological leaders. These men had prepared a code of six hundred and thirteen commandments. And of these they said: "The words of the Rabbis are to be prized above those of the law, for the words of the law are both weighty and light; but the words of the Rabbis are all weighty." In other words, they put the laws of their own making above the laws of God. And concerning the place of first importance among these commandments there was a never-ceasing, and, at times, a very bitter, controversy. The three classes of commandments, to the one or the other of which was most frequently given the place of preeminence, were those having to do with Sabbath observance, the rite of circumcision, and the offering of sacrifices.

The Jewish theologians seemed to think that by such learned discussions they met all the requirements of the Law. In the same way a great many people, in all ages, seem to think that when they, with much firmness and logical acumen, have defended certain orthodox doctrines they have met all the requirements of these doctrines on themselves. The simple truth is that the requirements of no Divine truths have been met on our part by the mere fact that we profess acceptance of them, nor by our arguments on their behalf, however ably maintained. The demands of Divine truth on us, whatever its particular character, are met only when that truth has become a living reality in our souls, only when it has become a part of our life, and controls our living.

We shall not spend any time in seeking to find the particular motive which prompted the Jews to ask this question of Christ. Our concern is with Christ's answer: "Jesus answered Him, * * * thou shalt love the Lord thy God with all thy heart, and with all thy soul, and with all thy mind, and with all thy strength." This answer of Jesus, who fathomed the law as no one else ever did, was not new. Indeed, it is almost as old as the giving of the Law itself, being found in Deuteronomy the fifth chapter. And we have here a glimpse of the fact that in early Old Testament times the basis of the relationship of man to God was on a nearer level to that of the New Testament than many casual students suppose. But the Jewish people of Christ's time had so completely lost sight of this fundamental truth that it came with the force of a new revelation. And let us learn anew the oft repeated lesson that Christ's answer emphasizes; namely, that the heart of Christianity, as of ancient Judaism, was not in observances or repeating formulas, not in defending theses or pronouncing anathemas. These things are all right in their time and place. But the heart of Christianity is heart relationship to God. And heart relationship means affection. The right relationship between God and man is that which exists between a loving father and a beloved and affectionate child. Not only by the Lord's Prayer, but by the commandments also, "God would tenderly invite us to believe that He is our true Father, and that we are his true children, so that we may, with all boldness and confidence, entreat Him, as dear children entreat their dear father."

Here a truth is expressed that is sought for in vain in any other religious system than that of Revelation. God is conceived of under various forms, and as sustaining divers relations to man. The true God alone is known as a God of love and mercy; as a Father who wants children, not merely subjects.

God is not satisfied even if we do not run after other gods, if the love which belongs to Him is withheld. That would be a strange mother who would be satisfied to have her children, the children she bore in anguish and nurtured at her bosom, the children by whose sick-beds she spent so many sleepless nights, for whose good she offered so many prayers; I say it would be a strange mother who would be unmoved to see these children lavishing all their love on some other woman, speaking all their words of endearment into her ears, while for the real mother there was never a word of affection, never a caress, never any token of love. And no normal mother would be satisfied even if these tokens were not given to another if they were also withheld from her. She wants them herself. Her mother-heart craves them. And she has a right to them.

God is a parent to us, our first parent; the one to whom we are indebted for more blessings than any other being in the universe. He gave us our being. He provides for our wants. He forgives us our sins, clothes us with the righteousness of His dear Son, and assures us of our heirship to all His riches. Earthly parents sometimes prove false to their children; human, or, rather, inhuman, fathers sometimes fail to provide for their offsprings; even earthly mothers have been known to forget and forsake the children nursed at their bosoms. But our heavenly Father never forgets or proves false to His children. And being a Father in deepest reality as well as in name, He wants not only our formal allegiance, but our affection. "Thou shalt love the Lord thy God."

God is not satisfied that we love Him with a cheap, nondescript love. He demands the highest love of which mortals are capable. He wants a love in which the highest and farthest reaches of a truly enlightened mind play their part. God does not want to be loved with a superficial emotion. He wants our affection to be based on an understanding of His nature, attributes and disposition. There are, no doubt, many poorly informed Christians who are saintly in their simplicity. This, however, does not gainsay the fact that their lack of information detracts from their sainthood. God wants us to love Him because we know from the witness of our minds, as well as from the witness of the Spirit to our spirits, that He is supremely worthy of our love. We get this understanding of God's exalted character from His Word in which He has most clearly revealed Himself. So definitely, so prominently should this knowledge of God's nature and works be impressed on the whole content of our minds that all power, all beauty, all goodness, everything, indeed, which inspires by the loftiness of its character, should lead us on to Him who is yet far beyond all that human mind has conceived of power and beauty and goodness; the original and source of all these reflected rays which reach our mortal minds.

Have we met this supreme requirement of the Law of God? Have we given to God a love in which is concentrated all the highest powers of mind and heart? Have we given Him such a love without interruption? I know the answer that I, with shame and regret, have to give; the answer which God's Word says we all have to give. We have all failed, and most of us are conscious of having failed, miserably failed. Only One akin to us in our fleshly nature dwelt in the perfect love of the Father, and returned a love, perfect in nature and degree, to the Father. It was Christ Jesus our elder brother and Saviour. And as it is with all specific commands, so also with this summation of all commands, Christ's fulfillment avails for us when Christ Himself becomes ours by faith. And then, taught by Christ, and ever prompted by the new spirit He imparts to us, we begin to awaken, more and more, to the love of God for us, and to love Him more and more both for what He is, and for what He has done for us.

Using God's Name Reverently

To love God aright is the only guarantee that men will reverently use His name.

As it is with the first part of the first great commandment so it is with the second. As God is not satisfied when men worship no other gods, so He is not satisfied when men do no more than refrain from taking His name in vain. The requirements of the Second Commandment are not met by a dumb and unfeeling silence. A bunch of mummies or a hall filled with human statues carved from stone would be silent enough. You would hear no profanity there. But God's requirement would not be met thereby. There are men and women in goodly numbers who have advanced far enough to know that it betrays vulgarity and a general lack of culture to use profanity. Prompted by a certain elementary self-respect, and a desire not to transgress the generally accepted conventions, they refrain, usually at least, from profanity. It is to be conceded that it is better to be decent from a faulty motive that not at all; but a mouth not polluted by this gross profanity, if this is the only motive, is as far from bringing its possessor within the circle of those who truly keep the Second Commandment as the dimmest star-light is from equaling the splendors of the noonday sun.

God's holy name is profaned not only by uttered profanity; but by profane silence, by contemptuous indifference. He wants His name to be enshrined in loving hearts, and to fall reverently from the lips of those in whose hearts it is thus enshrined.

In Paradise, before that awful tragedy, man could no more have kept from devoutly speaking God's name, nor from speaking to Him, than he could have kept from breathing the perfume laden air of that earthly reproduction of heaven. If we loved God to-day with all our minds and souls, our hearts would overflow with songs of praise, and our lips drop melody freighted with His blessed name, as naturally as the birds sing when the warmth and brightness of spring returns to woo them with its caresses; as naturally as the angels around the throne find their delight in such service.

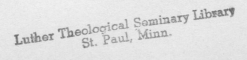

Why is it that we are so slow of speech when it comes to speaking about God and Divine things? Parents can usually speak to their children with a great deal more freedom on almost any other subject. We scold them for doing wrong, but do we show them that our chief hurt is because they are offending God, our God and theirs? We become incensed at the injustice which prevails in the world, we are filled with disgust at the thought of the filth in which men and women wallow. But what is the chief element in the offence we take? Is it not this that they bring disgrace on the race of which we are part? that they violate our sense of the proprieties? that they add, in a number of ways, to the burdens of those who would think right, and live right? How much of our offence comes from this that all such conduct is an insult to the holy name of God, a dragging of His name in the mire, that it is a campaign of destruction waged against the highest and best loved of His earthly workmanship? Our blood is inclined to boil, and our face to be suffused with the scarlet flush of rising emotion, if the revered name of an honoured father, a beloved mother or any dear friend, is used in a way to reflect on its bearer. If love for God sat enthroned supreme in our hearts, the honour of His great, holy name would be the first consideration in all things.

The Becoming Worship of God

"Thou shalt love the Lord thy God with all thy heart, and with all thy soul, and with all thy mind." Thus does Christ explain the measure of our highest duty toward God. If anything approaching this degree of love dwelt in our hearts, what a transformation would be wrought in our lives with respect to the observance of the Third Commandment — "Remember the Sabbath day to keep it holy."

We profess to be God's children; to stand in such relationship to Him by faith that we daily and richly receive forgiveness of our sins, and thus to be heirs of heaven and its glory. This relationship, however, does not only secure us blessings, it imposes obligations as well. To His children God has given a book through which, by the Holy Spirit's aid, we may be led into the possession of all needed truth. This book is the Bible, and with respect to it God says: "Search the scriptures, * * * for they are they which testify of me." We have seen people lost in reverie as they pored over the yellow pages of letters penned by the hand of some loved one no longer in the land of the living, but to whose memory the living one was loving and leal. If we loved God more after this fashion, with the full rich love of an enlightened mind and devoted heart, would we not often eagerly take up His letters and devotedly ponder them? And this all the more because we know that God, through this Word, gives us the power progressively to realize the ideals He therein sets before us. But to how many professed Christians the Bible is practically a closed book. And many who do occasionally turn to this Book of books, matchless in its beauty as well as in its power, do so with little real interest, turn its pages with leaden fingers, and listlessly follow some brief portion of its message with eyes in which there burns none of the light of love.

That we may be for a time divorced from the engrossing cares of the earthly life, God has given us a special day of rest and leisure; a day of opportunity in which to repair to His temple, there to replenish the diminished fountain of the higher life of our souls by feasting them on the bounteous beauties and blessings which He has spread for our delectation in its sacred ministries. When we have been forced for a while to be away from home and loved ones, with what eager haste we turn our steps toward that magic place — home, where live those to whom we are bound by all the ties of loyalty and love. Some of us truly love God's house, the place where His honour dwelleth. But do we feel the same warmth of affection for it that we do for the earthly home? And the conduct of many, yea, many professing Christians, proves that they cannot honestly say: "I was glad when they said unto me, let us go into the house of the Lord." "How amiable are thy tabernacles, O Lord of hosts. My soul longeth, yea, even fainteth for the courts of the Lord; my heart and my flesh crieth out for the living God. * * * For a day in thy courts is better than a thousand" (Ps. 84).

What we all need as the real propelling force of our lives, urging us on and on toward these and all other God-given ideals, is a greater measure of love, love for God, and the things of God. This love does not come, nor increase after it has begun, by vaguely wishing for it. It comes through the gateway of the knowledge of God, of trust in God, and of fellowship with God in all that is good and true.

In this first commandment, or rather explanation of all commandments, Christ shows us how high the ideal is which is set before the Christian. God's Word and our own experience teach us how far short we have come of fulfilling it. And failure in the supreme duty is the supreme failure. The greatest of all sins is the failure to love and trust God aright. Mere human power can never make good this failure. Jesus Christ has atoned for the sin of lovelessness and faulty love as well as for all other sins. He did this because He loved His heavenly Father supremely, and his brethren, the children of men, supremely. In the school of Christ we learn to trust and to love.

THE CHRISTIAN FAMILY

"The Lord God said, it is not good that the man should be alone; I will make him an helpmeet for him. * * * Therefore shall a man leave his father and his mother, and shall cleave unto his wife; and they shall be one flesh." — GEN. 2, 18, 24.

"Ye stand this day all of you before the Lord your God; * * * your little ones, your wives, and the stranger that is in thy camp, from the hewer of wood unto the drawer of water; that thou shouldst enter into covenant with the Lord thy God, and into His oath, which the Lord thy God maketh with thee this day; that He may establish thee today for a people unto Himself, and that He may be unto thee a God, as He hath sworn unto thy fathers; * * * lest there should be among you a man, or woman, or family, or tribe, whose heart turneth away from the Lord our God, to go and serve the gods of these nations; lest there should be among you a root that beareth gall and wormwood." — DEUT. 29, 10-13, 18.

WE are now ready to take up the study of the Second Table of God's holy Law. This Second Table, beginning, according to our division, with the Fourth Commandment, deals with man's relation to his fellowman. But let us not forget that, though these commandments treat of human relations, they are still God's laws. And equally well let us remember that the violation of these commands, while a sin against man, is, primarily, a sin against God Himself.

In taking a general survey of this Second Table of the Law, even the most cursory student could scarcely fail to notice that there is one institution which lies at the very foundation of more than half these commandments, and is not excluded from the others. The Fourth, the Sixth, the Ninth and Tenth Commandments presuppose directly the family relation. And we shall never get the bearing, or the real significance, of many things spoken of, or referred to, in the Second Table of the Law until we have a fair idea of this fundamental human relation, — the family. As an introduction, then, to this second part of the Law let us consider —

The Christian Family

I. The family is a Divine institution. God Himself established it. The family existed in Paradise before ever sin made its appearance on earth. These facts give us sufficient evidence of the holy nature of the estate, and of the sacred and important ends God intended to have accomplished through it.

The family is not only the first institution of earth as to time, but it is the first also in importance. It is the fundamental institution for the perpetuation and development of the race. It is the radiating point of all the influences which affect the children of men. As the family is, so, largely, the State is going to be, and the Church. The ideals which prevail in the family circle, and are imbibed there, become the actuating motives of those who grow into manhood and womanhood there, and will dominate them when they go out into the wider circles of business and social life.

Reformatory efforts, whether they look to improvements in the Church, the State, or the general social conditions of mankind, shall fail, and fail miserably, if they do not look, first of all, at the correction of the family life. The family is the first unit in all human relations. It is the fountain head of human existence. And no stream can rise higher than its source.

No man can build a house which will stand, especially when the storms rage and the floods surge, on a foundation of sand. And a flourishing Church, a sane and prosperous State, a wholesome, brotherly social and business life, cannot be built upon a family life which is not sane, and wholesome, and spiritually minded. We do not have healthful, flourishing, fruit-bearing trees where the roots are cramped, or rotten. The tree surgeon may trim such a tree so that it will look very symmetrical, and fill up the decayed places with medicated cement; but if the soil conditions are not good, if the roots are slowly dying, other branches will continue to die, and other decayed places will continue to appear in the trunk, and soon there will be a dead tree. But if the soil is such as the tree needs, if the roots are sound, and perform their functions, there is good prospect of warding off the enemies which attack the trunk and branches; of continuing the life of the tree, and keeping it fruitful. This is a fair illustration of the relation of the family to other human institutions. It is the root, they are the branches. And the health of the branches depends on the health of the root. This is a truth which is being more and more recognized, and emphasized, by those who are not teachers of religion. Let us who are not only members of families, but members of the Church of God, not fail to learn, or having learned, not fail to profit by this lesson.

As the basis of the family relation we have marriage, an ordinance of God's own establishment. It was He who said in the words of our text: "It is not good that the man should be alone, I will make him an help meet for him." It was God who brought the first lonely man a companion. It was God who united them, one man and one woman, in the indissoluble bonds of love, of unity of purpose, and of hearty co-operation, for life. And God is still the maker of marriages when people, in the fear and love of God, seek His good guidance. But when parents have no other thought than to be matchmakers, in order to get their children off their hands, and well settled in life; when young people, who have never had a serious thought in all their lives, rush into marriage with never a thought of its real responsibilities, with never a thought about the decisive bearing this step cannot fail to have on their own lives for time and eternity; with never a thought about the bearing this union will have on the Church, the State, the race; under such conditions marriages are not made in heaven, but in the other place. And only a miracle of grace can prevent them from being failures in every sense of the word.

Marriage! Marriage an institution of God's ordaining, sacred in all its relations! Marriage an institution through which God is to be continually glorified, and humanity to be blessed! What thoughts these terms provoke! What a noble relationship! But would right thinking people want to apply these terms, or any one of them, to a union which is the result of a thoughtless, foolish escapade? Would we want to call that a Divine union where a man only wanted a housekeeper, and the woman only wanted to escape what is sometimes foolishly spoken of as the stigma of spinsterhood? I glory in the woman who, rather than sell herself for a name, or a home, or surrender herself to a man whom she can neither respect nor love, will courageously shoulder the responsibility of carving out her own career, and live and die unmated. And my advice to the young man is that, if he cannot find something better than an animated clothes-rack, or one of those empty-minded giggling nonentities who has never had a higher thought than eating chocolate bonbons, having a never-ending good time, escaping every form of work and responsibility, and keeping a man eternally in debt, then he had better follow suit, and live and die unmated; or hunt up one of the sensible, unspoiled bachelor maids and see whether he cannot get her to change her mind. I am giving such advice, not because I disparage or would discourage marriage, but because I have such an exalted opinion of marriage and its fundamental relation to every human institution that I would a hundred times rather see no marriages than bad ones, which wreck and ruin human lives and human institutions.

The center around which the family life radiates is the home. Home, one of the sweetest words in any language! If we had hours instead of minutes in which to dwell on this thought we could come nearer to doing it justice. The word home is one of those which strikes deepest into the heart of the average man or woman. Aside from Divine overruling grace there is no influence on earth which does so much to make or mar humanity as the home.

A house is not necessarily a home. A palace, with costly tapestries, statuary, and every product of art, may still be no real home. To have a home there must be the contact of loving hearts, there must be fellowship of those of kindred spirit, there must be that which draws out and strengthens the best of which human nature is capable.

If we could only get people to think more of being home-makers! It is a great thing to be a land-owner, and produce live stock, and grain, with which to feed hungry people. It is a great thing to be a big business man, producing for men, or conveying to them, the necessities of life. It is a great thing to be an honest toiler of any kind, and to know that thereby one is contributing to the good of humanity. But the greatest work of all is that which has as its conscious object true home-making. Here, as nowhere else, minds are trained, characters developed, and destinies of men and nations fixed.

II. Because of these undeniable facts, I affirm that Christian Family Life is the only Hope of the World.

In our second text, which is a part of the account of God's covenant made with his people on the occasion of the giving of His Law, God Himself tells us what the consequences are when men, whether as individuals, or families, or nations, depart from the Lord. He tells us that it means the introduction of "a root that beareth gall and wormwood." Such people bring on themselves, justly and inevitably, the wrath and punishment of Almighty God. And, sooner or later, it means the downfall of that man, or family, or nation. And this fall comes because men themselves despise and neglect the elements which make for safety and perpetuity, and allow the introduction of the elements which can ultimately end only in decay and dissolution.

The family circle is the primary training-school for the cultivation of all the virtues. "Finally, brethren, whatsoever things are true, whatsoever things are honest, whatsoever things are just, whatsoever things are pure, whatsoever things are lovely, whatsoever things are of good report; if there be any virtue, if there be any praise, think on these things" (Phil. 4, 8). I ask you where is the first place, and the most effective place, for teaching these things? There is but one answer, in the home. And they will not be taught, they cannot be effectually taught there, unless the fear and love of God rules in the home, unless the spirit of Christ reigns there. It is the Church's exalted duty to teach these things, but one reason why the Church's teaching does not produce any greater results is that they are not practiced in the home as they ought to be. None of us are perfect, we all have enough faults; but it is certain that if these things are not taught and practiced in the home, they will not be practiced out in the world.

It is in the home that human beings are brought

into the closest, the dearest, the most responsible relationships in life. The Divine ideal is that humanity is to be a great brotherhood, mutually considerate and helpful. "None of us liveth to himself," saith the Lord. Now the very center of this great complex of human relationship is the family circle. Here is where the real heart-beats of humanity are felt. If here there is a true spirit of mutual love and helpfulness, if here there is willingness to make sacrifices one for another, if here the spirit of self-control is exercised, if here the spirit of selfishness is banished more and more, then it may be reasonably expected that, with proper encouragement, this spirit will be carried out into the larger relationships, into the community and the Church. But if parents are themselves supremely selfish, if they are not willing to make any sacrifices for the common good, if they constantly seek to escape responsibilities, if they are full of impatience with one another, if their children are always in the way, and everything done for them is done under protest, what is to be expected when such people get out into the world? Is it any wonder that they regard the world only as an orange to be squeezed for their own pleasure? And if children learn none of these primary virtues in the home circle, if each one lives only for himself or herself, if each one is an Ishmael with his hand against every one else, if each one lives only to get and be served, but never to give or to serve, then there is but little hope that they will ever effectually learn these lessons. By the grace of God there will be exceptions. Just as the water lily grows up in beauty and fragrance out of the mud and miasm of a stagnant lake, so an occasional child, reared in the godless and chilly atmosphere of an unchristian home, will develop into beautiful manhood or womanhood, because the warm rays of Divine grace beam upon it from other sources than the home. But the odds are greatly against this.

How shall the one picture we have drawn be escaped, and the other be realized? How shall the root which bears gall and wormwood be destroyed? How shall the curse which means the blotting out of our names from under heaven be avoided? Only in one way, by turning to the Lord our God, by having the fear of God before our eyes, by making the Law of God the rule of our lives, by opening our hearts to be filled and ruled by the Spirit of Jesus Christ; and by making the home the first and greatest school for the teaching and practice of these heavenly virtues.

Blessed are the men and women who came out from homes where unassumed and unassuming Christian piety reigned; from homes where the only law was the law of righteousness and love; from homes where the grief of one was the grief of all, and the joy of one the joy of all; from homes where the richest heritage was a godly father's counsel, and a sainted mother's prayers. Such a home is earth's vestibule to heaven. In such a home love is a law of life, and kindly deeds are love's legitimate fruitage. If, because of human frailty, there is offence given, there is also ready reparation and forgiveness. To such a home as this the inmates will flee, as to a haven of rest, from the wearying, vexing battles which are waged in the world by warring human passions. And when to the members of such a home inevitable sorrow comes, bowed and burdened hearts are comforted and cheered by love both human and Divine. From such homes come nearly all the men and women who bless the earth with their presence and their work. The names of such homes are kept sacred in the records of heaven. And their influence shall never perish from the earth.

Brethren, on bended knees, and with hearts filled with gratitude, let us thank God if we have the memory of such homes. Their sweetening, corrective influence on our lives will never be entirely obliterated. But the only safe thing to do, for ourselves and others, is to perpetuate such homes. Let us make our homes Christian homes in the full, rich meaning of that term. Let us make God a party to our home life. Let His Word be the daily manna of our life. Let us endeavor to put its principles into practice in the little everyday things of life as well as the great. Without this it is meaningless prattle to talk of a regenerated society, of a noble citizenship, of self-effacing, self-sacrificing officials, or of a spirit of brotherhood manifesting itself in the marts of trade. Without this it is useless to talk of a Church filled with power which shall conquer the world for Christ.

The family and the home are threatened in our day by an ever-growing and powerful list of enemies. The growing congestion of city life, the crowding of families into apartments where real family life is next to impossible, the rearing of children in the midst of the most unfavorable environment, the increasing stress of competition which breadwinners have to face, and the multiplication of temptations for children and adults, have led students of economic and social conditions to ask the question: Can the family, the home, survive? It behooves those who love humanity, and are interested in the coming of the Kingdom of God, to bestir themselves to the end that it shall survive; not alone in the sense of substantial dwellings, but in the sense of men and women of God mated in love, Divine and human, who will live their religion in their homes, and beget and rear children who will follow in their footsteps. Then shall the root which beareth gall and bitterness find no soil for growth in our homes. Our land will be safe and prosper. And the Kingdom of God take on new vigor. As of old the called and professing children of God, with the nation at large, are standing at a critical point in our history. What shall our answer be to God's proposals? Let the answer of each be that of the man of God of old: "As for me and my house, we will serve the Lord."

THE DUTIES CHILDREN OWE THEIR PARENTS

"Honour thy father and thy mother; that thy days may be long upon the land which the Lord thy God giveth thee." — EXODUS 20, 12.

"Children, obey your parents in the Lord; for this is right. Honour thy father and mother; which is the first commandmant with promise; that it may be well with thee, and thou mayest live long on the earth." — EPH. 6, 1-3.

WE have, in a measure, prepared the way for the consideration of this Fourth Commandment by our meditation on the Christian family. If all families were Christian families, if all parents lived and wrought in the midst of their families in the fear and love of God, and made it their chief concern to have their children follow them in this, then we should have the least possible trouble in having the Fourth Commandment fulfilled. Lovelessness and disobedience will never entirely perish from the earth so long as humanity carries about with it its sin-tainted flesh and blood, but they flourish least in the atmosphere of a true Christian home. And in such a home honour for parents, and loving obedience also flourish best.

It would be difficult, indeed, to exaggerate the importance of this commandment. It is the connecting link between the First Table, which looks directly Godward, and reminds us of our relationship to Him, together with the duties this relationship makes obligatory on us, and the Second Table which tells us of our relationship to our fellowmen, and the duties we owe them. This commandment urges, at the very fountain head of human life, and in those early years when the tendencies of life are most easily formed, the implanting of those principles of human conduct without which nothing in human society can be either permanently peaceful or prosperous.

Young people, give earnest heed to these words. They are not mine. They are not the words of any mere man. They are God's words. And their truth is attested by all the thousands of years of human history. Only by obedience to them can you ever hope to come to that which is holiest and best in life, here or hereafter. This is one of the special precepts of the Lord in the keeping of which there is great reward. (Ps. 19, 11).

And those of us who have come to maturer years may still profit by paying close attention to these words. There are lessons here for our good, lessons which we cannot afford to ignore.

May the great Master, who took the little children up in His arms and blessed them, and gave His sanction to the ancient Mosaic commandment by inspiring this great Apostle to record it in the New Testament, may He guide and bless us in the renewed study of this holy law, which sets before us:

The Duties Children Owe Their Parents

We will consider what these duties are, the spirit in which they are to be discharged, and the blessing which they bring.

I. The first thing for us to do is to get a clear understanding of what the duties are which the Fourth Commandment requires of us.

In no sphere of life is consistently correct conduct to be expected from those who have not been instructed as to the nature and extent of their duties. Nor is it to be expected from those who have not been given the proper motives for the discharge of such duties. This truth applies to children. And without wholly excusing disobedient children, it must be said that herein parents and others are often largely at fault. They expect from children what they have not taken the pains carefully to teach them. And sometimes when the teaching has not been wholly neglected, the spirit is faulty. As soon as children are old enough, and that means while they are still at their mother's knee, they should be carefully instructed as to their duties, and given to understand why they should perform them.

The duties of children the Law of God sums up in the words: "Honor thy father and thy mother." It is important for us to remember, however, that the Word of God, by word and example, interprets the word parents to mean more than the natural father and mother. Of course, it means those in the first place. But it also includes all those who, in any way, take the place of parents; such as foster-parents, step-parents, grandparents, teachers of every class, representatives of the government, old people in general, and employers. And this shows us that we must proportionately widen the meaning of the term child. When the Lord says:

"Honour thy father and thy mother," He is speaking not only to the little ones led about by the hand. He is speaking to every one of us who have a parent, or parents, living. He is speaking to every citizen, every employee. I shall speak, however, chiefly of children in the narrower sense. If children would remember that they are required to honour and obey as children, only as their parents and others who may be over them are required to honour and obey as citizens, it would do much to soften and destroy that spirit of resentment which is so quick to arise in the human breast, especially when one gets the notion that he is a representative of the only class which is required to render honour and obedience.

Now that we understand who are included in the term parents, let us inquire what the duties are which we owe them.

One of the first and most important duties which children owe their parents is obedience. It appears that the Lord Himself makes this the primary duty of children when He leads his inspired Apostle to introduce the New Testament version of the commandment with the words: "Children obey your parents in the Lord, for this is right."

Obedience is a virtue the character and importance of which we all need to learn a great deal more. So many regard it as a virtue only in the menial, and that obedience gives evidence of such a character. This is a great perversion of the truth. The true spirit of obedience is learned only by those of great mind and exalted character. Obedience is one of the first and best preparations for places of trust and power. No one is fit to rule till he has learned to obey. He who obeys accepts discipline. And by discipline men grow. To obey is to confess a superior power, and as obedience is the proper spirit of the pupil, it is the way to power.

The real test of obedience is in the little things. We make preparation for state occasions. The spirit of the occasion gives the sustaining power. It is in the little things, and when our own inclination runs counter to the duty confronting us, that we exhibit the true obedience, and get the most benefit from it. Here is where the true discipline which builds up a strong life comes in.

Children! Young people! Do not get the idea that the requirement of obedience is a provision made just to take advantage of you, because you are young and comparatively helpless. If true love fills your hearts such thoughts will never suggest themselves to you. Your parents are not lording it over you. The Fourth Commandment is a provision made first of all for your good, then the good of the home, and society in general, in the State and the Church. We all have to learn that there is such a thing as authority in the world, and learn to order our lives in conformity to it, before we can find our right place in the larger social complex, and fit ourselves harmoniously into it. And experience proves one thing conclusively, the young people who never learn obedience, never make good citizens, good business men, good husbands or wives. And God in His goodness has provided that our parents, those who love us better than any one else in this world ever will, and have our real interests at heart as no others ever will, shall first exercise this authority over us. If you have not thought much on this subject, you may not be able to see this clearly at present; but all the centuries bear witness to the wisdom of this provision. In time, unless you close your eyes, you will come to see it. In the meanwhile trust the Lord's wisdom and goodness — and obey.

The word honour, however, my young friend, means more than simply to obey; that is, to do what you are told to do. To honour means to put the one honoured in the place of superiority, so that the one honouring looks up to the one honoured. It means, to hold this person in high esteem. There must be a spirit of reverence in a person's heart for another before he can show this honour. This also, this especially, does the Lord require. And above all does He require it of children for their parents.

We know, boys and girls, we parents know, not only from our experience with you, and others like you; but we know by looking back to our own early years, that the mind and heart of youth is often inclined to resent being told so frequently that they are to be subject to authority, that they are to be guided by the wishes of their elders. As human nature is now constituted, and unless it is early brought under the moulding influence of God's Word, it is quite natural for the boy, before he puts on a man's clothing, to think that he is as wise as his father; and for the girl in the middle teens to think that she is as well acquainted with the problems of life as her mother. But it is a great mistake, nevertheless. Because your parents have toiled and sacrificed they may have been able to give you advantages they never enjoyed. And before you were fifteen you may have learned some lessons from books which they never learned. But facts from books do not constitute human life. Your parents have learned in the school of experience what it is impossible for you yet to have learned. And all the added advantages your parents, from love of you, have sacrificed to give you, are another reason which obligates you all the more to love and respect them. Not to do so marks you as an ingrate.

Children, young people, do not grow restive under parental guardianship. It is God's gracious plan for your good. If you can see no other reason for compliance, recall that it is God's own command. By this arrangement you are relieved, in a measure, of responsibility and care until your character has become somewhat formed, and you have obtained a maturer judgment. Believe that God was planning wisely for you when He made these arrangements, seeking only your good. By the grace of God keep down the feelings of insubordination, the exhibitions of which are so plentiful all around us. To give room to the spirit of disobedience means to have in your breast one of the most prolific breeders of discontent, a spirit which will set many dangerous pitfalls for your feet all along the future paths of life.

The history of all the ages proves that the paths of peace, and general well-being, are those trod by the feet of those who recognized legitimate authority. Go to the reformatories, the prisons of all kinds; go to the majority of those who have made shipwreck of life: and very many of them will tell you that their downfall was closely associated with disobedience to parental authority. On the other hand, most of the great and good men and women of the world are known to have been obedient and respectful to their parents; and not ashamed to own it before the world. Some of our most honoured and best loved presidents were not ashamed to show their love for their aged mothers before the multitudes which witnessed their elevation to the highest office in the gift of the greatest nation on the face of the earth.

Depraved heathenism was distinguished by the lovelessness and disobedience of children. But the better class of these people recognized the beauty of filial obedience and the binding character of the obligation. We are told that Titus, who commanded the armies of his father, Emperor Vespasian, was falsely accused of plotting against his father. When this report came to the ears of Titus he was so distressed at the thought of the pain it would give to his honored father that he left his command, and, with all speed, hurried back home, burst into the presence of his father, with the cry: "I have come, father, I have come." This example could be multiplied manifold from the pages of heathen history. We call ourselves Christians and profess ourselves governed by Christian principles, but are often very much lacking in the virtue of loving obedience.

Think of the way the Bible emphasizes the necessity of obedience, and its blessedness. From Genesis to Revelation, by word, and by example, it is taught. Think of the conduct of Joseph, not only in early youth, but when he sat on the second throne of a great nation. There is one example which, if there were no other, ought to settle for all time this question of honouring parents. We are told that the youth Jesus, after the time when the larger visions of His divine relationship and His great mission began to dawn upon Him, went down with his parents to their humble Nazareth home, and was subject unto them. Young people, let me tell you, you cannot be followers of Jesus, you cannot enjoy His blessing, now or hereafter, unless the spirit of obedience to parents which He taught and exemplified, dwells in your hearts.

Then think of the misery disobedience to parents has brought, and is bringing, to the earth. And this misery is not confined to broken-hearted parents. Children cannot fail to share it. Unless they have hearts of stone, the suffering they cause their parents will recoil, and strike into their own hearts. And if this is not the case disobedience to parents is going to bring misery and wretchedness to those guilty of it before they get out of this world.

I sometimes wonder whether the Lord did not, in a sense, make this Fourth a special Commandment because of His own experience with disobedient children. The eternal Father Himself, who sits enthroned at the heart of the universe, knows what it is to have disobedient, rebellious children in the family nearest the throne. Some of the fairest and brightest of the sons of the morning, the angels in heaven, spurned His Fatherhood, and sought to overthrow His rule. And here was given the first instance of the truth that parental authority cannot be thrown off without serious consequences. As a result of this disobedience we read those words which almost make the blood chill in one's veins: "And there was war in heaven. * * * Michael and his angels fought against the dragon and the dragon fought and his angels, and prevailed not, neither was their place found any more in heaven." As the direct consequence of this disobedience in heaven we have that tragedy of disobedience in the Garden of Eden, to which we must trace all our ills. And all the way down the ages, the pages of history are blotted by the tears of broken-hearted parents. Listen to the lament of David. He loved his children. When one of his little babes was sick unto death, strong man though he was, he fasted, and wept, and prayed. But now in later years, his beautiful and beloved, but wilful and wayward son Absalom rebels against him. Again David weeps, but they are tears tenfold more bitter than when death claimed his babe. The barbed dart of filial rebellion pierced his heart. And in the bitterness of a crushed and bleeding heart he cries out: "Oh, my son Absalom, my son, my son Absalom! would God I had died for thee. Oh, Absalom, my son, my son."

Many of you recall the story of King Lear, in which Shakespeare has depicted, with his usual mastery, the story of childrens' ingratitude. When his heartless daughters, Goneril and Regan, to whom the king had given so much, turned so completely against him, the old man, broken-hearted, and crazed with grief, cried out: "How sharper than a serpent's tooth it is to have a thankless child."

Children, we expect, we have a right to expect, better things than this of you. You have not only been taught to know better, but the grace of God has also been given to you to make this knowledge effective. You are not only the children of your parents, you are the disciples of Jesus; you have been taught what His will is as revealed in His Word, you are to be the imitators of His example through the power of His indwelling spirit. This was, in part, the meaning of your baptismal covenant. This is included in the promises you made, or are to make, on the day of your confirmation.

II. There is also something to be said now of the spirit in which the obedience required by the Fourth Commandment is to be rendered.

Let us not forget that it is God who gives this command to honor father and mother. In discharging this duty we are serving God as well as our parents, and in refusing to comply we are offending God as well as our parents. Indeed the real grievousness of the offense is that it is a rejection of God's authority, a spurning of His loving guidance. Luther, therefore, rightly explains this commandment by showing that obedience to it must proceed from fear and love to God. If our hearts are right toward God, if we own His fatherhood, if we are subject to His authority, if we love Him for what He has done for us in body and soul, then we will gladly be subject to our parents. This is what our text means when it says that our obedience to our parents is to be "in the Lord." We are members of Christ's body, citizens of his Kingdom, and to conduct ourselves as such is to be our chief consideration.

As God is not to be served simply because we are afraid of His power and punishment, but from love, so our parents are not to be obeyed in a sullen manner. Our parents are not slave masters, they do not exercise authority over us only because they are older and more powerful than we are. Parents love their children, and counsel and correct them because they love them, and wish their good. And children are not to obey like slaves, who move only when driven: they should respond out of love, they should obey willingly, and thus gladden the hearts of their parents.

The time will come when the duty of obeying, in the strict sense of the word, that is, of doing just as we are told to do, will largely cease; for when we become men and women, and have learned the lessons which are to affect all our after life, we must go out into the world, and assume responsibility for our own conduct. But the time will never come when we are relieved of the sacred duty of listening respectfully to the advice of solicitous parents. And in later years, possibly when it is too late, you will appreciate, as you do not now, the privilege of carrying your perplexities to the loving hearts of those to whom you will always be their boys and girls. And be assured, O youths and maidens, that, if you turn out to be the right kind of men and women, you will have few greater sorrows in your later life than the memory of any unloving, undutiful conduct of which you may have been ignorantly or thoughtlessly guilty toward your parents.

Did you ever read the story of Dr. Johnson, the noted English author? Johnson's father was a book-seller. In those days book-sellers often had stalls in the market-places, much as our market people have now for other things. One day the father was ill, and he asked his son to go to the market and manage the book stall. The boy was usually obedient, but on this occasion his pride got the better of him, and he refused to go. He said, in later years, that, so far as he could remember, it was the only instance of direct disobedience to his father of which he had ever been guilty. But he never could forget it, or forgive himself for it. And fifty years afterwards, when he happened to be near that place, he hunted up the old market stall, and stood there bareheaded in the rain, subject to the sneers of the passing crowds, because he felt that he ought to do some kind of penance for that act of disobedience.

Did you ever read in history the story of James IV. of Scotland? In his early youth he was led to join in a rebellion against his father. He afterwards became king, but could never forget how he had broken this Fourth Commandment. His whole life was a bitter and unending remorse for his lovelessness and disobedience. And he, also, did penance. He wore constantly, next to his flesh, an iron chain. And every year he added to its weight. This was a Roman Catholic superstition, but it does not invalidate the sincerity of his contrition.

Boys and girls, men and women, if our memories were as good as those of Dr. Johnson and King James IV. of Scotland; if our consciences were so keen to reproach us for lovelessness and disobedience to parents, would not life probably be unbearable to some of us? We cannot atone for such misdeeds by exposing ourselves to ridicule, nor by punishing our bodies. The only way to find pardon and peace is to fall down before the throne of the heavenly Father, who was outraged much more by such conduct that even our earthly parents, and there confess our sin, and seek forgiveness for Jesus' sake.

How much lack of respect, how much lovelessness, we hear in the very speech of young America. It is seldom that we hear the good old words "father" and "mother." It is "governor," or "the old man," and "the old woman." This shows that we have lost something of the fineness of culture as well as religion out of our lives.

Again, how often do we see growing boys and girls, and young men and women, who know their parents are wearing themselves out for the family good, but never offer to assist; and when asked to help do it with a scowl, and then no more than they must. This is the class of children who allow their parents to exhaust themselves for them, and then when they become old and feeble, turn their backs on them, and allow them to suffer, or go to the poor-house. As far as the heavens are above the earth is such conduct from the spirit of the Fourth Commandment. And whatever their professions, such people are not, and, in such condition cannot become, children of God.

The Word of God teaches us that children should show their love for their parents in a practical way. The prevailing idea seems to be that parents should spend their lives in providing for their children. There is often but little recognition of a kindred obligation on the other side. But it exists. Natural affection teaches it. And Revelation confirms it. The Divine admonition to children is: "Let them learn first to show piety at home, and to requite their parents, for that is good and acceptable before God" (1 Tim. 5, 4).

There is a difficulty which presents itself to some when they consider the spirit in which the obedience required by the Fourth Commandment is to be rendered, namely, with reverence and love. Many are wont to excuse themselves by saying that love does not come at one's own bidding. And sometimes children, especially when they get somewhat older, will excuse their ill spirit by saying that their parents are not lovable. Shame on the child that will try to hide its faults behind such a subterfuge. Suppose our parents had reasoned so about us when we were helpless charges depending on them! Some of us were not extremely lovable, I am sure. We were not all little angels, either for goodness or for looks. Some of us were dull, and most of us quite troublesome,—but our parents loved us, and cared for us, and found good points in us that no one else could see. It was the relationship. We were their children. God had given us to them. Because of this they loved us, and did their duty by us. And it is to be the same way with us. They are our parents, God put them over us. They have watched over us, spent sleepless nights on account of us, shed tears because of our ills, toiled to the point of exhaustion for our good; therefore we have ungrateful, unchristian, inhuman hearts if we do not love them.

A German preacher tells the story of a fine young man who was standing on the street, watching a band of prisoners march by in charge of a guard. Suddenly he ran out to one of the prisoners, took his hand, stooped reverently, and kissed it. An official who witnessed the act spoke of the unseemliness of a young man like him kissing the hands of a criminal. "Oh, but that criminal," replied the youth, "was my father." The father had disgraced him, he had brought the blush of shame to his cheek, but still the son loved him. The love of a true child, a child that has the love of God in its heart, is, like father-love and mother-love, stronger than death.

III. There is a promise attached to this Fourth Commandment which is well worth careful consideration. "Honor thy father and thy mother; that thy days may be long upon the land which the Lord thy God giveth thee."

All the commandments have promises attached to them, if not explicitly stated, yet implied. But this is the only one which has a special promise, one which refers to the present life. This shows how much importance God attaches to this commandment. He has a right to command, and with respect to the great commandments of the First Table that is all that He does, so far as the words of the commandments themselves are concerned. But here He encourages by this special promise. This shows how much God is interested in having children walk in His ways; and how much He thinks of fathers and mothers and the duties they perform, that He would help them in this way.

This promise of long life, so far as it applied to the Jewish people, had reference, in part, to their existence as a nation. And the history of the Jewish people, and of every other nation, proves that the people which fears God, holds the family life sacred, rears its children to habits of obedience, industry, and frugality, becomes and remains the nation of strength, and perpetuates itself on the earth.

The cornerstone of an enduring nation is the hearth-stone of its God-fearing families, the families where the fear and love of God rules, where children are trained to honor and usefulness, where children grow up to honor their parents and all authority.

But this promise of long life belongs also to the individual. I know there are difficulties in explaining it thus, but no more, I think, than in applying it to nations. The fact that St. Paul repeats the promise, changing the wording slightly to meet changed conditions, is convincing proof that it is a promise that God will add length of days to those who religiously keep the Fourth Commandment. There are exceptions, of course. Often the good die young: when God takes them thus, it is to make them partakers of greater blessedness than earth can afford. But the rule holds, Christian boys and girls, that if you honor, love and obey your parents, you shall add to the length of your life.

There is a calmness, a quiet power, that inheres in a character reared in a Christian home, where God rules, where parents rule in love and are obeyed in love, that tends to prolong life. Insubordination, on the other hand, has in it the elements of feverishness and rashness which tends to cut short the tenure of life. Obeying Christian parents results in the formation of habits which tend to lengthen one's days. The prodigals and the Magdalens, the boys and girls who think that home, and the advice of a Christian father, and the proprieties of a godly mother, are pitiable evidences of a lack of up-to-dateness; and insist on going out into the world to join in its giddy experiences, and sip of its forbidden sweets, these are the ones who are sowing the seeds of remorse for the mind, and of swift decay for the body. And then comes, unless there is sincere repentance and forgiveness, endless darkness and despair.

The God-fearing, father and mother loving child misses many of the frivolities of the world. And how much better off they are having missed them. In place of them they have won many blessings. It is no small thing to go through life with the blessing of father and mother resting on one's head. And to have the peace that comes from having faithfully discharged the holiest of all duties pertaining to earthly things — those having to do with one's parents. And then, in the evening of this life, comes the larger, the endless life, in a better land — the heavenly land. God grant it to us all, for Jesus' sake.

PARENTAL RESPONSIBILITY

"Ye fathers, provoke not your children to wrath, but bring them up in the nurture and admonition of the Lord." — EPH. 6, 4.

THERE is no commandment addressed specifically to parents. But no one can study the Fourth Commandment with discernment without seeing that there are many things required there of children which can have no existence without the discharge of a corresponding obligation on the part of parents. And in this sixth chapter of Ephesians St. Paul so connects this admonition to fathers with the Fourth Commandment as virtually to make it a part of it.

No doubt, those of us who are parents were glad to hear the Fourth Commandment explained and applied to the younger people. It is a subject which, it is widely recognized, needs to be given a new emphasis in our day. We no doubt hoped that it might be of personal advantage to us by way of reminding our children of their duties, and giving them a new impulse toward discharging them. But now we are going to turn the tables, and tell the parents of some of their duties. We shall speak on the subject of Parental Responsibility; its nature and extent, and the manner in which it is to be discharged.

I. One of the first things parents ought to know is the nature and extent of their parental responsibility.

It is one of the greatest, one of the most responsible things in the world to be a parent. It means, in a certain sense, to take God's place, to be God's agent, in the perpetuation of the Divine mystery of human life. It is easily to be understood how people, who have no other light than that of nature, can worship this mystery, and its processes, as many of the wisest of the heathen have done. It is one of the greatest things in the whole round of human activities to take a human life, fresh from the hand of God, and be one of the decisive factors in fashioning it into a temple fit for the indwelling of God's Holy Spirit. It is a great thing, a great responsibility, to train a child for citizenship, — to give it the principles by which, ordinarily, it will be governed when it comes to manhood or womanhood.

In these days when men, and women, too, are going in crowds to colleges and universities, for the purpose of learning how best to raise live stock and poultry, it ought not need much argument to prove that it is a great thing, and should be considered one of the divinest things under the sun, to be a co-worker with God in the perpetuation of human life, and then to help train the lives of those who are to take our places, continue and improve our institutions, and finally move on, as we shall move on, to people another world, either of light or darkness. And yet there is plenty of evidence to show that there are any number of people who do not think as much of the real far-reaching problems of child-training as the average farmer does of raising pigs.

Let us imagine a crib before us, and in it

one of those tender, helpless little flowers of humanity. It might be a perfect stranger so far as kith and kin is concerned. But at the sight of it there is not a woman worthy of the name in whose bosom there would not stir something of that mother instinct which, more than anything else, makes woman what she is — the most loving, and the best loved, creature on God's earth. And there is not a man, in whose breast there beats a heart of flesh, who would not grow a little more tender, a little more thoughtful, as he stood in the presence of that greatest mystery of human life.

In that crib there lies a frail little body, so tender that a passing breeze might blight it. It is besieged by enemies from which it must be lovingly shielded. The necessities of life must all be provided for it. Its body must be guarded and guided in its development, so that, if it please God, it may grow up into sturdy manhood or womanhood, and enter the lists as a capable contender for the legitimate prizes of life. There is in that little body an embryonic mind, with, probably, not a single clearly defined conscious thought. But who knows what the potentialities of that mind are? Under favorable conditions it may develop the powers of a Newton or a Webster, a Kant or a Luther. Whatever is there, it is to be given its chance. Under the stimulus of interested and intelligent guidance it is to be encouraged to unfold. And in that little babe there is a soul. A soul so precious that before the worlds were God made plans for it. A soul so precious that for it the Son of God suffered and died. Yes, there is a soul there awaiting the transforming, renewing touch of the breath of the Divine Spirit, and the guiding, developing contact of other awakened souls, to make it, possibly, a most effectual champion of human rights, a leader in the ceaseless crusade for truth and righteousness; at any rate, a polished gem in God's eternal crown.

The first and most evident parental responsibility is that of providing for one's children, especially in their earlier years, with shelter, sustenance, and protection. And with respect to this the Scriptures say that he who does not do it "Hath denied the faith, and is worse than an infidel" (1 Tim. 5, 8). There are parents so completely lacking, not only in parental love, but in the milk of common human kindness, that they fail in this first obligation. But there are more who seem to think that this provision discharges all their responsibility. There are not a few who so pet and pamper their children that they give them the impression that the only purpose their parents are to serve in this world is to be slaves for them, and that the supreme object of the child's existence is to eat, wear good clothes, and have a generally good time.

The whole sphere of the higher responsibility of parents may be summed up in the one word "training." "Train up a child in the way he should go; and when he is old he will not depart from it" (Prov. 22, 6). This Word of God expresses the judgment of ancient Israel, which, as a people, trained its children more admirably than any other nation. When we, to-day, speak of training, we generally have in mind the process of education.

And, rightly understood, it is correct. But education means much more than the mere impartation of the facts of knowledge. It means the development of character, the cultivating of a life. It means giving sane, wholesome views of life, the world, and human relations.

We believe in educating the mind, a belief that ought to be shared by all parents worthy the name. But let us get away from the idea that all education must be for professional life. An education which will enable one to appreciate the beauties of literature and art should not make one ashamed to be a good carpenter or mason, a good clerk, bookkeeper or housekeeper. When education makes people proud and ashamed to work with their hands, and inclines them to live by their wits, at the price of honesty and the welfare of others, it is not a blessing, but a curse. The honest man, with a noble spirit, though he has but the rudiments of an education, as we ordinarily understand the term, is a gentleman and a prince in comparison with the polished loafer and trickster. Parents, let us not forget this while educating our children.

The high, far-reaching duty of parents is set forth in our text: "Ye fathers, provoke not your children to wrath; but bring them up in the nurture and admonition of the Lord." Before defining and applying our text in so far as it sets forth the duties and responsibility of parents in the training of their children, let us emphasize what it implies with respect to the position and conduct of the parents themselves. To bring up a child in the nurture and admonition of the Lord means more than mere obedience to implicit instructions. It means that in this work we are the Lord's representatives. It ought to have a most salutary effect upon parents to remember that we are not privileged to do as we please with our children. Here, as everywhere else in life, we are but stewards. The absolute ownership of our children rests in the Lord. The absolute will in conformity with which our children are to be reared is the Lord's will. In all positions of authority and responsibility, in the Church, in the State, in the family, the incumbents are God's representatives. And they have to give account of their conduct, not only to their fellow-men, but to God. But in no position of authority is man so wonderfully, so directly, so vitally God's representative as in the parental office. What God is to us older people, lover and law-giver, provider and controller, that we are to be under Him, to our children. Fathers and mothers! let us not lose sight of this consideration. It will do much to give us the clear-sightedness, and warm-heartedness, the firmness and perseverance, so necessary to the proper discharge of these holiest of duties. One of the first, most abiding, and life-controlling thoughts of every parent should be that expressed by mother Eve when the first born of the sons of men rested on her bosom. She said: "I have gotten a man from the Lord" (Gen. 4, 1).

In the light of these thoughts, let us consider the divine admonition of our text: "Bring up your children in the nurture and admonition of the Lord." We will pass by those primary duties which pertain to body and mind, already referred to, and which are, in our day, to most people self-evident.

God has given us children to be trained, not only to make a living, but, which is much more, to live. To live means more than having food and shelter or any degree of material prosperity. Merely to vegetate, to exist, is not truly to live. To spend an existence of isolated selfishness is not really to live. A round of useless or silly pleasures is a poor, shallow, unsatisfactory kind of life. The real measure of a man's life is the measure of his approach to the Divine ideal of what life should be. We live in proportion as we find our true place in the great complex of Divine and human activities, and fit ourselves, or allow ourselves to be fitted, into the harmony of this ordered system. In other words, we truly live only as we find, and consciously pursue, the true aims of life. Only thus, my brethren, can men have happiness. And happiness, rightly understood, happiness in its highest and holiest form of blessedness, is man's highest good, the end of his creation, in the possession and appreciation of which he most truly glorifies God.

This, parents, is the stupendous task to which God has put our hands, our minds, our hearts. We are to help God to mould human lives, to develop human character. Under Him we are to train our children to have the right outlook on life, to fulfill their part of the task of making this world a more livable place, and finally come to the right end of earthly life — eternal life.

On this foundation of a generally well-developed character, which, of course, is progressive, and continues through life, parents are to bend their energies to the building up of a symmetrical and useful active life. The virtues of industry and frugality are to be inculcated. Children are to be taught, not only to make a place for themselves in the world, but to stand in right relation to other people. They must learn, not only to respect the rights of others, but to have regard for the feelings of others, and to respect the needs of others. The kingship of self-control must be taught. In early life, we should begin the process of teaching the child that man is differentiated from the mere animal by this that he acts, not on the promptings of impulse or appetite, but as the result of reflection, on the dictates of an enlightened conscience, following the choice of a divinely cultured will.

This brings us to a point which needs a special emphasis. The Fourth Commandment, so far as the duties of children are concerned, rests on the principle of authority. Our boys and girls and our men and women need to learn that they are not, that they can not be, free lances in this world. This world is not built on the principle of do-as-you-please. Peace, progress, and prosperity are bound up with order. And authority begins in high heaven, at the throne of Almighty God, and runs down, step by step, through all the institutions and relations of men. We are living in an age when this lesson needs emphatically to be learned. Anarchy is in the air. In only too many instances it has invaded the home, the very first place where reverence for authority should be taught and established. Parents, it is not only our Divine right, but our Divinely imposed duty, to be the source of authority in the home and to make it such a sacred thing that it must be reverenced. Where it is not reverenced, and thus freely obeyed, there the sting of disobeyed law must be felt. We do not inculcate the rule of force in the home. In most cases the law of love is mightier than the rule of the rod. But where people, whether young or old, are proof against the allurements of love, there forcible measures must be used. The Divine Word itself says that there are instances when "He that spareth his rod hateth his son" (Prov. 13, 24).

There are many other specific parental duties which might be mentioned, and which will not be overlooked by the wise Christian parent. But there is one duty requiring fuller elaboration and emphasis. It is the duty toward which all others are to lead, into which all others are to merge. If we are Christian parents we know that our children have been given us to be trained for heaven. Christ tells us that we ourselves are to seek first the Kingdom of God and His righteousness. And the first great good we are to seek for our children is to make them members of God's Kingdom, and to train them to live as consistent members of it. No parent has discharged the full measure of parental duty, whatever else may have been done, until the child entrusted to that parent's care has been taught to look up from the earthly parent, and to add to the words "father" and "mother" the words: "Our Father who art in Heaven." We may be able to give our children but a start in the training of the schools; we may not be able to give them a rich dowry of material things, we may not be able to leave them the memory of parents signally distinguished; but if in these things we have done the best we could, and, by the grace and help of God, have brought our children to become heirs of the riches of God's Kingdom, we have done well by them. And God Himself will say: "Well done."

Some one may be thinking to himself, "This part of the Fourth Commandment does not concern me; I have no children, I am not even married." But I say, not so fast, my friend. You cannot excuse yourself so easily. If you never do get married, if you never become a parent, you cannot be excused. We learn from the Fourth Commandment that the obedience of children is not to be limited to parents in the strict and narrow sense of the word, but includes all those who are, in any way, in authority. The younger child owes something to the older one, especially if that older one is a true brother or sister — loving, considerate, helpful. It owes something to its teachers of every kind and class. It owes something to older people in general. If this be true, and it is founded on good sense, as well as thoroughly Biblical, then it follows that all older people have a responsibility with respect to all younger people. There is no one-sided responsibility in this world. It is all reciprocal.

You older brothers and sisters owe something to your younger brothers and sisters. You owe to them to second the efforts of your parents in their behalf. You owe to them to set a good example for their imitation. You owe to the little ones to treat your parents and one another as you would have them treat your parents, now, and when they grow up to be your age. You owe to the younger ones of your family to be the ideal into which they should develop. I ask you — you who are older brothers and sisters, are you such young men and women that you can be satisfied, without a prick of conscience, to have your younger brothers and sisters take you as the ideal of what a young man, or a young woman, ought to be?

And you teachers, whether in the church-school, or any other school; you teachers, who occupy one of the most responsible positions on earth, next to a parent, are you mechanical, uninterested, phlegmatic dispensers of information; or are you the incarnation of the living principles of truth, and righteousness, and love, without which the facts of history, the mastery of arithmetical principles, and all the other subjects with which general education deals, are but as dry bones? Is there in you, radiating from you, that warmth of life, that loving sympathy, that lively appreciation of the worth of all human life, which is not only the most effective element in arousing dormant mental faculties; but, which is still better, is the most potent factor, next to the grace of God, in penetrating to the oft-hidden fount of the best and noblest possibilities of the human soul, and arousing them to action?

Oh, yes, teachers, you have a great, a far-reaching responsibility with respect to the young. Do you recognize it? Are you living up to it? Are you yourself the pattern into which the plastic material of the young lives entrusted to your care is to be wrought?

And you, aunts and uncles, and others who come within the charmed circle of that larger family life, made up of all those kin to us and kind to us, do the eyes of the children brighten, do their hearts beat faster, when you are near? Or do they run away and hide when they hear you coming? Do you take a kindly interest in their affairs? Have you a word of counsel and encouragement for them? Are you adding a good part, though it may be a very small part, to the children's growing ideal of what human life should be? You, too, have your share of responsibility.

And you, who are only neighbors, casual acquaintances, who pass the children of the neighborhood only occasionally on the street, do not forget that you are adding your little part to the children's growing consciousness of what the men and women out in the larger world are. You, too, have your responsibility. By a casual word, by the smile or frown you habitually wear, by the very way in which you carry yourself, you are helping, though it be but in a small measure, to make or mar the life of the men and women of the next generation.

II. How can parents properly discharge the great obligations they owe their children?

If the responsibilities of parents are as great as they have been represented, this is one of the most important of questions. Nor can it be too strongly pressed home to the consciences of parents. Napoleon was once asked what he considered the great need of France, and he unhesitatingly answered, "Mothers." That is true of every nation. What America needs, what every land needs, is true fathers and mothers. Not merely progenitors, but fathers and mothers in the full, tremendous meaning of the words. More than tariff laws, more than a merchant marine, more than a plethoric national treasury, more than armies and navies, do we need fathers and mothers, God-fearing, humanity-loving, far-seeing, carefully-planning fathers and mothers. With these our future is secure; without them we face doom, and nothing can stem its tide.

To discharge the grave responsibilities resting on us parents we must, of course, carefully instruct our children. They come into the world with latent possibilities. They must be developed. For the more successful prosecution of this work we have our schools and our specially trained instructors. But, in spite of all this, the home, especially in the child's earlier years, is the chief school. Here, more than any other place, the ideals are set. Here should be the fount of inspiration. And the parents are the chief factors in it.

Parents should study their own children. They are not all alike. They do not all need, they will not all stand, the same treatment. They have their individuality, their personal traits. Do we parents know our children? Do we know the best way of reaching the heart and conscience of each one individually? Do we know to what treatment they will most readily respond? Let us not think that we are wise parents till we have learned somewhat how to act along these lines.

The same principle applies to the religious education of our children. We have turned this over largely to the Sunday school. If we had adequate Church schools there would be more reason in this. No school which meets but one day out of seven, and for but an hour and a half on that day, can meet the full requirements of a child's religious training. Think of it! five days a week, and five or six hours a day, nine months of the year, and this continued for from seven to ten or fifteen years to get ready for fifty years work. And one hour a day, one day of the week, for a varying term of years, to get ready for eternity. Oh, parents! here is the weakest place in all the provision made for our children; and if we truly love them, it cannot fail to concern us much. But even if we had the most ideal arrangement for having our children instructed, that would not discharge our obligations. Instruction in the Word of God by any one measurably qualified for the task, no matter where imparted, will not be in vain. But it will never bear its full measure of fruit unless the family circle is a church of the living God, with father and mother as priest and priestess ministering at the home altar in holy things, and with brothers and sisters as acolytes bearing the censers filled with the sweet incense of prayer and praise.

In moral and religious matters, especially, too many children simply grow; they are not reared, not trained. You have seen vines and trees which were never trimmed. Sometimes there is a riotous profusion of branch and foliage, but generally a noticeable scarcity of fruit, and that of inferior quality. So human life is inclined to grow. There are always showy nothings to attract the young; they are easily picked up, and after a while hard to be discarded. The child should be taught to distinguish the shoddy from the real, to love the one, to dislike the other. There are always evils the young need to be warned against. And they should not only be forbidden, but their true nature should be pointed out. The snares and pitfalls which beset the young along the path of life must be discovered to them, and their consequences so portrayed, and it can be done without exaggeration, that the young will recoil from them.

The good and the true must not only be urged upon the young; but their profitableness made so apparent, and their beauty so attractive, that they will want to achieve them, not as a matter of dull duty, but of eager desire. And the view children get of these things in their early years, the atmosphere they breathe in the home-life, the things their parents love and desire, will be a decisive factor in influencing the choices of the child.

I am speaking to Christian parents, to those who, while not despising other things, believe that Christian character is the most important thing in life. We believe all life, all endeavor, is to be dominated by distinctively Christian principles. To achieve this, nothing worth while, nothing permanent, can be accomplished without God's help.

"Without me," Christ says, "ye can do nothing." Assuredly we ought not to undertake a task which is to show results for the eternal ages without His helping presence. God's presence and help, for spiritual ends, are conditioned for us largely by the use of His Word. This Word is His power unto salvation to every one that believeth (Rom. 1, 16).

How we Christian parents ought to use this Word that we ourselves may be made wise and strong! And how wisely and lovingly we ought to apply it in the actual training of our children! The power which has tamed the fiercest savages, which has been the bulwark of the finest civilization, which gives a new heart to all who do not reject the Spirit who accompanies this Word — shall this power not be the most essential and beneficent factor in moulding the lives of our children?

No doubt, if we parents prayed more for and with our children we should soon see the result. We are taught that the effectual fervent prayer of a righteous man availeth much. What burden of prayer should be expected to come so naturally from our hearts as that in behalf of our children? And what prayers would be more pleasing to God; for are they not His children also? Monica prayed forty years for a wayward son, and won him, and the Church has the history of St. Augustine as the result. No doubt, if we prayed more faithfully we should keep more children from going astray.

So far I have spoken chiefly of active effort in the training of children. That is all very well. We can never entirely dispense with it. But it is not enough. We must illustrate what we teach by what we are. Fathers and mothers! we must be the pattern of what we want our boys and girls to be. We may fail even when we teach by both precept and example. The chances are many times greater that we shall fail if we have only the teaching and lack the example. Children are great imitators. They are all the time absorbing influences.

When we are urging character upon our children, telling them that they should love and choose the good and beautiful in life, that they should always tell the truth, and be pure in word and deed; we should be the concrete illustration of what all this means. When we urge them to shun the things which are little, and low, and mean in life, our lives should be the living commentary on what it means to be above stooping to deeds that Christ does not approve. As we have seen all along, this commandment hinges largely on the recognition of authority and obedience. By our own lives we can make properly constituted authority a thing to be reverenced, loved by our children; or we can make it a hideous nightmare. And it will depend more on our example than on our teaching.

With double force does the principle of illustrating by our lives the precepts we teach by words apply to the religious training of our children. How much importance will the child attach to our preachments about the importance of God's Word if they never see us use it? What will they think of our urging them to go to Sunday school and church services if we are indifferent, and easily find excuses for remaining away? And so through the whole category. We must honestly and earnestly practice what we preach. Children cannot long be deceived.

With our best intentions, and most honest efforts, parents will still make mistakes. That goes with human nature. In child-training one of the most common faults of the well-meaning is aloofness. Too many parents never get close enough to their children. Many a father who means well by his children, is a stranger to his boys, so far as real comradeship is concerned. And the same is sometimes true of mothers. While this condition exists, boys and girls will not take parents into their confidence. And they lose one of the best opportunities of being able to counsel and guide in the most critical affairs of their children's lives.

Another mistake often made by parents is in not making home the real center of attraction for their children. This cannot be done by mere ornamentation or wealth of furnishings; it is done by the cultivation in the home of the affections, tender comradeship, sweet Christian graces,—these make home the most attractive place on earth.

With the expenditure of the greatest possible wisdom and effort we shall meet with discouragements. There will be some failures. But such work given in God's name, and supported by His grace, will never be wholly in vain. It will be hard for the child reared in this way to go wholly to the bad. And if one should become even a prodigal or a Magdalen, the influences set to work in happier days may still bring them to their senses before it is too late.

Happy are the parents rich in the love and respect of godly, obedient children. If they have not succeeded in their efforts at child-training as they should have liked, they will at least be relieved of an intolerable burden if they have a good conscience, a conscience which tells them that they did what they could for their children's welfare. Most blessed of all are those parents who can come before the great white throne, and say to the King—Here we are, and the children Thou didst give us.

THE DUTIES OF GOVERNORS AND THE GOVERNED

"Honor thy father and thy mother, that thy days may be long upon the land which the Lord thy God giveth thee."—EXODUS 20, 12.

"Let every soul be subject to the higher powers, for there is no power but God: the powers that be are ordained of God. Whosoever therefore resisteth the power, resisteth the ordinance of God; and they that resist shall receive to themselves damnation. For rulers are not a terror to good works, but to the evil. Wilt thou then not be afraid of the power? do that which is good, and thou shalt have praise of the same; for he is the minister of God to thee for good. But if thou do that which is evil, be afraid; for he beareth not the sword in vain; for he is the minister of God, a revenger to execute wrath upon him that doeth evil. Wherefore ye must needs be subject, not only for wrath; but also for conscience' sake." — ROMANS 13, 1-5.

WE have learned from a former address that the Fourth Commandment includes in the term parents all those who are in authority. There are many Scripture passages in which rulers of various degrees of authority, and in various spheres of work, are spoken of as fathers. Indeed, the community, the village, the state, the nation is, in a sense, but an enlargement of the family. Each smaller unit is an epitome of the one next above it. As God has ordained that the parents shall be the source of authority in the family circle, and receive proper respect and obedience from the other members; so has He ordained that those who are called to positions of responsibility in any of the spheres of the larger human family shall receive their due meed of honor and obedience. For all human authority, whatever its particular sphere, is but an extension of parental authority.

The obligations in the sphere of government, however, are not all on one side. Just as parents have responsibilities with respect to their children, which they cannot shirk without incurring guilt, so those who are called to discharge the affairs of a community, the social or political family, have great responsibility resting on them, which they cannot pervert, or shirk without sinning.

The problem of government is a great one. What the ends to be achieved are, how these ends may be best secured, what the relationship is to be between those who rule and those subject to authority, these and kindred questions have been discussed ever since society has grown to such proportions that it has become impracticable for the fathers of families to exercise proper supervision over the affairs of the people as a people. And in every age some of the best thinking has been along the line of this problem of government. But unfortunately much of the social, economic, and political discussion of every age overlooks the most important factor — what does God say about these matters? What principles does He lay down for our guidance in the development of these affairs? He has said much; and we Christian people cannot afford to be ignorant of what He has said, nor to be indifferent with respect to it. Let us, then, as

Christian members of that larger family, the State, consider the duties of Governors and the Governed.

Government a Divine Institution

Before we can profitably consider the duties of either those who govern or those subject to authority, we must have an adequate conception of the nature and purpose of government itself. This is the proper point of departure in the study of the subject. Faulty and unworthy conceptions of the nature of government cannot fail to lead to unworthy conduct and carelessness on the part of those who exercise the rights of citizenship, likewise, to unworthy conceptions of their duties and to corrupt practices on the part of those who fill official positions.

We speak much of the dignity and responsibility of our citizenship. But why is there so much indifference on the part of many when it comes to discharging its duties? On the fourth of July, in campaign orations, in party platforms and pledges, as well as in inaugural festivities, we hear a great deal about the exalted dignity and far-reaching responsibility of having the franchise; also about the dignity of office and the effect upon the welfare of the people of the proper discharge of the duties of office. In view of all this, what explains the continued lethargy of so many voters, and the negligence and malfeasance of so many men in public office? The prevailing perversity of human nature accounts for much of it. But when we see so much of this culpable indifference among intelligent and, otherwise, well-meaning men, we cannot but conclude that they fail utterly to understand and to appreciate the true nature of government. They have evidently failed to grasp the fact that it is a Divine institution, that its obligations, both on the side of the citizen and the official, are a sacred trust, imposed on us by God Himself.

Our text from Romans gives us the gist of the whole great complex subject of human government. It tells us that this institution which we call government did not just happen to be. Nor is it a mere human development. As to form it has had a development, but its genesis was not human. Government is not a mere convenient mode of transacting public business. It is not a mere human compact whereby a certain individual, or individuals, are empowered to enact and execute laws for the common good. This is a feature of government, but it does not explain the final derivation of authority.

Government is an institution of God's ordination. "There is no power but of God, the powers that be are ordained of God. Whosoever, therefore, resisteth the power resisteth the ordinance of God." The real authority of government comes from the throne of heaven. Only in a secondary sense is it derived from men. The One who comes before us in the First Commandment and says: "I am the Lord, thy God; thou shalt have no other gods before me," He it is who stands before us in the sphere of government, and says, I am the King of kings. "By me kings reign, and princes decree justice" (Prov. 8, 15).

In our land we have separated Church and

State. And it is undoubtedly best that it should be so, for the ends sought are different. In the State the end is the preservation of order and the betterment of temporal conditions. In the Church it is the liberation and culture of the spirit. But, in our judgment, the matter of the separation of Church and State may be over-emphasized to the detriment of both Church and State. It has a tendency to lead men to consider government as but a contrivance of men, with the result that the devil often usurps virtual control of it. As government is of God, it ought to be in the hands of those who are God's children — those who have the mind of God, are able to discern the will of God, and are willing to do His work in His way. With this principle conceded, I am in favor of separation between Church and State. The State exists for the purpose of carrying on a distinct department of God's universal government: the securing of peaceable conditions and material prosperity. Under such conditions, government, though it exist as a separate establishment from the Church, will still be, as our fathers have ever declared it should be, a champion and protector of the Church. We do not believe in the leaders of the Church meddling in practical political affairs, especially when such interference has as its aim the aggrandizement of a particular church organization; but I positively affirm that the only stable foundation of any government is found in the eternal principles of truth and righteousness for which the Church of God stands, and which are set forth with clearness only in God's revealed Word. All things, in heaven and on earth, have but one legitimate ultimate aim, the glorification of God's name. And all temporal, as well as spiritual, good for God's creatures is best achieved and most secure when God's will is most truly done and His name thereby most truly glorified. When this condition prevails, then, whatever name men may give it, Democratic or Republican, in the truest sense we shall have a theocratic government — a government of God, the only one qualified to attain the Divinely appointed ends.

God's Word does not prescribe the form of human government. Nor does he designate the particular persons who shall discharge its duties, nor specify the extent of power they are to wield. These things are left to be determined by the will of the people, under the overruling providence of the King of kings. The forms of human government change as human conditions themselves change. Where there is but little general qualification for self-government, or the discharge of the duties of public life, there we usually find the exercise of governmental functions in the hands of the few who are strongest and wisest, if not always the best disposed. As the people become better qualified for participation in the affairs of government, they inevitably become more and more the rulers, until, as in our land, they become the real sovereigns, who delegate to certain of their compeers the right to make and execute the laws. But in all, and over all, and under all circumstances, God reigns the supreme sovereign.

This Biblical idea of government does not eliminate all the elements of mystery which perplex the human mind. Indeed, it seems to introduce some. But where do we not find these mysteries? The chief perplexity presented to the devout mind is that of the ever-present problem of evil. If government is of God, why so much perversity among those who rule? Why so much self-aggrandizement, so much grinding of the faces of the helpless? Why so much governmental activity that is not only not prompted by the Spirit of God, but even inimical to His cause? This is the world-old problem of sin. We find it everywhere. It crops out in the Church, among those who wear, not the royal ermine, but the vestments of the sanctuary. And this will continue till we come to the new heaven and the new earth, wherein dwelleth only righteousness. But in the meanwhile in the State, as in the Church, God overrules it all. Evil is ever contrary to God's will, but He uses even the perversity of men to chasten the perversity of other men, to keep us all humble, to show us all our sinfulness, and, where men will yield, to lead them back to the tried and safe paths of reliance only on the grace and goodness of God. These perplexities must not overmuch discourage the children of God. Much less must we allow it to induce despair. God, our God, still rules. Sin has not become God; it has not dethroned God; nor shall it defeat his ultimate purposes. As in the Church so in the State, which is only one sphere of God's general government — God's will shall finally be supreme. God's Word assures us of this, and that is enough for us. But the true philosophy of history corroborates this. It reveals a slowly but constantly progressive movement which builds on all the ruins caused by sin a higher civilization and more beneficent institutions. And it must be so to the end, for the supreme governor is Almighty God.

The Duties of Those Who Govern

With this understanding of the nature of government in itself, it ought not be difficult for us to come to some very definite conclusions with respect to the duties of those who bear rule in governmental affairs. Indeed, God's Word settles the matter, at least as to its general principles.

What a different aspect the governmental affairs of the world would present if those in high places remembered that they are not independent lords, that they are not privileged to do as they please; but that they are God's representatives, and that they have not been elevated to do what is expedient or easy, but what is right. And God's decrees alone make right.

If men had this conception of the purpose of government, politics would cease to be a mere game played for the excitement and the gain it affords. If the true idea of government prevailed, the great problem of politics would not be what it too often seems to be; namely, the problem of getting one party out of power and another party into power. In that case public office would not be prostituted to the low level of being, primarily, a system of rewarding political henchmen and of enriching the incumbents of office as speedily as possible.

Government! Much that goes by this name is

rather misgovernment. It is too often a system of spoliation; a system whereby the strong keep down and fleece the weak. That this is frequently the case is a well-known fact. But it is by no means new. This is a school in which men have long been adepts. Of the officials in the Roman Empire under Constantine it is said that the majority of them were bent only on their own advantage, accessible to every one who had a new scheme of corruption; they were striving only to raise themselves to large incomes, and brilliant positions, to the utmost possible nearness to the imperial sun, the dispenser of benefits. This sounds as if it might have been taken from a modern newspaper, but for the fact that very few of them would dare thus to tell the truth, because they are members of the political plunderbund, and feeders from the dish of political pap. And this is so because our governments conform in vital respects to heathen standards. This and kindred evils will be corrected only when we get to the right principles that government is of God, that governors are His representatives, to rule according to His will.

Government exists for the good of the people. Our text tells us that the ruler is "the minister of God to thee for good." Being the minister of God, and having as the aim of his ministry the good of the people, the ruler, whether he exercise his office in the smallest municipality or in the highest place in the state or nation, should be the wisest and best man that can be found — one whose qualifications are not only intellectual, but also moral. And there is but one true basis of consistent morality, and that is religion. The bearer of office should be a broad-minded, far-seeing man. He should be a man of the strictest integrity. But more than this, he should be a man whose heart goes out to the people. He should be a real father to the people. As the father of a family thinks and plans not only for himself but for the welfare of his children, so every one who has to do with governmental affairs should think and plan for the good of those he serves. We have no sympathy for the doctrine of the Divine right of rulers when it means more than proper respect and obedience when they do what is right, but we do believe with all our hearts in the Divine right of the people to get a square deal. It is said of ancient Confucius that as a magistrate "he cultivated virtue, tempered justice with mercy, and made the people's good his chief concern." This sort of conduct we cannot expect from many in present official life, because, as to character, they are not even decent heathen.

Government exists, our text tells us, for the purpose of preserving peace and order among men. Rulers are to make and execute laws with this end in view. Peace-loving, industrious citizens are to be encouraged and protected, that they may enjoy the fruits of their efforts. The turbulent and unruly, who aim to live chiefly by preying on others, are to be made to feel the strong hand of the law.

Let any one who knows anything about existing conditions compare this picture of what rulers, governmental officials, should be, and the ends they should serve, with what we find in reality. There are, thank God! noble, upright, God-fearing, man-loving men in public office. But there are far too many who are characterless and conscienceless; too many who are even steeped in filth. And as to the welfare of the general citizenship, that is the last thing in the world about which many of them think. Indeed, the heaven-born prerogatives of government are not infrequently prostituted so as to become in their hands the instrument of plunder and oppression. And the fault is largely our own. If the people generally, instead of being blind partisans, wanted good men, men of integrity, brotherly men, they could get them. The demand would bring the supply.

What a terrible reckoning awaits many of those who sit in high places. St. James speaks of those who keep back, by fraud, the hire of the laborers who reap the harvests, and he tells us that the cries of these reapers enter into the ears of the Lord of Sabaoth. And, as a result, the riches of these oppressors become corrupted, and their garments moth-eaten. Their gold and silver becomes cankered, and the rust of it shall eat their flesh as it were by fire (James 5, 2-4). If this result shall follow the oppression of one person by another, what shall be the portion of those who do these things, as it were, by wholesale, as is the case with corrupt and oppressive officials?

Think of the vice which flourishes in many cities with official connivance, if not by official sanction! Why? Chiefly because it fills the pockets of political henchmen with gold. Many live in ignorance, contract disease, endure suffering and death as a result of conditions that could be remedied. Why is it not done? Why is there no legislation looking to the correction of these evils? Or, if there is legislation covering it, as is often the case, why are the laws not enforced? Because of the influence and the sharing of the spoils, of those whose purses are filled through the prostitution of government to corrupt personal ends. Furthermore let us think of the cities and villages reduced to ashes by the ravages of war, of the battlefields reddened by the blood of vigorous young manhood, of the wives that are widowed and the children that are orphaned, of the civilization turned back a century, of the burdens of taxation an already weakened people will have to bear for generations! Did the people invite these measures, so fraught with hardship to them? They but imperfectly understand the motives back of them. The pride of rulers is at fault, and the greed and envy of those who control them, and will fatten on the carnage. How terrible must the reckoning be! Is it not plain that men have forgotten that government is of God; and that its one legitimate object is to bless mankind?

The Duties of Those Governed

All of the responsibility for existing conditions, however, does not rest on those who govern; part of it rests, justly, on the shoulders of those who are governed. And nowhere is this truer than here in our own country. This will become clearer to us as we consider the duties of subjects.

The chief and comprehensive duty of those under authority, as it is set forth in the Fourth Commandment and in the Apostle's directions to the Romans is that of obedience to law, of respect for those legitimately in authority; in other words, of being, as we usually express it, law-abiding citizens. And this duty exists not only where laws meet our approval and the officials are of our party, but even where the laws do not specially favor our interests, and when those who interpret and apply the laws have been put over us without our approval. Only when those in authority do that which conflicts with the Law of God, and curtail our rights and duties as his children, do we have, not only the right, but the bounden duty, of protesting. In such cases we must say as did the Apostles when they came in conflict with those in authority: "We ought to obey God rather than men" (Acts 5, 29).

The spirit of anarchy is entirely too prevalent everywhere. There is something of the anarchist in every natural man. He does not like to recognize any authority but his own will. Only the Spirit of God working in man can change this. He brings us to recognize that authority is primarily from God, and that its exercise is intended for man's good. Men are inclined to forget that there can be liberty only where there is law, and on the part of those only who have brought themselves into harmony with rightly constituted law. The anarchists, those who fight against law, are the ones who are endlessly in conflict — and not only with men, but with God. "Whosoever therefore resisteth the power, resisteth the ordinance of God; and they that resist shall receive to themselves damnation."

Our constant aim as citizens of two kingdoms,

a temporal and spiritual, an earthly and a heavenly, should be to cultivate more of the law-abiding temper, and to aid in its cultivation in others. We should begin with this in the home and the school. And nothing will so much help this as to keep mindful of the fact that government is of God, and that the making and administration of law, though in the hands of fallible men, and often perverted, is still, in its great fundamentals, of God.

Our responsibility as American citizens is so much greater in these matters because we have so much to do with the government. The ideal of this government is that it is a government of the people, by the people, for the people. This is a beautiful theory not yet by any means fully realized, but more fully no doubt than anywhere else on the earth. This ideal will be realized fully only as the people awake to their responsibility. As long as people ignorantly sell their votes for a few dollars, or allow scheming politicians to lead them like sheep by inflaming their party prejudices, or indolently refuse to exercise the privilege so many thousands have died to win, so long this talk of a government by the people, for the people, will be a lovely sentiment backed by very little reality. With an intelligent electorate, which lives up to its privileges and its duties, this ideal will become more and more a reality.

In our country the responsibility of the governed is so great, because of the fact that the character of the general public makes the character of the average law-maker and administrator of law. If the people of a community have lax ideas with respect to honor, truthfulness and honesty, not much more can be expected from those who administer their governmental affairs. It is because our American people, as a class, are greedy that we have scheming, grafting officials. A stream does not rise higher than its fountain. If the people generally come to entertain high ideals of character, to reverence authority, to have proper respect for those who administer the affairs of the government, then we will have officials of the same stamp, men who will bring honor to any office.

Brethren, we must cultivate nobler ideals with respect to all governmental affairs. We must recognize the part which each one of us is to play in this work. We ought to be ashamed to confess that we have failed to vote, or to discharge any duty which rests on us as citizens. We must get away from the idea that this is playing politics. Government is God's business. And in this land He has put it into our hands. And in its time and place it is just as sacred as going to church, or any other duty. It is a matter concerning which, as the Scriptures often tell us, there should be earnest prayer.

Listen to what the Lord says through the mouth of St. Peter: "Submit yourselves to every ordinance of man for the Lord's sake, whether it be unto the king, as supreme, or unto governors, as unto them that are sent by Him. For so is the will of God." If we are to submit to the requirements of the government as a service to God, then, assuredly, if we are privileged to have a part in the ordering of these affairs we ought to appreciate it, and discharge it as a service rendered to God. We owe it to ourselves, to our fellowmen, and to God, to do this.

When Christian men, and women, too, get to see this matter in the right light, and act accordingly, then we are going to have a better government, better administered. The good of mankind will be better served. God will be more fully glorified, for His will will be more nearly done on earth as it is in heaven; for even through the secular government we will have been contributing something toward the more complete realization of the larger Kingdom of God.

THE SACRED MYSTERY OF HUMAN LIFE

"The Lord God formed man of the dust of the ground, and breathed into his nostrils the breath of life; and man became a living soul." — GENESIS 2, 7.

"Thou shalt not kill." — EXODUS 20, 13.

THE Second Table of the Law starts out, in the Fourth Commandment, by throwing a safeguard about the very fountain head of human life, and human society. It sets before us the family, parentage, and the reciprocal relations of parents and children. In that first commandment of the Second Table we were brought face to face with the great problem of human life; a problem of which no thoughtful, pure, reverent soul can think without being devoutly stirred to the depths of his being. In the Fifth Commandment, which we are next to take up for consideration, we have a statement of that Law of God which gives emphasis to the sacredness of human life, and throws about it the protecting shield of His care.

The Fifth Commandment has not become antiquated, or outgrown. The world has made much progress in certain forms of appreciation of human life; but this law is still needed, badly needed. It has been wrought into the organic law of every civilized nation. But there is still a great deal of reckless and needless jeopardizing of human life.

"Thou shalt not kill" is a prohibition which, because of present conditions, shocks the moral consciousness of a goodly portion of our people, and which ought to burn like a branding-iron into the consciences of princes and of thousands of others. The flower of the manhood of many nations is being cut down in the prime of life by the hundreds of thousands. Some one, or some coterie of persons or interests, is responsible. Would that in every drop of spilled blood they might have to read, in letters which burn, the words: "Thou shalt not kill." Would to God that in the groan of every wounded man, and in the shriek of every shell they might hear the voice of an outraged God, saying, "Thou shalt not kill."

Yes, in spite of the way men usually prize life; in spite of the advances made in the study and appreciation of life; in spite of the hoary age of the law against the taking of human life, we constantly need to have it impressed anew. Before we take up, in a direct way, the prohibition of the Fifth Commandment, we shall consider to-day the more general and preparatory subject of the Sacredness of Human Life.

The Mystery of Life

What a wonderful, awe-inspiring subject we approach when we take up the problem of human life. Life there is all around us, life in various forms, life without intelligence, life differing widely in degrees of intelligence, life serving widely differing purposes in the great complex which makes up this universe.

Life! The savage bushman, almost as fierce in his disposition as the tiger which shares with him the jungle, has some faint, shadowy conception of the wondrousness of life. In spite of the fact that, in practice, the life of his fellowman may not be held sacred by him, he has, nevertheless, a certain superstitious reverence for the phenomenon of life itself.

Life! The greatest sages of all ages, those who have looked lovingly and with keenest discernment into the deep problem of the causes, nature, and tendencies of things, have stood with bowed head before this profoundest of earthly mysteries, — life, especially human life. If anywhere in the realm of nature there is a shrine before which men might bow with some show of justification, it is in the presence of this mystery of life. But great as is the mystery of life in its general aspect, it is raised and intensified a thousandfold when we follow it from its lowest and insensate forms to its most perfect form — in man. There are wonders to challenge the intellect and to call forth admiration and praise for the creative Cause when we view life merely in the vegetable kingdom. And what science has done, and is doing, in this sphere only helps to reveal such wonders, though there is still much here which no savant has ever fully explained. What we find in the vegetable kingdom we find also in the lower animal kingdom — the wonders of life, such as growth and self-propagation, and, added to it, sensation, a form of consciousness, mind. And what we find there we find in man, but something more, something so much greater that we find difficulty in expressing it without using the terms of infinity. The gap between the simplest protozoan and the most highly developed vertebrate is as nothing to the distance between the highest mere animal and man, between the life of the most highly endowed animal and the life of man, who is the image of God.

Human life — life which thinks, and wills, and loves, and hopes, and aspires, and struggles to realize its destiny; life which spans the ocean with cables, binds the earth with tracks of iron, skims the bottom of the pathless deep, and soars through the upper air as if on eagle's wings; what a wonderful object is this life! Think of its flight of imagination! It delves into the darkness of the lower regions, and paints such pictures as we have in Dante's Inferno. It goes back through the millenniums and gives us the sublime imagery of Milton's Paradise Lost. It pierces the untraversed and still unpolluted future and gives us a vision of Paradise Regained. In the sphere of reason it gives us such creations as those of Plato and Kant and Hegel. Besides these and other renowned products of the human mind in the sphere of the liberal arts, we have those sublime creations in the wide field of the fine arts. Think of the poems conceived in the souls of men like Michael Angelo and Sir Christopher Wren, and then wrought out in stone and metal. Think of the symphonies which the responsive souls of men like Beethoven and Bach have caught from the orchestras which God has placed all around us in the universe, and which they have translated into the language of mortals. Think of the masterpieces of such artists of the brush as Raphael and Rembrandt.

All this and much more is the product of human life. What a transcendently wonderful thing it is! In a score of ways, what a wonderful thing is life! And yet how little most of us think of it, at least in this light. We are so accustomed to the manifestations of life, so used to living, that the wonderfulness of life no longer makes much of an appeal to us. We have reduced life largely to a round of rather commonplace, and often sordid, activities. Let us make amends for this remissness. Let us think more of life, and, if need be, a little less of merely living, or making a living. But when we have done our best, life will still be largely a mystery! — but a mystery of which we shall think with more reverence, and of which we shall be more careful.

The problem of life has ever been one of intense interest to man. Philosophy has dealt largely with it, has tried to account for it, to define it. Modern science has tried hard to reduce life to its final elements, and compass it in the terms applicable to phenomena in other spheres. The devotees of science have attempted to uncover life with the scalpel, and compound it in the laboratory. While we are grateful for all real advances made, it remains true, as is said by one of the noted philosophers of the present time that, "The intellect is characterized by a natural inability to comprehend life." No mere human intellect has ever told us whence life came, no human research can discover to us the fountain out of which it streams, the goal whither it is bound, nor what shall be its final estate.

There is only one place where the great problem

of human life is given an explanation which really satisfies the spirit of man. This answer is found, not in the book of Nature, but in the volume of Revelation. All other lines of investigation have met with baffling difficulties. And what does Revelation tell us of life? It leads back along the pathway of history till we come to the point which is designated as the beginning. There we hear the uncreated Creator speaking the potent words: "Let there be!" By these words of God every living creature that moves was brought forth. And then we come to the boldest, and most pregnant words, so far as man is concerned, ever wrought into the language of mortals: "And God said, let us make man in our image, after our likeness. So God created man in His own image; in the image of God created He him."

We do not profess — it would be the height of folly to profess — that this record eliminates all the elements of mystery from human life. It does nothing of the kind, and does not profess to do so. Life is still mysterious. No man has ever seen it. We see only its manifestations. But this much it settles: we have learned to know our parentage. We do not owe our being to some tadpole which came to wiggle, somehow, in the primeval ooze. Nor do we count in our ancestral line some chattering chimpanzee which inhabited some prehistoric jungle. Nor are we, as individuals, the sporadic manifestation of some all-pervading, impersonal life element. Whatever others may claim, or be willing to accept, God, the great personal Father, the supreme Intelligence, the all-working Love, is the Author of our being. And He placed us here to work out, by His gracious help, a glorious destiny.

The Sacredness of Human Life

The origin of human life, coming as it did directly from the hand of God; its character, being created to bear the image of God; its destiny, being created to share the inner sanctuary of the universe in fellowship with God Himself for all the æons to come, these are the things which help to emphasize the real greatness, the sacredness of human life.

The nobler-minded of the heathen, though they looked at man with eyes enlightened only by the lamp of human reason, and measured human life only by the standard of his capacity for pleasure and present achievement, or in view of that for which they but dimly hoped, sometimes had rather exalted conceptions of the character of human life. But usually it was not so. With them, generally, life was held very cheaply. In ancient Rome multitudes thronged the amphitheatre, to witness, with every manifestation of delight, strong men hew each other to pieces. It is so wherever God has not been allowed to teach man his own true nature. It is the truth concerning human life revealed in God's Word which makes it so inestimably precious. And it is not only because we were created by God, but because of the relationship we are to sustain to Him. We are not only God's handiwork, but His children.

Throughout the whole history of the covenant

relationship between God and man there has been a progressive revelation of the sacredness of human life. So far as the revelation itself is concerned, it reached its climax in the coming and teaching of Jesus Christ. In the very fact of the Son of God becoming man we have a witness, greater than human language can ever express, to the worth and potential greatness of human life.

The worth, the sacredness of human life! Is it not foolishness to speak thus? If we open our eyes and look around us, is what we see not enough to disprove all talk about this greatness and sacredness of which men speak? Not to see much which makes earnest, thinking people sad at heart is to be blind and obtuse indeed. The blush of shame must often mantle the cheek as the result of what one sees and hears. All around there are lying, drunken, selfish, beastly, besotted men and women; those who scheme and plot, and are cruel in carrying out their plans. Everywhere there are those who, like bats, love the darkness, and fatten like vampires on the blood of their fellows; those who leer and gibe and mock at everything holy, whose looks and words are salacious, who live in a moral and spiritual charnel house. All this is only too sadly true. But all this, and all that might be added, does not disprove our contention, nor quench our optimism. What we see is not human life as God brought it forth. It is a wretched caricature of it. Sin has terribly disfigured the handiwork of God as it was shown in human life when it left His hand. But the groundwork, the potentiality, is still there. It is when we see the Spirit of God at work in man, when he has come forth a spiritually new creature, loathing sin and struggling to be liberated from it; when we see him a humble suppliant at the throne of grace, walking humbly with God, and going forth with the light of new faith and love in his eyes, strong in his determination to count no cost in the service of God and of God's other children, — then we begin to catch glimpses of that other man, the true man, the man made in the image of God.

You have heard, have you not, of the lost portrait of Dante? This portrait was painted on the walls of the Bargello, at Florence. For many years, I know not how long, it was supposed that the picture had been destroyed, so completely had all traces of it been lost. In the course of time there came an artist who had hopes that it might be found, and with determination to spare no pains in the attempt to find it. The place where tradition said the picture had been painted was a lumber room, filled with all kinds of litter. The walls had been heavily coated with whitewash. Undaunted, the artist had the place carefully cleaned. Then he began, cautiously, to remove the whitewash from the wall. After a while lines and color began to appear. And after much careful, painstaking work had been done, there was to be seen, in much of its original strength and beauty of execution, the picture of the grave, noble face of the great poet. A striking illustration this of the work Christ did for the restoration of humanity. Man is lost, but he is lost only because he originally belonged to God. Man is a prodigal, but a prodigal is still a son, and there is still a place for him in the Father's house. He may dwell among the swine, and may have developed many swinish propensities; but he is not one of them. He is capable of being brought to his senses, of recalling his Father's house, of appreciating his Father's embrace, and of wearing with growing grace the new raiment the Father provides. The image given him has been disfigured, but it is capable of being restored. Life, as it is now by nature, is sadly disjointed; but it is capable of being again articulated. Man is a guilty sinner, but God is willing to pardon, and man is capable of reconciliation and growing holiness. This is all God's work, but even God could not do it if the possibility were not in man. Thus, does man, even in his worst estate, give evidence of the greatness and sacredness of his life.

The final word as to the proof of the worth of human life is found in this that, to accomplish that of which we have been speaking, the Son of God did not only become man in order to give the world another glimpse of a real, true man in his beauty and power; but to die for mankind. And what is the central meaning of this inexpressibly great sacrifice, if not to show us that God Himself counts no sacrifice too great to pay for the redemption and restoration of a human life?

The Christian Attitude Toward Life

The supreme practical question of Christianity is that of man's attitude toward life. The question of our attitude toward life is virtually one with that of our attitude toward God. We cannot have right thoughts about life and wrong thoughts about God. We cannot serve God acceptably and neglect or abuse life. Ignorance of life, its origin, nature, and destiny, is back of much of the waste and abuse of life. It is this which must be corrected. Because of sin and consequent weakness, man's achievement is always many degrees behind his vision and desire. We can never, therefore, expect men to show their appreciation of life in any adequate degree till they have become impregnated through and through with the idea of its dignity and worth.

We see this principle illustrated in every sphere of life's activities. Men struggle for the things which they think most worth while. They scramble for money, position, fame — a variety of goals dominated by the much abused term "success." We must put something of this principle into practice with respect to life, but we must fashion it from the viewpoint of God's Word and will. The first step is the cultivation of a consciousness of the true worth of life. Life is not the mere fact of living, nor the struggle to get and enjoy; it is the God-given gift of life itself of which we speak. When this has been accomplished, a motive will have been established, more powerful than any other, for the proper care of life.

The Christian attitude toward life is one of keen discrimination. The child of God knows that his body is worth taking care of, for his physical life also is God-given. Because of this he cannot with impunity abuse or weaken it. It is the instrument by and through which he is to work. He is obligated, then, to take the best possible care of it. It is a sin against God unnecessarily to weaken or injure the body, and thus to lessen the scope and character of the work which might have been done through it. Much of this is constantly being done by ignorance, but the ignorance itself is a sin; for we have no right to be ignorant of such important, far-reaching matters. Ignorant, careless children are not usually entrusted with pieces of mechanism delicate and costly. The very fact of our having life ought to lead each one to make a study, as thorough as possible, of its nature. If we take life, care for it, use it as a gift of God, it will crown us with blessings. If we handle it carelessly, degrade it, abuse it, it will curse and slay us.

The highest worth of the bodily life lies in this that it is the vehicle, or instrument, of a higher form of life, that of the soul, or spirit. There are too many, not only in the world, but in the churches, who give evidence that they understand by life chiefly that of the body, and even such fragmentary conceptions do not always move on the highest plane. They pamper the body, gratify all its desires and call this caring for the body. Nothing is further from the truth. The body must often be kept in restraint, and its desires crucified, if the inner life is to flourish. Indeed, Jesus Himself teaches us that circumstances may arise which call for the sacrifice of the bodily life, and that only by so doing can one inherit the larger life. It is the soul-life, and its salvation, which is the matter of supreme importance, according to the Biblical, Christian view.

It is eternity, and man's eternal relationship to God, the author of life, without whose presence and favor no life can be blessed, which gives its vital importance to the great problem of human life. And this earthly span of existence is the school in which we are to receive the training for the great beyond. God has done all that infinite wisdom, power, and love, working through a Father's heart, can do to make our schooling a success. He has sent a Savior to make it possible for us to profit by our schooling. God is still sending His Spirit to open our blind eyes, to touch and revitalize our dead hearts, to enable us to receive Christ in whom we have forgiveness of sin and new life, and to be our constant teacher and comforter. And God's aim, in all the disciplining processes of this school-life, is to prepare us for eternal life. And eternal life is by no means the same as an endless continuity of life. No human life shall ever cease to be, so the Word of God teaches us. But eternal life is eternal holiness, eternal blessedness, eternal glory, eternal fellowship in all these things with God Himself.

In the enlightened Christian view of life there is no room for the question, "Is life worth living?" That is settled by the premises which condition life itself. Life here may be but poorly provided with the things which minister to comfort; it may be heavily handicapped by weaknesses, and burdened with pain; it may be hard beset by trials and temptations; but it is still the gift of God, and if it is submitted humbly, believingly, to Him, its discipline will be only such as will fit it for its glorious destiny. And none of those who have caught the vision of what life is, and of that radiant angel of life who beckons us on and gives us, ever and anon, glimpses of the life which is to be, will count the cost of the discipline too great.

Let us prize life! It is Divine in its origin, mysterious in its nature, magnificent in its possibilities, utterly beyond the full comprehension of any merely human mind, as it is beyond the complete control of any human power. What obligations this puts upon us to take proper care of it, and cultivate it! If any one of us had a casket of gems, would he not exercise every precaution to preserve them? The value of life, of each individual life, is beyond computation in the terms of material things. It is the only thing with which we shall stand in the presence of God. When we come into that presence may we stand adorned with the righteousness of Christ! That righteousness, possessed in faith, is eternal life here and now, and the pledge of it in its final beatific fullness and majesty.

THOU SHALT DO NO MURDER

"Thou shalt do no murder." — EXODUS 20, 13.

"Whoso sheddeth man's blood, by man shall his blood be shed." — GENESIS 9, 6.

"All they that take the sword shall perish by the sword." — ST. MATT. 26, 52.

GOD'S WORD provides the lenses through which we get to see human life in the right light: what it was originally, what it has become, what it may yet become. It shows us that life not only came from God, but that it had impressed upon it the very image of God the Maker, Himself. It shows us that, in spite of all that devils and men have done to mar, to destroy, the image of God in man, its potential elements are still present in such manner that its restoration is possible. This Word, moreover, shows us how desirous God Himself is to have this image restored, and tells us what He has done and is still doing to have this restoration realized. Further, this Word helps us to visualize the endless career which stretches out before the children of men, a career which means either an endless groping in darkness and self-loathing or an endless fellowship with the spirits which inhabit the celestial realm and walk in company with the Eternal Father Himself. Only when we thus view life, are we capable of appreciating aright its sacredness and begin to realize the full import of the command of the great Author of life, "Thou shalt do no murder." Influenced by right conceptions of life, we will want to keep our hands free from the stain of blood, not only because we are afraid of becoming entangled in the meshes of the law; but because we appreciate what life is, and cherish it as God's greatest gift.

Gross Forms of Murder

When we speak of the usual forms of murder of the gross kind we need spend no time on definitions. We know what is meant by this species of murder, whatever may be the particular manner in which it is committed or whatever the weapon or instrument used in its commission.

It might seem that there is but little need of speaking against this kind of murder to the average audience of intelligent, humane, not to say, Christian, people. Are not the only classes who need instruction on this subject those who have fallen into the clutches of the law, and are gathered into our jails and other penal institutions? Unquestionably the average man and woman detests the crime of murder. But there is, nevertheless, much reason why the men and women of the law-abiding class, yea, why the men and women who sit regularly in the pews in our churches should hear the voice of God thundering from Sinai, "Thou shalt do no murder." If for no other reason, we should hear it because we are a part of the common, or social, body, bearing our share of the responsibility for the conditions which prevail in our citizenship; for, with respect to the crying sin of murder, conditions are far from good in our country.

The late Andrew D. White, one of the most

capable and painstaking students of American criminology, has shown that in spite of our boasted advance in the art of living, the number of murders in proportion to the population has been steadily increasing. He called this the most disgraceful evil in our national life. This shows us that for the proper safeguarding of human life merely intellectual culture and the inculcation of merely humanitarian considerations is not enough. Men must be impregnated with the thought of the sacredness of human life as God's Word presents this truth. The Spirit of God, who alone teaches men rightly to cherish life, their own and that of others, must dwell in their lives as the most potent influence.

We sometimes hear this increase of murder explained by attributing it to the influx of people of foreign birth, many of whom are of an undesirable class. But the point of this argument loses most of its force when we are reminded that in no other civilized country in the world are there so many murders in proportion to the population as right here in our own land. Even southern Italy, where the Camorra and Mafia societies flourish, has many less murders to a given population than we have here. And just beyond the border in Canada, where there is just as much of a mixture of nationalities as we have here, there are far fewer violations of the Fifth Commandment than on this side of the invisible boundary. Whether we will have it so or not, this condition puts part of a grave responsibility on us; for we are a part of the society in which this state of things exists, and we are not free of the blood of the slain till we have done our utmost to rectify conditions; nor free of the blame till we have done all we can do to have proper laws enacted and then fearlessly and impartially executed, whether the offender be a prince of the intellectual realm or the merest lout, a millionaire or a pauper. We are our brothers' keepers.

Capital Punishment

This discussion brings us to the important subject of capital punishment. Capital punishment is the legally enjoined punishment for the crime of murder. It is the conviction of many that the enforcement or non-enforcement of this penalty has much to do with the attitude of our people toward the Fifth Commandment, the first requirement of which is not to take human life. Notwithstanding, there are a great many who consider this punishment as contrary to the spirit of the age and of Christianity.

That capital punishment, namely, the taking of human life as a punishment for murder, was sanctioned by God's Law of old can not be questioned. Such taking of life was not murder. Nor are those murderers who, to-day, execute the just decrees of the law. Murder is the taking of human life on one's own initiative, from the desire of revenge or other evil motives. The Fifth Commandment prohibits the taking of human life in this way. Language cannot be clearer and more absolute than the words, "Thou shalt do no murder" (Rev. Ver.). Where the Scriptures speak of the taking of human life by due process of law and as a punishment for a crime deserving such treatment, another word is used. This removes the objection of those who appeal to the inclusive and peremptory character of the Fifth Commandment as an argument against capital punishment.

Some of the modern advocates of the abolition of capital punishment remind us of certain of the ancient sectaries, such as the Manichæans and others, who pressed the Fifth Commandment so far that they thought it sinful to pull for food a growing turnip or to kill a troublesome flea.

So insistently did God's ancient law decree the penalty of death for the murderer that no sanctuary sufficed to shield him from this fate. You recall that God had cities of refuge appointed to which those who unwittingly, by ignorance or accident, took human life might flee, and be safe from those who still desired to wreak vengeance on them. But the one who, with malice and purpose, took life might be taken from the very altar and put to death. God established this law of retribution, to be executed by the proper tribunal instituted by Himself, not only to emphasize the sacredness of human life, and the inalienable right of the inoffensive man to life and liberty; not only because it was the punishment best befitting the crime committed, but, unquestionably, because it would serve as the most effectual deterrent to those who would be restrained by no other consideration. And, notwithstanding all arguments to the contrary, experience has proven that it is the most effectual check on those who recognize no law but their own angry passions. In other lands, for instance in the British Isles, where murderers are far less likely to escape the penalty of the law than in our land, murder is of much less frequent occurrence than with us.

Those who argue for the abolition of the death penalty for murder generally do so on the ground that we should get away from the barbaric blood-thirstiness of the dark ages, or base their plea on the character of the New Testament. The plea for mercy, even for the murderer, has an appeal in it which it is hard for some natures to resist. There is no normal man who does not recoil from the thought of having anything to do with the taking of human life. But shall all the mercy be shown the criminal who takes human life, and none the law-abiding citizens who must live in fear of being deprived of life? The law takes cognizance of mitigating circumstances, and this is right. No man's life should be taken when any doubt exists as to his guilt. It is even questionable whether the death penalty should ever be enacted on merely circumstantial evidence. But where it is clear that men with malice aforethought or in the course of other crime, commit murder, then the society that sets them free makes itself a partner in that crime, and no less so in the future crimes they may commit.

Some Christian people argue that the New Testament, if not the Old, breathes a spirit which precludes the idea of taking human life as a penalty, even by due process of law. They say the spirit which Christ taught his disciples is opposed to it. If that is true we say yea and amen. But we have failed to find this spirit in His teaching. We grant that the ideal toward which the Kingdom of God is to move is the reign of the Gospel of peace and good will. But the ideal has not yet been attained. As long as men persist in resisting God's goodness and refuse to live on the Gospel plan and perpetrate crimes, they are under the law, and must accept the penalty of outraged law.

The passage in which Christ tells Peter, who would have defended his Master with carnal weapons, to put up his sword, because "they that take the sword shall perish with the sword" (St. Matth. 26, 52), is adduced as evidence that Christ prohibits capital punishment. It is much rather a reproof of Peter's failure to realize that Christ's Kingdom cannot be furthered by weapons of carnal warfare, because it is not a kingdom of this world. It was to Peter a reminder of the law which forbade the individual taking the law into his own hands. By so doing he would make himself subject to the law of the land, which could put him to death for such rash conduct. In reality these words, instead of disproving capital punishment, rather sanction it.

In Romans thirteen, which we considered a few weeks ago, we are told that government is of God, and that rulers are for the punishment of those who do evil. If men are not to be adequately punished for murder, if justice is to be a lost virtue, why not apply the same principle to the thief and every other law-breaker?

The trouble is that men are turning away from the Word of God. The old Biblical doctrine of sin and punishment is distasteful to them. They prefer the doctrine of development, of reformation. We all want reformation, but let such reformatory effort be put forth before men have become murderers and inoffending citizens' lives have been sacrificed. We stand by the Word of God, which teaches the right and duty of those in authority to punish evildoers. The truth set forth by St. Paul, in Romans 13, is affirmed by St. Peter (2, 14) and by St. John (Rev. 13, 10).

I have dwelt on this subject at some length because of the periodic and persistent agitation for the abolition of the death penalty. It seems a very strange condition of things that the legal execution of murderers should be about the only form of taking human life that draws upon itself, to any great extent, the protests of the sentimentalists. Are we not known throughout the civilized world as the nation where murder most abounds? And is there not much complacency about it? We have heard of no campaigns started for the correction of the evil. Only one murderer out of four in our land is ever brought to trial. Only one out of every ten of those brought to trial is even sentenced to prison for the crime of murder. Only one accused murderer out of every eighty is executed. With this condition staring us in the face, a condition at which the world points the finger of scorn, there is but little outcry about the sacredness of human life, about the inalienable right of man to life and the pursuit of happiness. The only class which elicits the sympathy of our sentimental reformers is that of the murderers. This uncalled-for outcry against the death penalty has had much to do in bringing about the condition we have described, and which is constantly getting worse. It is because we have lost our respect for the sovereign majesty of the law. It is because we fail to seek the good of the many who are law-abiding citizens, and have turned our misguided sympathies toward the few who have elected to be anarchists, knowing no law but their own perverted will and passions. I believe it is the solemn duty of every Christian to vote against the abolition of capital punishment, and to use every opportunity for lifting up his voice, and to bring all influence to bear on the strict enforcement of the law, whether it be against murder or any other violation of law.

War and Murder

The subject of war properly comes up for consideration under the Fifth Commandment. All the more does it press for careful treatment at a time like this, when our brothers across the sea and to the south of us are drenching the ground with the heart-blood of their bravest and strongest.

A great cry of anguish is going up to the throne of heaven, not only from the wounded and dying, not only from the widows and orphans, not only from bereaved fathers and mothers; but from all those who know and feel anything of the ties of the general brotherhood of man, from all those who believe in a Kingdom of God on earth, and who work and pray for its upbuilding. Everywhere the declaration is made that this must be the last great war. We pray that it may be so. That is the Divine ideal. Jesus came to make men brothers. War compels them to act as fiends. War is one of the most dreadful evils that can be visited on a people. In addition to causing the loss of life and property, it sets back civilization greatly. Human ideals of the more spiritual kind are greatly hindered. Every constructive movement is arrested in its progress. Both victor and vanquished suffer in this way. If all rulers and those who help to make their policies were really Christians, and were not so often consumed by insane jealousies and equally insane greed, the prophecies descriptive of the Messianic Kingdom would be nearer realization: "They shall beat their swords into plowshares, and their spears into pruning hooks; nation shall not lift up sword against nation, neither shall they learn war any more" (Isa. 2, 4). But we entertain no sanguine expectations that present conditions shall be speedily and radically changed. Still more certain are we that universal peace will not come as the result of humanitarian Peace Congresses, or international treaties. Present European conditions—a curious commentary upon the boasted twentieth century culture—are sufficient proof of this. These movements have some influence; as an educational propaganda they will not be fruitless; but they prove no effectual barrier against the spirit of national aggrandizement, racial antipathy, and the burning desire for commercial supremacy. The only guarantee of a real brotherhood, which shall no longer learn the arts of war, is to get the nations to hoist to the very pinnacle of their flagstaffs the pennant of the King of kings, and make subordinate to that the emblems of all parties and interests. But to bring this about, the majority of the people everywhere, and especially the leaders, must be children of God, not only in name, but in reality.

God must be the acknowledged sovereign of men's hearts, before the real brotherhood of man can be inaugurated.

The contention is not Biblically correct that all warfare is necessarily wholesale murder, though I do believe that in every conflict of the mailed fist some person or party will have to bear the guilt of wholesale murder. We have reached a stage where calmness, sanity of judgment, and methods of arbitration should be allowed to settle all difficulties. But as the State is bound to defend society against a murderous person, so it is bound to defend its people when another State arises against it. If patient, brotherly pleading will not deter the aggressors nor bring them to just measures, those assailed may rightfully defend themselves. They should indeed be long-suffering; they should exhaust every peaceable means of securing justice; they should even be willing to surrender much, and endure much; but if driven to the wall they have the right to appeal to the arbitrament of the sword. Self-defense is a right of nations as well as of individuals. And Christian citizens need have no hesitancy in yielding obedience to the requirements of the civil power under such circumstances. This is proven by the fact that God Himself has more than once, and in more than one way, sanctioned war (Judges 20, 27 f.; I Kings 22, 6 ff.). If Israel had not been directed to make war upon the vice-eaten nations of Canaan, she would soon have been extirpated, and the establishment of the Kingdom of God would have been impossible. What was morally permissible then cannot be wrong now. The fundamental principles of morals never change.

If any change was to have been made we should have expected it with the founding of the New Dispensation. But we find no such prohibition of war. The right of waging warfare under certain circumstances is assumed. When soldiers came to the iconoclastic John the Baptist, asking what they should do to prepare themselves for the Kingdom of Christ, he did not stipulate as a requisite that they should lay down the profession of arms. The centurion, so highly praised by Christ, was a soldier; yet he received no censure. Another centurion, who received a heaven-sent vision directing him in his spiritual perplexities, and upon whom the Holy Spirit descended in miraculous manner, was allowed to remain in the service even of a heathen king (Acts 10).

Our God is not a God of war. He is no Christian Mars. He is a Father, a God of peace and good will. His aim is to cause wars to cease unto the ends of the earth. But His omnipotence extends even to the sphere in which there is clash of arms. When the monsters of man's construction belch forth death and destruction, He is still God. And in the end He makes these chastisements, which are the fruits of wickedness, to praise Him.

Self-Murder

Another dark, gruesome subject that must be treated under the Fifth Commandment is that which deals with self-murder, or suicide.

The increasing prevalence of this crime renders the consideration of this subject imperative. In the past half-century suicide has increased in European countries four hundred per cent., while the population has increased only sixty per cent.

Self-murder has ever been prevalent among heathen people. This is explained by the twofold fact that they have no true conception of the sacredness of human life, and that among them living conditions are less tolerable than in those lands where the beneficent rays of love, Divine and human, are shed abroad among men from the page of Revelation. But even clear-sighted heathen discerned the cowardice of self-destruction. Plato, for example, described suicide as a desertion of the post of duty.

It is a sad commentary on the religious condition of most professing Christian countries that suicide is alarmingly on the increase. We have about ten thousand suicides annually in the United States. In ten years an army greater than those which decided some of the great battles of history ushers itself, uncalled, into the presence of God. It makes one shudder to contemplate this awful fact. In a number of European countries the condition is still worse. This is attributable to two correlated causes. The chief one is that men are losing their faith: their faith in God and their faith in their own eternal destiny. We are not surprised that men like Hume, Gibbon, and Ingersoll should argue in behalf of man's right to end his own life. It is because virtual infidelity has taken hold of so many people that life is held so cheap. This is shown from statistics. In Germany a few years ago, to every one hundred thousand of population there were seven hundred and thirteen suicides. Of these only sixty-eight were even nominally Christian, forty were Jews, and six hundred and five were non-Christian. I doubt not that the same disparity would be found elsewhere.

Through the loss of faith men become materialists. They live only for what they can get out of the present life in the form of material gain, honor, or pleasure. When these things fail, when disease or misfortune cut short their hopes of gain, the ties which hold them to life fail, and they end it all, as they say. Life, to them, is no longer worth living.

Ending it all! But it is not ending it all. "It is appointed unto men once to die, but after this the Judgment" (Heb. 9, 27).

Sometimes the stories of self-destruction are exploited in the newspapers in the language of heroics. In any case, it is nothing short of cowardly and contemptible for people to take their own lives. And all the more is this so when, as is often the case, the self-murderer leaves behind those still less strong and capable to fight alone the unequal battle with adverse circumstances.

The real instigator of this crime—of all crimes, indeed, but more directly of this than of many another—is the devil, who was "a murderer from the beginning," and the father of lies, especially the blackest and most damnable of all lies—those which deceive men as to the nature, purpose, and destiny of life.

The Fifth Commandment applies as well to the

self-murderer as to the murderer of any other life. "Do thyself no harm," is the admonition of Holy Writ. And another Scripture declares that "no murderer hath eternal life abiding in him" (I John 3, 15).

A question that injects itself into this discussion is that which has to do with the responsibility of the person who lays destroying hands on himself. It seems that a fully rational person could not be capable of such an act. Many, unquestionably, are not rational at the time the deed is done, but he who knows Satan's power over the soul deceived by him will not doubt that many commit suicide with full consciousness of what they are doing. And we dare not forget that responsibility may go back far beyond the time when the deed is committed. When, by the spirit of ambition or greed, one has been led to apply himself so strenuously as to undermine his health and dethrone reason, or if the same results are brought about by sin, such as drunkenness or lust, the responsibility for suicide remains, because a moral and spiritual collapse brought on that of the mind. This fact helps to emphasize how careful and prayerful we should be in watching the whole sphere of life.

The terribleness of the sin of suicide is augmented by the fact that, if successful, it ushers the perpetrator into the very presence of God with little or no opportunity for repentance.

In cases of suicide where the mind has become unbalanced, from sickness or other causes not superinduced by overt acts of sin, we may suspend judgment and leave the victim to the mercy of God, who deals rightly with all.

Race Suicide, Infanticide

One of the forms of murder which often ends, if not purposely, in self-murder, is that of race suicide, or child-murder. Of all the dark sins which blacken the pages of history, chiefly unwritten history, is that of the murder of unborn offspring. If there were no other evidence, this would suffice to prove that there must be a hell of some sort; otherwise this class of murderers would not get their desert. Of all the cruel, damnable things I think the darkest and most damnable is that which links the name which should be the sweetest and most sacred among men—the name mother, with one of the foulest of crimes, murder.

Race suicide, the refusal of men and women, especially women of a certain sort — selfish, luxury-loving, without patriotism, women who wish to be wives but not mothers, is bad enough, though no murder be committed. It runs counter to the highest laws of God and the noblest instincts of humanity. It is both a result of race deterioration and a decisive contributing factor to it. It marks a condition of social dry-rot. It helps to loosen the marriage bond. It is a fruitful parent of lust. But when, to avoid maternal duties, prospective parents, lacking the parental instincts native even to the tiger and the hyena, redden their hands and damn their souls by taking the life of their unborn children, language fails to be an adequate medium for expressing the feelings of loathing and condemnation which surge through the souls of right-thinking people.

Some of the most perplexing, heartrending problems I have ever had to deal with in my ministry were those brought by cases of this kind. What can be done, in a brief space of time, to help those in a spiritual way who, in perpetrating murder, give at the same time the thrust which speedily wrought their own destruction.

And of all those who deserve execration and contempt at the hands of their fellows, at the head, indeed, in a class by themselves, stand those who are called to minister unto life, who have taken the Hippocratic oath to defend and save life; but, for a few paltry dollars, debase their noble profession and become the instruments for taking the most innocent and helpless form of human life. If there were no hell, such men would not get their deserts.

The Punishment for Murder

Of the legal punishment for murder I have spoken under the caption of both capital punishment and of war; but there is a punishment for murder above and beyond that of human law. Murder shuts the door of heaven in the face of its perpetrator. "No murderer hath eternal life abiding in him" (I John 3, 15; Gal. 5, 21). There are venial sins, sins of mere thoughtlessness and weakness, the commission of which does not imply that the one guilty of them has ceased to be a child of God. But the one with the spirit of murder in his heart cannot be a child of God. He must cease to be a murderer, not only in act, but in spirit, before he can ever become a child of God. That this is possible for even the actual murderer is shown by the example of the thief on the cross, and by Christ's prayer for His own murderers.

There is another punishment for murder of which it is questionable whether any one can ever be fully freed. There is no other sin against another person which wreaks its own vengeance on the perpetrator as does murder. It comes through the conscience, that monitor within, which is but the God-implanted counterpart of that Law which He wrote on the table of stone, "Thou shalt do no murder."

The murderer can seldom rest. He feels that everybody knows his dark secret. Even inanimate objects seem to him to have tongues with which to tell of it. The spectre of his victim haunts him in the silent watches of the night. Perhaps you recall the first scene of the fifth act in Macbeth. Macbeth, at the instigation of his wife, had slain Duncan, King of the Scots, while he was their guest. The crime preyed on her mind. It made her sleep troubled. Every night she would rise in her sleep, take the lighted taper she kept in her room, walk back and forth, and go through the motion of washing her hands. But with all her washing the imagined stain would not disappear. "Yet here's a spot," she was forced to say. And then she cried aloud, "Out, damned spot! Out, I say! What, will these hands ne'er be clean? Here is the smell of blood still; all the perfume of Arabia will not sweeten this little hand." So works the voice of conscience, which is but the soul repeating the voice of Him who said, and still says, "Thou shalt do no murder."

There is but one agent can cleanse the hand and the heart stained with blood. Not the perfumes of Arabia, not all the penance the most determined spirit can perform; but the blood of Jesus Christ the crucified, received in penitence and faith. "Though your sins be as scarlet, they shall be as white as snow" (Isa. 1, 18).

INDIRECT MURDER

"Thou shalt not kill." — EXOD. 20, 13.

"If an ox gore a man or a woman, that they die: then the ox shall be surely stoned, and his flesh shall not be eaten; but the owner of the ox shall be quit. But if the ox were wont to push with his horn in time past, and it hath been testified to his owner, and he hath not kept him in, but that he hath killed a man or a woman; the ox shall be stoned, and his owner also shall be put to death." — EXOD. 21, 28, 29.

IN thinking and speaking of murder, the average person usually has in mind only the actual and direct taking of human life,—as, for instance, with poison, a revolver, a dirk or some similarly deadly instrument. This probably accounts for the complacency so many exhibit when it comes to considering the command which says: "Thou shalt do no murder." Most people, on hearing these words, will at once say—that does not condemn me. That is at least one command of the Decalogue which I have not broken. My hands are not stained with blood. Those who speak thus have only a superficial understanding of the requirements of God's Law. And if I succeed in giving a proper presentation to some of the thoughts I have gathered, as direct statements or unmistakable inferences, from the Word of God, our complacency will, probably, be pretty well shaken; for we shall learn that murder, in God's sight, is not only the actual taking of human life contrary to the will of God, but anything which injures or may shorten life—our own or that of some one else. And not only so, but that the malevolent emotions, hidden down deep in our own hearts and known only to ourselves and God, such as anger and hatred, are murder in God's sight; for they are the germinating seeds of murder in act.

In distinction to the forms of murder of which we spoke in our last lesson; the deeds which resulted in the more or less speedy extinction of life, we will confine ourselves, to-day, to a consideration of what we may appropriately call Indirect and Prolonged Murder.

Murder by Indirect Complicity

The laws of both God and man take cognizance of certain forms of complicity in crime. For instance, the man who plans a murder and then, by bribery, or other method, incites some one else to commit the deed, is considered as guilty, in some cases more guilty, than the actual perpetrator. David, who thus contrived the death of Uriah, was more a murderer than the soldier in the line of battle who executed the king's orders. And the men in high places, at the head of labor unions, political and other organizations, who, to gain a point or get revenge, plot against the lives of others, often deserve much more execration and greater punishment, than the minions they employ to carry out their bloody work. The latter are often men of but low mental and moral type, to whom a few dollars appear larger than a human life; while the men higher up are the ones who prostitute noble gifts and great opportunity to ignoble ends.

There are, however, other forms of complicity

in taking human life which are not so apparent and of which the law of to-day takes little or no notice. For instance, there are forms of carelessness which make those guilty of it responsible for the consequences resulting from it. The Law of God, of old, required that a vicious ox, which killed a human being, should be put to death (Exod. 21, 29). Human life was held above all property considerations. But if the animal was known to be vicious and the owner had been warned of this, but failed to keep it properly guarded, then, if the ox killed a man, not only was the ox put to death, but the owner also was considered guilty of murder and could be put to death. He was regarded as guilty because of criminal negligence.

If this law were in force to-day a great many respectable people would get into serious trouble. I, of course, do not mean that law literally interpreted and applied only to the ox and his master; but the application of the principle therein contained to present day conditions. If the man who had a vicious ox, but did not confine it, was guilty of shedding blood when it killed an innocent bystander, what shall we say of the railway and other magnates who, to boost dividends, keep their employees at work till they drop from exhaustion? When these men, overcome by the infirmities of nature, make mistakes which cost their own lives and, may be, the lives of scores of others, where lies the blame? Whose hands are red with blood? They are the hands of those who, for selfish and greedy gain, would push humanity beyond the point of endurance. The same principle applies in every sphere where similar conditions prevail. Laws have, in some instances, been enacted looking to the betterment of these conditions; but there is still room for much improvement.

The pure carelessness of employees, who have not a shadow of excuse for it, not infrequently makes them guilty of complicity in the death of others. If the failure to keep an unruly ox securely tied made the owner guilty of murder when a human life was crushed out by the enraged animal, how about the workman who recognizes a serious flaw in some piece of important work he is turning out, a piece of work on the strength and dependableness of which the safety of human lives are to depend; but who, because he does not wish to lose a little time or money, fills the flaw with a little putty and covers it over with paint? When that piece of machinery or whatever it may be gives way under the strain, and precious human lives are left mangled and bleeding as a result, who is the guilty person? Who is the red-handed murderer? None other than that careless, inconsiderate, selfish workman, whose own life, by right, ought to pay the forfeit for his criminal carelessness.

If the owner of a vicious ox became a murderer through the acts of that animal, when he did not use proper precautions in confining it, what name shall we give to those who, for the sake of a little added profit, adulterate food products; not only with a cheaper grade of material, but not infrequently with matter which is decidedly injurious to health? Are they not murderers, also? Yes, and murderers of a very coarse and brutal type. And yet this thing was so frequent in this enlightened, cultured land of ours that the federal government had to take strong measures to prevent it.

The sweatshop owners of the North and North-east; the cotton mill owners of the South and South-west; and all those everywhere who exploit women and children or men either, for that matter, for the smallest possible pittance, for less than it takes adequately to support life in the plainest, most self-denying manner; and do this in order to pay big dividends on watered stock, that the favored few may roll in luxury on an unearned increment;—all these are guilty of an indirect, prolonged form of murder. Hood's poem on the seamstress has a real application to-day. The poet was not narrating fiction for his day, and it is nothing if not realistic to-day:

> "O, men, with sisters dear!
> O, men, with mothers and wives!
> It is not linen you're wearing out,
> But human creatures' lives!
> Stitch-stitch-stitch,
> In poverty, hunger, and dirt,
> Sewing at once, with a double thread,
> A shroud as well as a shirt."

The tenement owners who build dark, damp, ill-ventilated, unsanitary dwellings for the use of the poorer classes, because they cost less and will return larger profits; those who own and control places where men's bodies as well as their souls are destroyed; all those, indeed, who, from a spirit of greedy selfishness, produce or maintain conditions whereby the lives of their fellowmen are unnecessarily endangered and finally destroyed, all these are, in a degree and often in no inconsiderable degree, guilty of murder. And those who do not do all they can to correct these evils become guilty of contributing to the wrongs perpetrated.

There are still many other ways in which men become involved in indirect murder. I cannot begin to enumerate all of them and will mention but a few of the more common ones. How frequently children, by inconsiderate, ill-advised conduct, not only blight their own lives; but break their parents' hearts and hasten their end. Parents sometimes do the same thing for their children, and married people for one another. This is one of the most cruel kinds of injury. It is often worse than the thrust of a sword. Recall the heart-broken lament of Jacob when his unfilial sons brought back Joseph's bloody coat. "And Jacob rent his clothes, and put sackcloth on his loins, and mourned for his son many days. * * * And he said, I will go down into the grave unto my son mourning" (Gen. 38). Jacob lived to learn the truth and to be comforted, but I very much doubt whether he ever fully recovered from this blow. And it is certain that multitudes of parents and other people go down to their graves with broken, bleeding hearts, and that their going is much hastened by the unnatural conduct of those who ought to be the staff and comfort of their lives.

If men become guilty of murder by contributory negligence or when they only abet those who take life, what shall we say of the governmental officials who allow certain citizens of our country to help perpetuate the bloodiest war of all history? And what shall we say of the men themselves who, having lost all feeling of humanity, having steeled themselves against the groans of dying thousands, and the wails of other thousands of widows and orphans, robbed of their providers and defenders, prolong the carnage only for the one purpose of enriching themselves? For one thing, it proves that our country's affairs are not really in the hands of the men elected to represent the people and work for their interests, not only in a financial way, but socially and morally; but in the hands of the money barons who, by threats of panic and all other kinds of dire disaster, coerce our officials, of all parties, into accepting or at least enduring their schemes of frenzied and, as in this instance, bloody finance.

Never before has the world seen such an example of the triumph of conscienceless commercialism, at least not in a so-called Christian country. That the whole procedure is in direct contrast to what our government has done before is well known. That it has the right, as well as the power, to put an end to it now is not disputed. That the whole bloody business is outraging the moral consciousness of hundreds of thousands of our best citizens is becoming better known. And no American whose conscience rebels against this iniquitous traffic should cease his efforts till this bloody, unneutral business is stopped, and stopped for all time. No good will ever come to our country from the treasuries swollen with the money that bears the smell of the blood of our brothers beyond the sea, which blood cries out to high heaven. As for those who are directly responsible for this dark, bloody blotch on the pages of our national history, we may well leave them to the judgment of God, whose sentence they will not be able to escape, though they do succeed in subverting human governments. What real enjoyment can they get from this staggering wealth of blood-money? And even before they leave this world they shall have to reckon with this decree of Almighty God: "As I live, saith the Lord God, I will prepare thee unto blood, and blood shall pursue thee; since thou hast not hated blood, even blood shall pursue thee" (Ezek. 35, 6).

We must not forget, in this discussion, that the results of evil actions cannot be confined, wholly, to the actors. It inevitably reaches out and draws others into the stream. In this indirect way many a one has been killed toward whom no violent hands were ever raised. Murder is not only actual blood-shedding. There is a murder that begins with the hearts of men, a man-slaughter not recognized as such by the legal statutes. God knows, this old world has been thoroughly drenched by actual blood, but this is by no means all of the dark, gruesome story. Whoever breaks a heart or blights a life or destroys a soul's vision of hope is a murderer. Let us not boast too quickly that we have never broken the Fifth Commandment. Let us hold up our hands to the searching white light of God's holy Word and we shall very probably find them spotted with the crimson hue which spells murder.

Murder by Neglect

It is no doubt a new thought for many people to be told that they become guilty of murder by contributing, even in an indirect way, to the causes which bring about human hurt, or shorten human life. But this is the interpretation that God's Word puts on the Fifth Commandment. Our next thought takes us still a step farther, on to higher ground. The Scriptures show us that we may become guilty of a person's death where we have had nothing at all to do with producing the conditions which brought to the person suffering his mishap. This is the case when we fail to help him, according to our ability, when he is in need of assistance.

If we were in company with a person who happened to fall into the water and could not swim, could we help having a guilty conscience if that person drowned because we did not attempt his rescue? If we could have saved his life, but did not do so, we are assuredly guilty of that person's blood. The same principle applies to all cases of need. And not only to cases of accident; but in sickness, poverty, and every kind of need.

Luther, in explaining this commandment, in the Larger Catechism, says: "When you allow to go naked one whom you could have clothed, then you permit him to perish from cold. When you see one suffering from hunger and you feed him not, you let him starve to death." He then further quotes the words of Christ in St. Matthew 25: "I was hungry, and ye did not give me to eat; I was thirsty, and ye gave me no drink; I was a stranger, and ye took me not in; naked, and ye clothed me not; sick, and in prison, and ye visited me not;" and says: "That is, you would have left me and my followers to die from hunger, thirst and cold; to be torn by wild beasts; to decay in prison; and to perish from want. What is this but an accusation that they were murderers and bloodhounds?"

According to this interpretation of murder, wealthy Dives, who enjoyed his perfumed baths, lolled around in the raiment of royalty and feasted sumptuously every day, while unfortunate Lazarus, full of sores and covered only with rags, lay starving just beyond his gate, was a murderer. His hands were red with blood. And he went where all those who die as murderers go—he lifted up his eyes in hell.

According to this interpretation, the priest and the Levite, though they were ministrants at God's altar and were just on their way from this holy service, were not free from the guilt of murder when they passed by the sorely wounded fellow-countryman whom they found on the public highway. True, they had not wielded the instruments by which he had been brought low; but they had found him weltering in his blood. They knew he badly needed their help; that if he were allowed to remain as he was during the night he would, in all probability, die before morning. As the event proved, though it came from other hands, a little care would save his life. But the priest and Levite did not give the help for which the man's need called. They went on their way, concerned only about their own safety; and their hands were covered with blood.

They were just as guilty of murder as if the man had died as the result of their indifference.

What a terrible reckoning some people will evidently be eventually called on to make. They have never been called before any earthly tribunal, they are regarded, probably by most of their fellows, as people of clean hands, as exemplary citizens; but what revelations will be made when they stand in the presence of the Judge who is the discerner of hearts. To many of these the Judge will say: I gave you an abundance of the good things of life; you lacked nothing which could minister to creature wants. How about the widows and orphans you allowed to go hungry? How about the aged and infirm you refused to succor? How about the forsaken, the lonely, the broken-hearted you would not condescend to help raise and cheer? And they will be speechless. And though they may have held themselves far above ever actively raising a hand against a fellow mortal, yet their hands will be suffused with crimson, and the word murder will be written all over their narrow, self-centered souls.

Anger as Murder

If we have begun to lose our complacency as a result of the advancing revelations God's Word makes as to the nature of murder, shall we not tremble to learn that there are still other ways of becoming guilty of this crime, and ways which involve still more people? A person may become a murderer in God's sight, by a word, a look, a movement of the heart.

The Saviour tells us, St. Matthew 5, that by

unrighteous anger men subject themselves to the same condemnation which is visited upon the manslayer. And St. John clarifies the matter when he says: "Whoso hateth his brother is a murderer; and ye know that no murderer hath eternal life abiding in him" (I Jno. 3, 15).

There is potential murder in anger, in hatred. It is the germinating seed which bears murder as its ripened fruit. If the inward passion were always repressed the outward crime would always be prevented. Even the heathen moralist understood this, for he declared that men become murderers before ever their hands become stained with blood.

The tongue is the first and handiest weapon of an enraged mind and a burning heart. And many are the bloodless wounds it makes. And many are the more serious physically conflicts for which it prepares the way. No wonder the inspired writers called the tongue a sharp sword and a piercing arrow.

How many people have been murdered by eyes which looked daggers; by tongues which cut and slashed; by hearts which, burning with consuming hatred, wished all manner of evil to the people disliked. And are we altogether guiltless of this indictment? Have our hearts never been filled with the venom of hatred? Have our tongues never hissed with the sound of the serpent? Have our eyes never glowered, showing through these windows of the soul the dark passion burning within?

Prolonged Self-Murder

Indirect, slow murder may be of oneself as well as of another. By excessive and uncontrolled anger, by overwork, worry, intemperance in eating and drinking; by the excessive use of intoxicants and of tobacco, especially on the part of immature lads; by secret excesses, many people are reducing their mental and physical efficiency and shortening their lives. This is nothing less than slow suicide. It may all be done in ignorance, but ignorance does not excuse. We have no right to abuse our bodies in any way. They do not belong to us in the sense that we can do with them as we please. They belong to God, who gave them. Speaking in a special sense of the sin of personal impurity, the Apostle says: "What? know ye not that your body is the temple of the Holy Ghost which is in you, which ye have of God, and ye are not your own? For ye are bought with a price: therefore glorify God in your body, and in your spirit, which are God's" (I Cor. 6, 19, 20).

The strenuous character of our modern American life is telling on the physical condition of our people. This kind of life often begins with our children. The youth of today is often as old as his father, as old in experience, as old in the tenseness of his living, as old in his knowledge of the ways of the world and, if given to much dissipation, as old in the stiffness of his joints. We are crowding weeks into days in the feverish chase after dollars and pleasure. In a way perhaps not meant by the prophet, the children of to-day may die at the age of a hundred years (Isa. 65, 20). When the pace, however laudable the object of pursuit, wears out the body faster than it can recuperate, thus weakening the body and exposing it unnecessarily to the ravages of disease, it is a sin against the body and God who gave it.

This strenuous life is affecting rapid improvement in many directions. But is the game worth the candle? We are paying a big price for the gain. The number of sudden deaths is rapidly increasing. We are fast becoming a race of neurotics. And the accompanying evils of suicidal mania and insanity are making rapid increase. A machine, capable of standing a certain degree of pressure, if taxed beyond that limit is soon strained, weakened and made less efficient. The same is true of this most wonderful piece of mechanism—the human body. This weakened condition affects the body in many ways, predisposing it to many ills. One of the worst is when the mind gives way. And statistics show that the rate of increase in mental ailments has more than doubled in our country in the past twenty years. And much of it is the result of not taking proper care of our God-given bodies; the result of haste and worry and vice. And we will have to give an account to God for all this.

Soul Murder

Soul murder, as the murder of the body, may be direct and gross as well as subtle and indirect. The person who seduces another from the path of virtue often becomes guilty of destroying both the seduced person's body and soul. This is especially true where the violation is not only that of a moral principle, but at the same time of the laws of personal purity and health. A soul, however, may be murdered where the body is left temporarily to flourish. Whenever one person tempts another to commit an act or to a course of life contrary to God's holy will, the tempter becomes guilty of one of the greatest of sins. If God says of the murderer of physical life, "no murderer hath eternal life abiding in him," what think you shall be the punishment He will mete out to those who maim and kill the souls of men?

Many there are who are doing the work of destroying souls under the guise of feeding them with the Bread of Life. They are those who tear the word of God to pieces, deny its most fundamental teachings—the Divinity of Christ, His atoning work, the doctrine of the Sacraments and whatever does not happen to meet with their approval. There were such people in the Old Testament time and God had a word to say about them. "Behold, I am against the prophets, saith the Lord, that steal my Words every one from his neighbor. Behold, I am against the prophets, saith the Lord, that use their tongues, and say, He saith. Behold, I am against them that prophesy false dreams, saith the Lord, and do tell them, and cause my people to err by their lies, and by their lightness; yet I sent them not, nor commanded them" (Jer. 23, 30-32).

God wants us to be personally clean and believing, and what we have He wants us to pass on to others. To act otherwise is sin. Whether it be in the form of false teaching, or wicked example, or direct enticement for another to join us in the commission of evil, God's command is, "let us not therefore judge one another any more; but judge this rather, that no man put a stumbling block or an occasion to fall in his brother's way" (Rom. 14, 13).

There is still another way in which we may have to bear the guilt for the loss of another man's soul, and that is when we have failed to do what we could to save it. Jesus Christ has made it obligatory upon His Church to carry His Gospel to the ends of the earth and to keep it constantly before the children of men. "Go ye therefore, and teach all nations, baptizing them in the name of the Father, and of the Son, and of the Holy Ghost: teaching them to observe all things whatsoever I have commanded you: and, lo, I am with you alway, even to the end of the world" (St. Matt. 28, 19, 20). This means that part of the responsibility for doing this work rests on each one of us individually. Have we discharged this duty according to the measure of our ability? Have we fulfilled Christ's command: "Pray ye the Lord of the harvest, that He would send forth labourers into His harvest?" (St. Matt. 9, 38). Have we carefully considered the question as to whether one of our boys or girls ought not to be given as a missionary? Have we given what we should have given for the spread of the Gospel? Have we spoken to the unchurched and unsaved around us about their souls' salvation? If not, we are not guiltless.

Finally, let us not forget that we can destroy our own souls as well as our own bodies. If we do not feed our souls by reading and meditating on

God's Word, if we neglect to attend the preaching of the Gospel, if we do not live a life of prayer, if we do not put into practice what we hear from God's Word, we are robbing our souls of needed nurture and exercise. And if they die it is our own fault; we have murdered them.

Is there one here, Christian though he be, who has never been guilty of any of these things? God pity us all! The meshes of the Law, the wide ramifications of this Fifth Commandment, have caught all of us in its folds. We all stand convicted of complicity in murder — of men's bodies and souls. And there is but one way in which we can be cleansed.

"There is a fountain filled with blood,
Drawn from Immanuel's veins,
And sinners plunged beneath that flood
Lose all their guilty stains."

THE UNSPEAKABLE SIN

"Thou shalt not commit adultery." — EXODUS 20, 14.

"It is a shame even to speak of those things which are done of them in secret." — EPHESIANS 5, 12.

WE HAVE come now to consider a lesson which it would be much easier to pass by untouched. Some people, when there is little or no call for it, like to speak of such salacious subjects as are condemned by this commandment. For my part, I have never been able to bring myself to speak freely of these things, even to men, and I hope never to lose that innate reserve that causes me to shrink from such conversation. The difficulty is much increased when the occasion comes to speak of these things to a congregation. But we have no authority to pass this commandment by with its lessons untouched; no right to shun its difficulties. This is one of God's holy laws. Jesus Himself and his holy apostles treated of it. And there is certainly abundant reason for believing that the world in this day is still in crying need of having this age-old commandment hurled at it with the thunder-voice of Sinai.

It might be suggested that, however much this commandment may be needed by the world, it could, with safety, be passed by so far as Christian congregations are concerned. St. Peter did not think so. He said to the Christians to whom his first Epistle was addressed: "Dearly beloved, I beseech you as strangers and pilgrims, abstain from fleshly lusts which war against the soul." We, too, need to be on our guard. In spite of the loathing which this subject brings to pure, modest souls it is a seductive sin. The world makes light of it. It smiles complacently at the violation of the law of chastity. Because of this, as well as for other reasons, we need to watch and pray that we be not led into temptation.

If a man were gifted with the tongue of an angel, he would need the gift in order to speak on this subject with appropriate delicacy, and yet with such faithfulness and fearlessness as to give to the unknowing an adequate conception of the fire of hell with which those play who walk the primrose path of dalliance.

In view of the many things comprised in this commandment of which we can speak only by way of inference and allusion, we follow the suggestion of St. Paul, and call the wide subject treated of in this Sixth Commandment The Unspeakable Sin.

Marriage

There is a close logical sequence in the line of thought followed by the commandments of the Second Table of the Law. The Fourth starts out with a treatment of the family relation, that fountain out of which flow, and to which return, all human relations. The Fifth throws its safeguard around the life for the creation of which God has called the family into being. The Sixth Commandment has as its object to guard from pollution the fountain itself from which, under God, the stream of life flows.

As I have spoken somewhat generally of the marriage relation when I treated of the Christian family, in connection with the Second Table, I will speak here only of a few points not dwelt upon there.

Marriage is God's own institution for the primary purpose of perpetuating the sacred mystery and perpetual miracle of human life, and for the disciplining of the individual life so as to fit it as an orderly, working unit in the great social complex. Marriage being God's own conception, and the working out of His own plans, must needs be holy. For God is not, and can not be, the author of anything unholy.

From the earliest Christian centuries there were semi-Christian philosophizing sects which taught that marriage was a less holy state than celibacy. This teaching was based on the false assumption that evil is inherently and essentially connected with matter, that God is not the author of matter, and that, consequently, man was not a pure creature when God invested him with a body. I need not tell Bible students that this is not Biblical. God created matter; and man, as to his whole being, including his body, was pronounced by God very good. Notwithstanding this, a great Church has taken up this heathenish notion, and holds that marriage is a condescension to human weakness, less holy than celibacy. All that we ask you to do is to compare God's Word with the teaching of these people on this subject. When God created man He said of him, he is very good. Of this man God further said, "It is not good for the man to be alone." God Himself created the first bride, brought her to the first bridegroom, and performed the first marriage ceremony which made these twain one. On this Edenic marriage God pronounced His blessing. Throughout the whole Old Testament marriage is considered the normal state of man, and the New Testament reaffirms the teaching of the Old Testament. St. Paul, in the Epistle to the Hebrews, in which are presented some of the most sublime conceptions of the spiritualities of the Kingdom of God, says: "Marriage is honourable in all, and the bed undefiled" (13, 4).

No stronger confirmation of the sanctity of the marriage relation can be found than this that throughout both Testaments marriage is made the symbol of the holiest relation between God and his people. The prophet Isaiah says: "Thy maker is thy husband" (54, 5). Again: "As the bridegroom rejoiceth over the bride, so shall thy God rejoice over thee" (62, 5). In the vision of the peerless Revelator the Church is called "the bride, the Lamb's wife" (21, 9). In the same chapter the completed work of salvation, the gathering together of the finally saved, is described as the marriage supper of the Saviour.

To guard the integrity, the sacredness, of this institution, and to obviate the thwarting of its primary purpose and the poisoning of the stream of life at its very fountain head, God gave this commandment. For this reason every Christian, who loves God, and the things of God, and is, therefore, desirous that God's plans should not be perverted or frustrated; every one who loves humanity and is desirous that it may work out, in health and peace, a glorious and eternal destiny, should pray earnestly and work vigorously, that men, as individuals and as nations, may learn the lessons taught by the Sixth Commandment, and learn them before it is too late.

Divorce

One of the deadly evils which is doing much to destroy the sanctity of marriage and to reduce it to the level of a mere legal contract, to be broken at the whim of one or the other of the contracting parties or by the connivance of both, is divorce. This evil has grown to such proportions and is increasing with such rapid strides that not only churchmen but statesmen as well have repeatedly expressed their alarm. This evil threatens the very foundations of society: the family, the State, the Church. It is the deadliest thrust that can be made at the home, the sacred centre of human relations. As the experience of all history proves, it insures, sooner or later, the downfall of the State. And it is bound eventually to blight and blast the Church.

A generation or two ago divorces were comparatively rare. Now, throughout our land, there is one divorce to ten marriages. In Hamilton county, in our state of Ohio, which, in this respect, is one of the worst in the Union, there is one divorce to every three marriages. At this rate, it takes no seer to tell what the end will be before many more generations have passed.

The divorce evil is but one of the many evidences of a general decadence of morals. Even among the ancient pagan nations divorce was virtually unknown till luxurious living tainted the hearts and poisoned the lives of the people.

Many people still affect abhorrence of the plural marriages of the Mormons. But as a result of our modern easy divorce laws, married life, to many people, becomes but a species of consecutive polygamy. It is an easy way, at least for the rich, of gratifying wandering desire. But in this way the very ends aimed at by the Sixth Commandment; namely, the preservation of the sanctity of the family and the right of children to be born into a family and to be reared by parents who are interested in them and fit to rear them, is defeated; and society is paying, and will increasingly pay, the price of its folly in transgressing this Law of God.

The Word of God recognizes but one ground for securing a divorce, and that is the breaking of this Sixth Commandment by one of the parties to the marriage contract. In the Sermon on the Mount Jesus says: "Whosoever shall put away his wife, saving for the cause of fornication, causeth her to commit adultery, and whosoever shall marry her that is divorced committeth adultery" (St. Matt. 5, 32). In the case of divorce under such circumstances there can be no Divinely legal re-marriage for the guilty person. There is another Scripture passage which, speaking of marriage, says: "If the unbelieving depart, let him depart. A brother or sister is not under bondage in such cases" (1 Cor. 7, 15). On the basis of this passage there are those who hold that wilful desertion, which is virtually a divorce, is a sufficient warrant for a legal divorce on the part of the one deserted. Recognizing both of these as legitimate grounds of divorce, how great is still the difference between the teaching of Scripture on the subject, and its human legal status and the practice of many people.

Some concerted action ought to be taken to improve matters with respect to this crying evil of our times. The Church ought to take decisive steps to this end. I am afraid we cannot look for any material aid in the way of helpful legislation so long as the laws are largely made and executed by men who have little regard for the laws of God and but little favor for its strict morality. They will take no such steps till they are driven to it by public opinion. Our only hope, then, lies in the cultivation of the public conscience. And we must begin with our own people. We must get them to think more sanely and devoutly on the subject of marriage. The parents who have come to think more seriously must instruct their children. Our young people must be induced to recoil from the thought of taking this life-making or life-breaking step as a leap in the dark. They must be taught to refrain from thinking of marriage and from making marriage engagements till they have sense enough to know what marriage means. When people marry for love and not from lust or from a foolish, romantic impulse; when they have a modicum of solid, Biblical sense on the subjects of marriage and divorce, we shall have eliminated one great factor from which springs much of the evil of which this Sixth Commandment treats.

Personal Impurity

The Sixth Commandment having, as its primary aim, the preservation of the sanctity of marriage and the integrity of the family relation, speaks specifically of the sin of impurity on the part of married people. This was probably due in a measure also to the fact that, in that ancient time, marriage was almost universal and obligatory at an early age, so that this sin was largely confined to those who were married. But this commandment condemns also every violation of the law of personal purity, and on the part of every class of people. God's "thou" here includes men and women, married and unmarried, old and young; its demand is chastity for all.

We might prepare a kind of salve for our own consciences, and pharisaically wash our hands of complicity in the whole matter, by hurling our denunciations solely at a certain well-known class of offenders against this commandment, the public panderers to lust, — the white slavers and that vast army of women of easy virtue who live by prostitution. Language fails us in the attempt to give adequate description of this filth. Indignation chokes the utterance when decent people come to speak of this leprous blotch on human nature.

The face of every pure woman must burn with a consuming shame, and she must grow sick at heart, when she learns that in every metropolis, like New York and Chicago, there is an army, yes, a veritable army of possibly fifty thousand or more of these shameless, brazen-faced procuresses for the chambers whose doors open wide to the slippery path which leads to hell. In every city and hamlet throughout the land there is an equal proportion of them. And yet these all have our common nature. They, too, have that nature which left the hand of God bearing the impress of His own image. The time was when each one of this vast army was a little child, like your children and mine. The time was when each one of these was a mother's darling, a father's joy. How forcibly such a condition brings home to us the poem, Lincoln's favorite: "Oh, why should the spirit of mortal be proud."

Do not think, however, that all my scorn and denunciation is reserved for these blinded unfortunates. They would not be what they are nor where they are, if there were not a cause for it,—if there were not a demand for their devilish service. Many of these women are truly unfortunate, being where they are because of the devilish duplicity and bestiality of the men they trusted, not wisely, but too well. This great army of leeches, crying for blood, and more blood, is supported by those who are just as brutish and besotted as they have become. The great difference is that frequently those who have made these women what they are, and keep them at their devilish trade, move in good society, have access to the best of homes, and often pay acceptable court to pure women. Not infrequently these men, with their foul, disease impregnated bodies, become the husbands of pure women and continue the fiendish work of breeding disease, and heartache, and hell where love, and health, and peace should reign. I wish every one, especially our younger men and women, knew some of those heart-rending, wrath engendering stories of these things every practicing physician can tell!

This double standard of morality, which eternally brands and ostracizes the guilty woman, while the equally guilty, and sometimes more guilty, man goes scot-free, is a damnable piece of business of the devil's own contrivance. Nevertheless the truth remains that womankind has to bear much of the responsibility for this condition. They are not infrequently the most severe and relentless in dealing with their unfortunate sisters and often correspondently lenient in dealing with their guilty brothers.

Frightful and revolting, to all thoughtful people, as is the picture we have just considered, we should be glad if we could stop here. But we can not; truth forces us further. All the adulterers and fornicators do not by any means live in the undisguised houses of ill-fame or frequent them. There are others, far too many of them, both men and women — living in good homes, moving in respectable society, who are more or less habitual violators of the Sixth Commandment. There are women who are supposed by the general public to be faithful wives; there are men who are the fathers of families and at the head of public affairs who have so little regard for the thunder tones of Sinai, so little respect for themselves, so little regard for the troth they have plighted, for the children they have begotten, for the sanctity and happiness of homes, their own or those of others, that they allow themselves to be led by their lusts like the cattle of the field. There is scarcely a community where such conditions are not known to exist.

Only an angel, like Uriel, who knows how rightly to hurl the thunderbolts of God's wrath, is capable of painting in such colors as the subject deserves the damnable blackness of this sin. And all the blacker still is the sin when men, on set purpose, and with plans carefully wrought, creep, like worming serpents, into homes to destroy their purity and peace (2 Tim. 3, 6). And, though we say it with greatest reluctance, there are women who ply all the arts and wiles of womanhood to accomplish the same base ends.

If any distinction can be made in evils all of which are so despicable, I, for one, think that this latter class have blacker hearts, and viler characters, and are more to be feared, than those public characters whose purposes and manner of life are known and may thus be more easily shunned.

There are other forms of this sin into the sickening details of which I have neither the time nor the heart to enter. There are secret and solitary vices by which men and women, especially young men and women, pollute and destroy themselves in their whole being, body and soul; evils to which there is no approximation even among the beasts that rave in the wild. Excesses, destructive of body, mind, and soul are perpetrated under the sanction of the marriage license. These also come within the scope of the prohibition contained in this command.

We may have heard all this and still not be much disturbed, but I am not yet quite through with my subject. Suppose we have never lent our members to such gross, revolting things as we usually think of when the Sixth Commandment is mentioned. This does not mean that we are thereby altogether exonerated. Jesus, that perfect master of all the intricacies of the human life, says: "Out of the heart proceed evil thoughts, murders, adulteries, fornications" (St. Matt. 15, 19). Have we always kept that inner shrine of human life unsullied? Have we never had thoughts we would not dare to breathe into words? Have we never harbored desires which would have brought the scarlet tinge to our cheeks if we knew that some one was reading the hidden content of the heart? This same searcher of inner thoughts says again: "Ye have heard that it was said of them of old time, Thou shalt not commit adultery. But I say unto you, that whosoever looketh on a woman to lust after her hath committed adultery with her already in his heart" (St. Matt. 5, 27, 28). The lust of the eye here condemned applies to the feminine sex as well as the masculine. Have our souls never looked out of their windows carrying elements which could not bear, unrebuked, the searchlight of God's eye? As we have looked out into the world and beheld its suggestive sights, have our glances never recoiled upon ourselves laden with contaminating thoughts and desires? Let each one of us answer these questions to his own soul as in the presence of God!

Paying the Price

The world will have its fling. Men and women will sip of the forbidden sweets in which there is disguised the poison of perdition, and they call it pleasure and often gloat over their conquests. It is hard to get them to believe that the day of disillusionment will come. If they do know something of the bitterness which lurks in the lees of the cup they quaff, they hope against hope that some fortuitous circumstance may make them an exception to the rule. But the day of disenchantment inevitably comes. And, Oh! the bitter mockery of it all. How remorse, like the vulture at the liver of Prometheus, does gnaw at their vitals!

We may think ourselves secure, but we are not secure unless we are wise and well fortified; for thoughtlessness and levity provide no armor. Young women, go up the street to the Crittenden home, and learn the lesson of shame and remorse. There you may see how the seducer has torn the rose from what may have been the fair forehead of an innocent love, and set a blister there. Death would be many times preferable to the lot which is theirs. Nor is the suffering and shame theirs alone. Think of the mother's and father's hearts left to bleed in silence and loneliness. Think of the brothers' and sisters' eyes which are made to fall in shame. And once, no doubt, some of these young women only laughed at the thought that they might be in danger, and felt that they had little need to heed the admonition to watch and pray. There are others who do not have to bear the burden of transgression in such apparent fashion. It may be that no one but themselves and God knows their guilty secrets. Ah, but how about the silent watches of the night, when alone with their consciences and God? Do the galling tears of humiliation and self-reproach never flow? But if they do, streams of tears will not avail to wash away the stain or to draw out the serpent's tooth festering in their breasts.

Young men, you may possibly count yourselves fortunate that vile conduct does not recoil upon you in a form so severe as upon your sisters. But if you are a violator of this Law of God, you can not go free. Go to the infirmaries and see your brother-men polluted, decaying from head to foot, as a result of having played with the siren of lust. Look at the men who are the frequenters of the low saloons, and their usual annexes; note their bleared eyes, and shambling gait; — it is part of the price men have to pay for an immoral life. Go to the insane asylums; listen to the unintelligible jargon and the wild ravings of those whose reason has been dethroned, and then ask your physician how many of these are paying the price of unbridled passion.

Suppose you have not gone so far on this road and avoided hitherto its heavier penalties, you have not altogether escaped. As long as the Sixth Commandment is God's Law, its violation can not be without penalty. God's Word says: "Who committeth adultery * * * lacketh understanding, he that doeth it destroyeth his own soul. A wound and dishonor shall he get, and his reproach shall not be wiped away" (Prov. 6, 32, 33). If there are no other present consequences, the man who still has a living conscience, a vision of things pure, and aspirations for the nobler life, can never escape the inner pangs, the self-loathing, which accompanies the consciousness of having prostituted one's God-given manhood to base ends.

We must, however, look beyond the consequences to the individual. This sin is like a deadly epidemic, it affects nations and races. The voice of history proclaims the fact that no other single cause contributes so much to the downfall of nations as the sin against the Sixth Commandment. Nations everywhere remain strong, capable and progressive only so long as they remain chaste. With lasciviousness always comes growing effeminacy and progressive paralysis of all the powers that make for real greatness. Thus comes the inevitable eclipse of glory, and downfall. We have this story, not only in the Biblical history of Sodom and Gomorrah; it is also written on the pages which tell us of the fate of Persia and Egypt, of Greece and Rome. And the evidence of the destructive power of this sin is not wanting in modern nations.

The present physical consequences of these vices, grievous, far-reaching, and terrible as they often are, by no means tell all the story. They quench the Spirit and destroy the soul. These impure, corrupted souls will have to appear before the God of all purity and be judged with respect to the things done in the body. And this is what His Word proclaims: "Be not deceivers; neither fornicators, nor idolaters, nor adulterers, nor effeminate, nor abusers of themselves with mankind * * * shall inherit the kingdom of God" (1 Cor. 6, 9, 10).

The Remedy

Is there a remedy for this scourge of the nations? Can there be a remedy for an evil of such magnitude that its current history tells of chambers of horrors which rival those of the Inquisition, and recounts a cumulative assortment of bestialities more nauseous than the Augean stables? They are taken from every stratum of human society; not only from the dives, the pigsties of social filth, but from honored seats of learning, from the salons of the rich and cultured, and, to some extent, even from the ranks of those called to minister in holy things. Must not this social ill be — like leprosy, its nearest physical prototype — without a known remedy? There is a remedy for it, and it ought to be vigorously applied. Not all will accept it, but good will be done by proclaiming it to the world.

Some good may be accomplished by education. We must learn to know this evil and its train of terrible consequences. But we must go farther. We must acquaint ourselves with the whole great problem of this side of our life. Man, know thyself! is a good precept to apply here. We must acquaint the young with these truths. Most parents have been criminally negligent in this respect. We have allowed our children to get their knowledge of these matters by chance, and, only too often, in perverted form and from polluted sources. In many instances we said nothing because we ourselves lacked authentic information on the subject.

Some have been held back by a reticence falsely called modesty. In either case we are inexcusable. There are good books to be had on the subject, written in chaste, intelligible language. Let us instruct ourselves. And then, if we will carefully, prayerfully, instruct our children, when they come to the proper age, we can prevent them from growing up into young men and women who will look wise and smirk, when, of necessity, such subjects may be discussed. On the contrary, they will come to regard these matters pertaining to a very important side of our nature as, in very truth they are, sacred mysteries of God's own ordaining. When this is accomplished we shall have taken a decided step in safeguarding the purity of the coming generations.

This commandment is a negative one, it prohibits something; but its purpose is a positive one, — to preserve and foster purity of life. The way to build up life is not only by expurgating the evil; something good must be put in its place. We can never rightly hate the evil till we have learned to know and love the good and the pure. Luther tells us that the aim of this command is to induce us to "lead a chaste and decent life in word and deed." Let us, then, build up our own and our children's character. We must learn to know what the pure, the noble, the upbuilding, the helpful things in life are; and learn equally well to know that purity is the true sphere of the life hidden with Christ in God, and the only one in which true, lasting happiness can be found. Having first well learned this ourselves, we must, by teaching and example, weave this into the warp and woof of our childrens' being.

The inner secret of growth in purity of life is not mere strength of will. Purity does not come by simply going out, with high resolution, as did the knightly warriors of old, to meet and vanquish the foes which lurk and lure. It is not, to any great extent, the result of some elaborate process of building up the powers of the inner life. The real secret lies in this that we open wide the doors of the heart to let Christ, the Saviour, into our lives. With His coming, and in proportion to His coming, old things pass away, and all things become new. With His eyes we shall then see the evil and hate it; with His eyes we shall see the pure and good, love it, appropriate it. With Christ in the heart, like that shining example of purity chronicled in the Bible, we shall be able to say to the sirens who would lure us into the entangling, destroying meshes of impurity: "How can I do this great wickedness, and sin against God!"

If any, through ignorance, or weakness, have fallen it is not too late to rehabilitate the injured character. The bitter memories, and the lurid scars, will probably remain; but of the certainty of God's mercy, and the cleansing efficacy of Jesus' blood, there can be no shadow of doubt. David fell as the result of a sudden temptation, but the arrows of remorse pierced his heart, and caused his eyes to swim with the bitterest of tears. His prayer was: "Create in me a clean heart, O God; and renew a right spirit within me." And it was heard, for David became once more a man after God's own heart. Even the poor fallen woman, whom the self-righteous, because undetected, Jews would have had slain, received the consoling message from Him who is as merciful as He is pure: "Neither do I condemn thee; go, and sin no more."

WAY STATIONS ON THE ROAD TO PERDITION

"Thou shalt not commit adultery." — Exod. 20, 14.

"Watch and pray, that ye enter not into temptation; the spirit, indeed, is willing, but the flesh is weak." — St. Matt. 26, 41.

IN our first discussion of the Sixth Commandment I dealt with the evil of unchastity itself. In language as plain as my sense of propriety would permit, I endeavored to set forth the nature and results of this great sin. Of one thing I am confident; no exaggeration was used. If the words of those whose work has led them to make a special study of social evils may be taken without discount, and I see no reason for discounting them, it would be difficult to exaggerate either the extent or the hideousness of this evil.

I continue this morning with the Sixth Commandment, but my aim is to present a treatment which will be of the nature of a preventative. I consider that prevention, in every respect, is better than cure.

Years ago many of the districts of our southern country, and of Central America, were veritable plague spots. Malaria was constantly in the air. Yellow fever and other epidemics were liable to break out at any time in virulent form. But experts were put to work. They drained the swamps; they cleaned up the cities; they introduced methods of sanitation. The causes of ill-health were removed; and to-day these districts, many of them at least, are as healthful as those found elsewhere. There is not one where health conditions are not immeasurably better than they were before. This is, incomparably, the better way of fighting disease.

This principle applies to the subject in hand. Unchastity is a noisome disease and highly infectious. We must combat the disease itself. We must do all we can to stay its ravages. But even where it is cured it is bound to leave some scars. It is a hundredfold better to prevent it: to drain the filthy lowlands, to destroy the reeking cesspools, to clarify the moral atmosphere. How may this be done? By a process of moral sanitation: by abolishing, as far as possible, the causes which produce the evil; by removing the temptations; by making our people acquainted with the dangers besetting them; by getting our young people into a more healthful atmosphere; by fortifying them with the grace of God.

It is probable that some of you will not agree with all I have to say this morning, at least not till you have had time to think it over carefully. Starting from the same premises, we may not all be able to arrive at once at the same conclusion. Inclination has a good deal to do with our processes of thinking. But, whether you all agree with me or not, I must speak my mind. I must tell you the way I see things in the light of general experience, and especially in the light of God's Word, which is the best of all commentaries on human experience. If I did not do this, I should be, in the language of this holy Book, a dumb dog. On the Judgment day you would have the right to charge me with having failed to do my duty, and your condemnation, if it came to that, would, in part, be laid at my door. However, if I faithfully warn and people do not heed, the fault is theirs, not mine. Even if you do not at first agree with all I say, do not too lightly cast it aside. It is the part of wisdom to weigh the evidence. But bear in mind that where the Word of God speaks, the weighing has already been done. God has done it Himself. We may endeavor to ascertain the reason for the decisions rendered; but from them there is no appeal. They are absolutely final.

You recall that Christ speaks of the course of life through this world as a way: the broad way and the narrow way. With special emphasis do the inspired writers speak of those who live in violation of the Sixth Commandment as followers of a way, a wicked way. In the second chapter of Proverbs we read these words of warning concerning the strange woman, who has forsaken the guide of her youth and forgotten the covenant of her God: "Her house inclineth unto death, and her paths unto the dead. None that go unto her return again, neither take they hold of the paths of life." Again, in the seventh chapter we read: "Hearken unto me now therefore, O ye children, and attend unto the words of my mouth. Let not thine heart incline unto her ways, go not astray in her paths. For she hath cast down many wounded; yea, many strong men have been slain by her. Her house is the way to hell, going down to the chambers of death."

With words like these in mind, I shall speak

to-day of some of the Way Stations on the Road to Perdition.

A way station, bear in mind! is a point which serves as a kind of recruiting place, on the main line of travel. There are many such places on the path to perdition. Of some of these, which have to do especially with the violation of the Sixth Commandment, I shall treat this morning.

Evil Companions

I have spoken in my former address of some of the grosser violations of the Sixth Commandment in which people become entangled. I hope those words were not especially needed by us, save as a general warning, sufficing to keep us on our guard. To-day, in speaking of those things which contribute to the breaking of this commandment, I shall not dwell on the vile saloon, the dive, the wine room, or kindred things. These so clearly bear the trade mark of hell that young people and others who have been reared in the atmosphere of the Sunday school and Church ought not need any special warning against them. There are, however, other sources of temptation which are not so clearly recognized as evils, or at least not as such evils as they often prove to be. Here is where we probably most need our warnings.

I will start with the subject of evil companions. Evil companionship is the starting-point of the downward path for many a young man and woman. And not infrequently there is no intention of departing from the path of decency. Evil companions are among the devil's best recruiting-agents.

Companions have a great influence for either good or ill. If they are pure-minded, aspiring, active in good works, their influence for good is great and far-reaching. If they are evil-minded, smutty in conversation, and full of evil suggestion in demeanor as well, their influence is just as great for evil. St. Paul lifts to the dignity of Divine authority a saying that had long been a proverb among the observant Greeks: "Evil company doth corrupt good manners." One can not remain long in a smithy without becoming black, nor handle hot iron without getting one's fingers burned. Just as impossible is it to become a companion of persons of impure minds and unclean lips without becoming smudged. Nor is the blackening process slow: the poison acts quickly.

It takes years of work and painstaking care to bring a tree to the fruit-bearing age; but it may be destroyed in a few moments. So the life and character of sons and daughters, for the upbuilding of which parents may have worked hard and prayed long, and to the cultivation of which the young people themselves may have given much time and energy, may be quickly ruined. But, in spite of what is at stake — despite the warnings and pleadings of parents and others, how often do young people seem to gravitate toward the most coarse-grained, flippant, and irreverent companions they can find. Do the young people not know what they are doing? Do they not know the dangers to which they are subjecting themselves? Do they not realize that they are thus giving a revelation of their own real, inner character? If coarseness, vulgarity, and lack of devoutness attract people, is it not an unmistakable evidence that, despite all their training and opportunities, there is a streak of coarseness and vulgarity in their own makeup? And if they have any regard at all for themselves, any hope for their future, is not this in itself a trumpet call for them to be all the more on their guard, to watch and pray?

With the greatest care and deliberation we should choose our companions. We exercise precaution in selecting our clothes. We have laws the object of which is to protect our bodies, our physical health. Into what glaring contrast does this throw our frequent carelessness with respect to the contagion which threatens our characters, our souls. We are careful to root out of our gardens and flower-beds the weeds which hinder the growth of our plants. Especially do we try to keep down all poisonous growths that might injure man or beast. But the person whose presence poisons the moral atmosphere and scatters the seeds of moral and spiritual contagion everywhere is often welcomed, especially if there are present some of the attractions of physical beauty, wealth or education.

How often do young men seek the company of perfectly strange young women on the streets and elsewhere; and, to their shame be it said! young women not infrequently court such approaches. Such companionship never promises anything good. Young people may possibly come out of such escapades with their characters unsullied by taint of actual impurity, but the elements of danger are there. Such a step may be thoughtlessly taken without a conscious thought of impurity, but the fact that a young person is guilty of such conduct shows thereby not only lack of good breeding, but reveals the further fact that there is a weak spot in their character which needs most careful watching to prevent it from going to worse things. No young man who is habitually guilty of such conduct has real respect for the woman he seeks to meet in this way, and usually his intentions are evil. No young woman who allows such approaches or encourages them, has due regard for her own virtue or reputation. This is playing with fire, and the natural result is to get one's fingers burned.

One of the accompanying evils resulting from keeping bad company is the unrestrained, improper speech which often passes between such companions. The boldness and indelicacy of speech of many young people in our day is a matter of frequent remark. Not only is there much flippant reference to things sacred, but uncouthness and vulgarity is everywhere in evidence and constantly furthered by evil companionship. Of all this the Word of God says: "Let no corrupt communication proceed out of your mouth. * * * Neither filthiness, nor foolish talking, nor jesting, which are not convenient" (Eph. 4, 29; 5, 4). A pure heart and a filthy tongue cannot belong to the same person.

We often wonder what has come over some of our young people. Once they were interested in Sunday-school and Church services; they read their Bibles and said their prayers. After a while we begin to notice that these things have become distasteful to them. They are always seeking for excuses to keep from taking part in these sacred services. The trouble is that their hearts have become polluted, either by unbelief or some kind of impurity. There is great likelihood that evil associations had much to do with it. Young people, if you have made mistakes, do not go on with them. We want to help you. God wants to help you. Turn away from evil companions. "My son, if sinners entice thee, consent thou not" (Prov. 1, 10). "Flee also youthful lusts" (2 Tim. 2, 22).

It is said that if, during the summer months a canary is hung in its cage outside the house where the sparrows, with their noisy chatter, largely congregate, the sweetest songster will cease to sing before the summer is over and do nothing but chirp, much like a sparrow. The lesson, I am sure, you cannot fail to grasp. If we associate with scoffers and those who delight to retail vile stuff, we shall lose our singing and praying voice, because we shall have lost our faith and purity of heart.

Even where our companions are of the right kind, let us remember our human limitations. We all need to be constantly on our guard. Eternal vigilance is the price of our blessings, both so far as getting and keeping them is concerned. If we are God's children at all, there is some willingness for the things of the Spirit in our spirits, but the flesh is weak. Familiarity does not only eventually breed contempt; but, in the meanwhile, it often prepares the way for other, and still worse, evils. We need, indeed, to watch and pray.

Books and Reading

With the subject of books and reading I might have continued under the former topic, for they furnish only another form of companionship, but the uniqueness and universality of these companions is my warrant for giving them special attention.

The subject of books and reading is to most people a fascinating one. We might spend an hour or more in a profitable discussion of this topic alone. But we have time this morning for little more than a word of warning against bad books.

Good books ought to be in much greater demand. They are among the greatest and most accessible of teachers; among the best and most inspiring of companions. Men and women have testified that the reading of a single unpretentious volume in their early years gave direction and purpose to the whole of their after lives. What an opportunity we are missing if we do not love good reading. But, unfortunately, it is just as possible for one to read himself to death, morally and spiritually, in a very short time. One of the great and devout English ministers of a former generation tells us that while a student at college a companion gave him a book in which he read for only a few moments, but that in those few moments he imbibed a poison which was a source of bitterness and regret to him all the remainder of his life. The thoughts given him, the pictures which impressed themselves on his mind, in that brief period of time haunted him like foul dancing spectres till his dying day. Had he been a less pure-minded lad, and not so well fortified in the truth, he might have been attracted and destroyed by this filth, as is the case with so many thousands of men and women, young and old.

You have doubtless heard the old story of the man of letters in India, who went into his library to get a book. As he took it down from the shelf he felt a sudden sharp pain in one of his fingers, which he took to be the prick of a pin or needle. Soon, however, his finger began to swell, then his arm, and soon his whole body. He had been bitten by one of the many poisonous serpents with which the country abounds and which infest even the houses. And death soon ensued. There are many poisonous serpents hidden between the pages of attractive books and magazines. They instil into the minds of their readers, especially the young, doubts about sacred and divine things. They give perverted views of life. A large class of literature to-day speaks disparagingly of marriage, and flippantly of breaking marriage vows. They describe in attractive colors the story of illicit relationships. They paint virtue, especially that which has to do with the relation of men and women, as an old-fashioned dream, long out of date. From these disgusting recitals of lust and crime the young should be safeguarded as we would protect them from the attacks of a mad dog.

Young people, you who are old enough to know something of the dangers of which we speak, you who are beginning to realize something of the value of a good character, and the peace of mind and joy of heart that go with it, I appeal to you: avoid bad books and impure reading of every kind. It scathes and scorches the soul. It puts a blight upon the life, so that it will be hard for it ever to put forth the buds or bear the fruits of purity. Never look into a book which is known to be impure. Steel yourself against all prurient curiosity. Make up your mind that you will stop reading anything as soon as you recognize that it has a tendency to debase. Never drag your mind, that noble gift of God, by virtue of which you are so closely akin to Him, through the filth; and in this way make it a fit instrument and powerful for dragging your body likewise into the mire.

I have known of men, middle-aged men, who became so infatuated with the silly impossibilities of fiction that they neglected their business, and did nothing but read this debilitating stuff all day long and day after day. It is bad enough for people to bankrupt themselves financially in this way. But the consequences are still worse when people thus bankrupt themselves morally and spiritually. Excessive reading of fiction is likely to have this result even when it is not vicious in its teaching. It produces a form of mental intoxication and makes people irresponsible. It makes them dissatisfied with the every-day duties of the every-day life. And to live in a world of unrealities has a tendency to bring about a state of moral flabbiness. How much worse, then, will it be if the mind is burdened with a mass of fiction which is positively poisonous, because impure!

In the window of a bookstore in Cologne there was formerly a picture bearing the title: "A Bad

Book." It represented a young girl sitting at a table, eagerly reading a book. Behind her, looking over her shoulder, and smiling with fiendish delight, stood the devil, rejoicing that his work was being done so easily and effectively.

Young people, you who are the hope of the future, in Church and State, beware! If you read filth, your life will be filthy. Evil literature, especially a literature which is evil in the sense of the Sixth Commandment, weakens the mind, and destroys the will. There is no more pitiable, no more miserable creature to be found anywhere than the one who still has some vision of better things, a certain weak desire for them, but no will that God can use for cooperation with man for his rehabilitation. Young men and women, fill your minds with ragtime literature, conceived and written in the spirit of lasciviousness, and you prepare the way to become easy victims to the wiles of the first real tempter who comes your way.

Dress

Surely the teacher of morals, the one who is to point out the dangers that beset our people in the way of social impurity, cannot fail to mention the subject of dress. The field of fashion furnishes a sphere in which the devil is especially busy. It is one of the instrumentalities through which he is gathering many victims for the downward path.

Dress, much more than many people think, has always been a problem which had to do with morals. It was sin and shame which introduced the question of dress. Mother Eve and Father Adam fell into sin, but even when sin came they did not lose all their modesty. With the blush of shame which the sense of personal delicacy brought to their cheeks came the first desire for a covering for their bodies. In the course of the passing centuries many have lost much of this delicacy of feeling. Now one of the burning moral problems with which we have to deal is that of dress or, rather, in many instances, undress. To-day the idea of dress, with many, is not that of a covering. With clothes abbreviated at both the top and the bottom, the idea with some seems to be to get back, as near as possible, to the original fig-leaf style of dress.

We often hear it said, especially by the women: We might as well be dead as out of style. All we have to say is that if people cannot be happy unless they are following the fashions set by the demimonde of Paris, London and New York, they might just as well be dead for all the real good they will ever do in the world. It used to be said, with considerable cynicism but more than a grain of truth, that we imported our fashions from London, while London imported them from Paris, and Paris got them from hell.

Some one may say, Oh, it is to be expected that preachers will denounce fashionable dress. Not necessarily so. Most of us like to see people, men as well as women, well dressed. But it should always be the decorous garb of becoming modesty. That present fashions are largely not modest is the testimony of many who are not preachers. The chairman of the Chicago Vice Commission said some time ago that the prevailing fashions, which accentuate woman's form, has made women bolder, and increased the number of those who are careless of their morals. About the same time a woman well known in American public life, Mrs. John A. Logan, said of woman's dress that it was not only "hideous, but viciously indecent; an outrage upon the modesty of womanhood, the sorry sign of sorry times. * * * I think the exhibition is demoralizing. When I say demoralizing I use the word in a broad, serious sense. Anything which diminishes the modesty of women is a bad thing for the human race. And the fashions of to-day diminish, if they do not sometimes utterly destroy, the modesty of woman." These are the words, not of preachers, who are often thought to be unnecessarily narrow in their views, but of level-headed, thoughtful men and women of the world.

The styles have somewhat changed since the above words were written, but not appreciably for the better. Even the heathen Chinaman has his taunt for the fashionable American woman's dress. He says the Chinese women wear clothes to hide their forms, but the American women wear theirs to reveal them. To this he might have added that many of them are taking off their clothes to reveal their forms or using material which serves the same purpose. Our sensible women do not yield to these extremes, but the tendency is everywhere operative; for the nearer many can approximate these styles the better they seem to like it.

Women of the Church, do you realize what all this means? Some say that it means that women have become or are in the process of becoming emancipated; that they are being freed from the fetters of ancient conventionalities; that such emancipation from the proper conventionalities of dress is innocent because "to the pure all things are pure." I will tell you what it means. This striving for the nude in art, in literature, in dress has a meaning. It means that modesty is fast becoming a lost virtue; that the finest edge of pure womanhood is being lost. It means that the whole social body has become vitiated by moral poisons, which are still further corrupting the blood of the people and hastening the process of decay. It means, at least to those who are able to read the message written large on every page of history, that we are facing a historically demonstrated portent of coming disaster.

We should like to have time to make a plea for the emancipation of woman from the tyranny of fashion, to express the hope that the time shall come when individuality will be allowed to assert itself and woman will be adorned in modest but beautiful simplicity. The chief concern, however, is that they do not allow themselves to be gradually and insensibly robbed of the crowning virtue of their womanhood—their modesty. Women, you may question my opinions if you will; I can assure you that they are not different from those of many others, both men and women; but one thing you are obligated to do, and that is to listen to the words of the Master. He says, through the mouth of the holy Apostle: "I will therefore that women adorn themselves in modest apparel" (I Tim. 2, 9).

The Theatre

Another of the way stations on the road to perdition is the playhouse. It ought not to be so. It is not of necessity so. But that it is actually so, cannot be denied. Mr. W. D. Howells is not a man of puritanic bent of mind. But he declared, in one of the literary magazines of our country, a few years ago, that the modern theater is, in its general tendency, a school of immorality. He further said: "If from any pulpit vice were preached by mockeries of purity and appeals to lubricity such as are used in the theater; if lying were inculcated, and passion put above duty; * * * if adultery were treated as a comical affair; * * * somehow the law would reach that pulpit, although the state professes to have no relation with the church.

"In like manner, if in any private school or college the humanities were imparted by a chair devoted to the study of those authors whose works befoul literature, the law would somehow intervene to prevent the mischief. * * * The theatre, however, is left unmolested in almost any excess; ideas are inculcated if not expressed there which are simply abominable. We all know it; we can prove it at any time; it is undeniable."

In the Journal of our city, a few years ago, there was a lengthy article on the tendency of the modern stage. In it occur these words: "That there is a wave of immorality sweeping through the theatres of the country at our time, it is impossible any longer to doubt." This tendency toward immorality may be more pronounced in recent times, but it is by no means anything new. In every age the theatre has been in large measure of a character to debase and corrupt. The ancient heathen Plato said: "Plays rouse the passions and pervert the use of them; and of course are dangerous to morality." Ovid advised Augustus to suppress theatres because he considered them "a grand source of corruption." Rousseau, the French philosopher and skeptic, in his early life wrote for the stage; but in later life, when it was proposed to establish a theater in Geneva, he protested against it, declaring it to be "a school of vice." The gifted English historian Macaulay declared the theatre to be "a seminary of vice." Edwin Booth, the bright star of the American stage, because of his knowledge of it, would not allow his daughter to become an actress. And Macready, one of England's most gifted and noble actors, when he left the stage selected a home, it is said, far from London, so that his son might never see a theatre in his youth.

My objection to the theatre is not chiefly this that its object is to furnish amusement. Though it is specially liable to abuse, I believe that amusement or diversion, of the right kind and in such proportion as to be a relief to the serious and wearing business of life, has a legitimate place in life. The theatre could be such an institution. It could be an educative, uplifting force. My objection to it is based on the ground that it is an institution noted not only for its lack of positive moral teaching, but is notorious as a school of positive immorality.

In opposition to what has been said it is sometimes urged that the theatre is not wholly bad, that decent, yea, even religious, plays are presented. Yes, some men have seen the possibilities of the stage, and have tried to redeem it. Sir Henry Irving tried it in London, but his venture failed; Edwin Booth tried it in New York, but failed, and his theater was sold for a warehouse. Hannah Moore wrote good plays, full of noble sentiment, but they did not pay. Why did all these ventures fail? Because the theatre, as an institution, does not stand for that which is good. An occasional play which is clean and morally uplifting gets hold of a sufficient number of play-goers to make it successful, but they are in such a fearful minority that a moral stage appears to be out of the question, no matter how successful an occasional moral play may be. As a usual thing, even Biblical events are fearfully perverted when they are staged. The story of Joseph and his brethren presents in its Biblical setting the finest example of personal purity in all literature. And it does this without leaving a suggestive thought to rankle in the heart. But as it has been presented on the stage it should be called the story of Potiphar's wife. The temptation scene is acted out with every suggestion of vile passion that can surge from the depths of a heart given over to lust. No pure woman can behold it without wanting to cover her face for shame. And no virile man, who has struggled for purity, can behold it without trembling lest the suggestiveness of its appeal to his baser nature should get the mastery of his reason and his will.

There is but one reason why the theatre is so predominantly of this nature. It is so because the majority of those who frequent it want filth; and they get what they want. It is the only thing which will pay. With the world dollars are more than morals. The Christian people who frequent the theatre are not only endangering their own souls, but by their presence are encouraging the things for which the theatre preeminently stands; namely, looseness of morals and a depraved conception of life.

Young people, we know that there is something about the theatre which makes an especially strong appeal to the romantic spirit of youth. Beware of its fascination. You have heard how the snake charms the bird to its death. If the theatre did nothing else we should be very careful because it is apt to produce a form of mental inebriation, which gives one a distorted view of the things of life, and thus unfits one for the stern realities of this work-a-day world. And this is one step in the process of breaking down the moral character, a process which the teaching and the scenes of the theatre are nearly all calculated speedily to advance.

The Dance

Must the dance be classed with the dangers of which we have been speaking? Unquestionably! We know that the followers of Terpsichore plead that dancing is a fine art, that it ministers to grace, that it is the poetry of motion. We are not ignorant of all this. But we know also its purely sensuous nature and that there is but a narrow step, which needs very carefully to be guarded, between the merely sensuous and the sensual.

The real charm of dancing is the mutual attraction of sex. Separate the men from the women, and dancing will soon cease. The dancing of which the Bible speaks, to which its advocates oft refer as a justification of the art, was not promiscuous. The Bible dance was an exhilarating physical exercise, indicative of great joy, performed as a service to the Lord by men only or women only. Let people dance in this way, and there will be no one to demur.

Medical men have spoken much against dancing, on the score of physical injury, especially to young women. This is worth considering. Our bodies are gifts of God, and we shall have to give an account of the way we take care of them. But we shall leave this to the physicians: our chief objection to the dance is on the score of morals.

The real character and tendency of the dance cannot long be hid from any one who will give it a little serious thought. Nor need they be special guardians or teachers of morals to be able to see it. Police Inspector Byrnes, of New York, has said that a large percentage of the women on Blackwell's Island, a penal and corrective institution, started their downward course on the dance-floor. District Attorney Zabel, of Milwaukee, has declared that ninety per cent. of the cases of delinquent girls which came to the attention of the court started on their career of shame on the dance-floor. The more conservative defenders of the dance admit that the public dance-hall is not a safe place, all kinds of people meeting there. Not exactly all kinds: only the worst kind, and the simple ones who do not know its dangers. But why do the seducers of young women, and so many of the shameless young women, who have neither virtue nor shame to lose, hang around the dance-hall? Because they know it is one of the best places for the accomplishment of their nefarious purposes.

The pastor of a country parish recently told me that in a district with which he was acquainted there was a veritable epidemic of violations of the Sixth Commandment, with all its attendant shame and distressing circumstances. Investigation had revealed the fact that the whole trouble was traceable to the community dances, which had become the rage in that vicinity. By their fruits we judge of institutions, as we do of men and women themselves.

The tendency of the dance is shown in its development. The graceful minuet of our forefathers, so far as they were not Puritans, in which they touched finger-tips, and bowed with dignity to their partners, is no longer in favor. Instead of this dance, to which neither modesty nor grace can be denied, we have the grizzly-bear, the bunny-hug, the turkey-trot and other dances with equally suggestive names, all of which are equally proper and suggestive of the things described. It is all nothing but mad animalism. There is no more pruriency or lechery in the songs and dances of an Indian temple girl or a Japanese geisha girl, than there is in these pantomimes of lust. These performances bear the brand of bestial vulgarity. And these strong adjectives apply whether the performances are given in the annex of some cheap rum dispensary, or in the ball-room of some ultra fashionable dame.

The dance given in the home, in which only those participate who are known to each other, and where the rowdy performances with the animal names are debarred, is altogether a different thing. But I ask the young people, the Christian young people, whose desire is to do right, whether they want to be classified in the terms used by the best defenders of the dance. One of the most conservative of English papers, in a recent article defending dancing and mildly ridiculing the seriousness of those who oppose it, said: "Dancing is a rhythmical pantomime of sex, and the most haremish of pastimes." We know you do not want to be classed with those whose clinkered souls no longer know or care for virtue. But do you want to engage, as a pastime, in what its most cultured friends call a public exhibition of sex, and which bears the earmarks and radiates the atmosphere of the harem?

Young people, it is worth much to be aware of the snares and pitfalls which beset your feet, to know the forms of the allurements by which you will be tempted to forsake the paths of virtue. But this knowledge is not enough to insure safety. You must not merely know and drive out the evil, and set your face against it. Empty souls win no battles. They must be filled with the love of the good and pure. And this means above all things else that Christ must dwell in your hearts by faith and control your affections.

THE RIGHT OF PRIVATE PROPERTY

"Thou shalt not steal." — EXODUS 20, 15.

"Every good gift and every perfect gift is from above, and cometh down from the Father of Lights." — JAMES 1, 17.

THE life is more than meat, and the body is more than raiment." In these words Christ makes an appeal to his disciples to be concerned about the supreme things, life, character: the things which help us on toward complete manhood and womanhood. To all people these should be of chief concern. For the sake of the inner life, the mind, the soul, and the things which are exclusively the property of the inner life, honour, truth, faith, and the like, men ought to be willing, and many have been willing, to sacrifice the life of the body. This does not mean that the body is of no importance, and to be given no attention. It is of much importance. It is the instrument of the soul. It is the means whereby the spirit comes into touch with, and uses for its purposes, the things of the material world. The body is of much more importance than any or all of our external possessions, such as houses, lands, or merchandise. And we should use all reasonable care to keep it healthy and pure.

All this is very strongly emphasized, in an indirect way, by the divinely given order of the commandments. We have considered six of them, all dealing with the supreme blessing—life: the inner life and the outer life. The First Table, which tells us of God, our relation to Him, and our worship of Him, points out the first of all human duties—soul cure and soul culture. The next three deal with human relations which involve life itself, and, from one point of view or another, each emphasizes its sacredness, and the care with which it should be safeguarded and developed.

God puts His emphasis on the primary things, where it belongs; but he is not unmindful of anything that concerns his people. He says: "Seek ye first the Kingdom of God, and His righteousness;" but at the right time and with becoming eagerness, we may also seek the creature things, which, if used aright, will help us on our heavenward way, though they be but the perishing things of the earth. God created us with physical needs. He created this wonderful world in just such a way as to meet our physical needs and furnish us the opportunity of working out our Divinely appointed destiny. As God's children we are to use God's gifts for the purposes for which He has given them, and in accordance with the principles He has laid down.

We call these gifts of God our goods, our possessions, our property. The problem of getting into right relationship to these material things, of righteously acquiring a portion of them, of using them aright when we get them, of recognizing and respecting the rights of others to their share of them, is a difficult one for men to learn; but its importance is great. We shall defer to another time the prohibition of the commandment, and treat to-day of the underlying thought — The Right of Private Property.

There are two leading thoughts under which this subject may be treated: The right of private property is grounded in nature, for every good gift comes from God as giver; the relationship of man to the gift and the giver is that of a steward, which implies accountability.

I. God is the giver of all good. But this origin of the right to property is not universally recognized. Indeed, the right of private property; that is, the right of the individual to acquire such of the things of this earth as he can honestly get, and use it exclusively as his own, is generally taken for granted; but in most instances, probably, without much thought of how this right came to be. But it is a matter about which there has been much discussion on the part of those who have thought about it, and for the explanation of which many theories have been advanced.

The irreligious, materialistic theory of property, whether formulated in words or not, is that might makes right; that the strongest are the best, and are therefore entitled to take and keep what they can get. This theory is one which has largely prevailed in the world in later years. It has not always been proclaimed as a working theory; very many, nevertheless, have been acting on it in a quiet way as a principle of conduct.

Another view of the right of private property is that it is a creation of human law. This is the view usually set forth by jurists. Their statement of the case is that it was found expedient that men should be allowed the exclusive possession and use of the products of their own efforts, subject, however, to certain demands for the public good. And thus, in the course of time, laws were enacted guaranteeing to them their accumulated possessions. This unquestionably correctly states a series of historical facts. But it does not go back to the ultimate ground of the right of private property. The right of man to any legitimately acquired property antedates the enactment of any laws guaranteeing to him the undisturbed possession of it. Man's right to a fair proportion of the things of the earth, which men have not produced, and to the fruits of the investment of his own skill and industry, is a right founded in nature. It is a Divine right. This is implied in the Seventh Commandment itself. God has the right to impose laws respecting the use and treatment of property because He is the giver of it.

Man is a creature related to two worlds, the material universe and the world of spirit. On the one side of his nature he is raised above the limitations of the material world; on the other side he is dependent on it. The God who created man placed him here in the material world as the owner and master of it. It was given to him for the purpose of meeting his physical needs, and as a means of furthering his own and others' spiritual necessities. In this way, primarily, man came to have a right in property and power over it. It is a God-given right. Human laws were called for and enacted only because many men, as a result of sin, no longer respected or even recognized the originally implanted laws of God.

Property was given to man first of all to satisfy the needs of the nature God had given to him. But it serves other purposes besides those represented by the need of food and clothing. The acquisition and control of property is one of the disciplines of life, by which character is developed and strengthened. In this sphere, as in few others, do we get to see the real manner of man one is. We often get a better insight into a man's character when we see him at his work or in his place of business than we do by seeing him in church. In the latter place he has on his Sunday clothes and Sunday manners. In the shop or place of business, he is more likely to show himself as he really is. In the effort man puts forth to get food, clothing and habitation for himself and those dependent on him; in what he spends for the education of himself and family, for his own and their culture and amusement; in the way he dispenses hospitality and contributes for purposes of benevolence; in the measure of interest he takes and the efforts he is willing to invest for the general good of society; in his willingness or lack of willingness to consecrate his possessions to the furtherance of the higher good for himself and others, — in these things there is given to us one of the best portraits that can be drawn of the real nature of a man.

Property has still other functions to serve besides those of affording man the necessities of life, and giving him a needful training as he strives for it. Every man has particular duties to perform.

These duties have to do with his calling, his station in life, the rearing and nurture of those dependent upon him, and his relation to the general society of which he is a member. To meet these obligations he must have means which are his own, which he can use as the necessities of these demands require. Property, therefore, is not given merely as a means of self-gratification; it is not intended simply as something in the getting and control of which man is given the opportunity of exhibiting his mastery of things material; it is a God-given means through the proper use of which man is to reach his Divinely appointed destiny.

There are those who deny the right of man as an individual to hold property. Not all agree as to the degree in which this right is to be relinquished. The theories run all the way from belief in the public ownership of public utilities, to this that man has no right to any portion even of the product of his own labor; that even marriage should be abolished and the children of promiscuous desire be reared as the wards of the state.

There are certain things, advocated by some adherents of socialistic theories, upon which many of us Christian people look with favor. We believe that the general government could operate the railroad and steamship lines, the telegraph and telephone service, and perhaps other public utilities, as well as the mail service, to the advantage of the general public. Our cities could keep their railway, electric light, and other franchises, and operate them in the interest of the general public, to whom they should rightfully belong. We would get better service at cheaper rates. If the laboring people of all classes would stand together, they could carry on many co-operative enterprises to the benefit of all concerned, and correct many abuses which now exist. Undeniably many laws are enacted by the influence of the rich and powerful which inure to the benefit of the privileged few at the expense of the laboring people and the small property holders. But as long as political parties are able to throw dust into the eyes of the people, and lead them about by the noses, matters will not be appreciably improved. We must get rid of our prejudices, become better acquainted with these problems, and co-operate. Experience, however, has proven that communistic, or extreme socialistic, principles are impractical. They have been advocated in all ages, and tried in many; but never with success. For them to succeed there would have to be such a degree of disinterestedness, such integrity of purpose, such a spirit of altruism, as has never been attained on earth. From this point of view, common ownership of property would be a splendid ideal at which to aim. But the moral qualities necessary to the attainment of the ideal have never been seriously considered by the radical advocates of socialistic theories. On the other hand, their measures have been prompted by materialism gone mad. These advocates have generally been atheists, who believe that this life is all, and that they must, therefore, get all that ever is to be gotten out of this life.

The right of private property has not only been proven by experience to give impetus to the spirit of progress, but — a consideration far above this and every other — it is the teaching of God's Word in both Testaments. The patriarchs had their own property. When the children of Israel came to the promised land God had it divided and distributed, not only to the different tribes, but to the families. In the first Christian congregation at Jerusalem, under the spur of their first love, communistic principles with respect to property were practiced. They were not commanded, nor were they tried elsewhere in the Apostolic church. And communistic practice did not last long in Jerusalem. Hypocrites broke it up, among whom Ananias and his wife were the first and most flagrant. In this very narrative we have the proof of the right of private property. St. Peter said to Ananias concerning the property he had sold: "Whiles it remained, was it not thine own? and after it was sold, was it not in thine own power?" (Acts 5, 4). Everywhere in Scripture the right of a man to the product of his own skill and labor is taken for granted. No Christian, who has inherited property or by industry or thrift has accumulated something beyond the daily needs of himself and his dependents, need feel that he is acting contrary to the holy will of God.

We Christians recognize that the real title to all things rests in God. He is the absolute owner. He brought all things into existence. He gave to each created thing its peculiar nature. He controls it all. "All the earth is mine," said the Lord to his chosen Israel (Exod. 19, 5). And through his servant David He says: "If I were hungry, I would not tell thee; for the world is mine, and the fulness thereof" (Ps. 50, 12). This statement is repeated for us of the New Testament by the pen of St. Paul: "The earth is the Lord's, and the fulness thereof" (1 Cor. 10, 26). And our text from St. James tells us that every good gift, temporal as well as spiritual, comes from the Heavenly Father.

This is not the way the natural human mind is prone to look at the matter. With the unregenerate man the personal element, the I, is always emphasized. I have done this. My good judgment, my industry, my economy, have brought me these things. This is the usual language of all those who have not learned to know how absolutely all things depend on the power and goodness of God. Our life, our place in life, strength of mind and body by which we are enabled to play a man's or a woman's part in the world, all comes from God. In Him we live and move and have our being. Let us count up all that we have, let us consider all that we so fondly consider our contribution toward the acquisition of it — and then, that all unrighteous pride, all self-vaunting, may be dissipated, let us hear the words of the Master, which apply to every possession of man: "What hast thou that thou didst not receive? Now, if thou didst receive it, why dost thou glory as if thou hadst not received it?" (1 Cor. 4, 7).

This presents another thought needing enlargement and emphasis, namely, not only do all things come from God as the great original provider, but He still rules when it comes to the distribution of His bounty. "The Lord maketh poor, and maketh rich; He bringeth low, and lifteth up" (1 Sam. 2, 7).

There are many practical difficulties in connection with this subject which we, because of our sin-weakened condition, are not able to explain. It is well for all of us to recognize this disability, and not make things worse by attempting explanations that, perhaps, do not explain. One thing which often disturbs us is this, Why does God often allow wicked men, in wicked ways, to accumulate much property and enjoy so many of the good things of this world? We cannot explain it, at least not in detail. The other side is just as perplexing. Why does God often allow those who are devout and, at the same time, industrious and honest to be unfortunate so far as the things of this present world are concerned? We cannot explain this by specific reasons. But we do have a general explanation for it, a sense in which the secret of the Lord is with them that fear Him. We know that God does all things well, that He overrules all things for the ultimate good of those who love Him. If He allows us to be deprived of a temporary good, it is only to shield us from some worse evil, or prepare the way for a greater good. Let us do our full duty also in our temporal affairs, as God gives us light to see it and strength to perform it, and then let us trust God also in these things completely. God is God; He provides for our bodies and rules over our temporal affairs just as surely as He does in the sphere of spiritual things. And all that He does or allows to occur is right and for our good.

II. Men are but stewards of God's good gifts. From what has been said, it is clear that we can but hold in trust that which, in reality, belongs to God. We have our human titles and laws, in the light of which we may properly speak of that which is our own. So far as the use of it is concerned, within the limits of right, it is our own. And over against those who might wish to disturb us in our possession or deprive us of the things we possess, they are ours. But whatever the source from which our property came, whether by inheritance, labor, or purchase; whatever the nature of the title by which we hold it, we Christians recognize God's prior and inalienable title to it all. We own ourselves but His stewards. And what we acknowledge is true of all men. Many will not own it, but the denial, in either word or act, does not change the fact. Men may flaunt their abstracts and guaranteed titles as much as they choose; they are but stewards still, and will have to give an account of their stewardship to the great Householder.

This, then, clearly indicates that we cannot do just as we please with what we have in keeping. If we are to hear at the close of our stewardship the words of commendation, "Well done, thou good and faithful servant," we must make use of God's gifts in conformity with God's will. It cannot be used in a way to injure God's workmanship or detract from the glory of the giver. It must all be used in a way to further God's benevolent plans for the world. This includes our own physical as well as spiritual well-being, for time as well as for eternity.

To be careless, indifferent, lazy, is not the right attitude of one who is a steward. Work is one of the elements which makes for man's redemption in a physical and social sense. And God has ordained "that if any will not work, neither shall he eat" (2 Thess. 3, 10). God requires diligence, and promises that it shall not go unrewarded (Prov. 12, 24; 13, 4; 22, 29). There are many who would like to have and to spend, but they dislike the effort which it takes to get property and to improve it. It shows neither faith nor appreciation of God's bounty to approach, in any degree, the condition of the slothful man so strikingly pictured by Solomon: "I went by the field of the slothful, and by the vineyard of the man void of understanding; and, lo, it was all grown over with thorns, and nettles covered the face thereof, and the stone wall thereof was broken down. Then I saw, and considered it well; I looked upon it and received instruction. Yet a little sleep, a little slumber, a little folding of the hands to sleep. So shall thy poverty come as one that travaileth, and thy want as an armed man" (Prov. 24, 30-34). Not infrequently those who do the most complaining about the fickleness of fortune and the general unfairness of the distribution of things generally in this world, are the ones who have done the least to make a success of life.

There are honest and unavoidable misfortunes. There are people who, in spite of their best efforts, do not seem able to make things go, as we say. When such is the case, the true child of God is never really hurt. God overrules it all for the good of his children. Let us beware of the misfortune which comes because the doors and windows are standing wide open, inviting it to enter. But when unavoidable adversity comes, let us remember that God still rules; and that all these things must serve as stepping stones for God's people to mount to higher blessings.

Since we are stewards, not only of the gifts of mind and heart with which God has endowed us, but of every penny coming into our possession; and since we shall have to give an account of every farthing to the Master who once sat in the treasury of the Temple and observed what the people did with their money, down to the very widow's mite, how careful we should be of the things entrusted to us by God. That He does not want us to waste it is shown in the parable in which Jesus commanded the disciples to gather up the fragments, that nothing be lost. He wants us to use His gifts so that there will be a proper increase (St. Matt. 25, 14 ff). He does not want us to squander our patrimony, as did the prodigal son. Such squandering may be in the form of senseless luxury, as well as the way of actual transgression. We are living in an extravagant age. Many are spending for naught that which in the hands of our thrifty forbears would have been saved for the emergencies of life and secured to them a competency in old age. Most of us are living beyond our means. This, more than anything else, is responsible for the present prohibitive prices and the general restlessness and dissatisfaction of our people.

The constant consciousness of our stewardship of God's gifts will, on the other hand, preserve us from the sin of covetousness, which is idolatry (Col. 3, 5). As it is wrong to waste God's material gifts, so is it wrong to refuse to use them as God requires. As it is wrong to lack appreciation of these gifts of God, so is it wrong to make gods of them, and thus give to the creature the honor which belongs only to the Creator. We sometimes read of misguided creatures who live a squalid life — in rags and filth, denying themselves proper food and clothing, and all other things which contribute to the higher life; they sit and gloat over their possessions, their eyes dilate and their breath comes faster as they behold their bags of gold and silver. These are extreme cases, but there are many who are affected with milder forms of the same disease. Let us, by all means, take proper care of what God gives us. If we can discharge our duty to ourselves and those whom God has given to us as objects of our care, and still lay up something for the proverbial rainy day, let us do it. That is much better than to waste what God has given us, and then be dependent on others the moment some accident occurs or old age comes creeping upon us. However, the other extreme also must be guarded against. We must not love money, or any kind of property, for its own sake. We are to possess our property, and not be possessed by it. It is valuable only for what good can be done through it. What would a million dollars be worth if there were no food to be bought, none of the necessities of life to be secured? The only real good of any of these material gifts is the contribution which they make to life; the furtherance, the beautification, the enrichment of life.

There is a greediness which overreaches itself.

As we have seen, God rules also in the distribution of earthly things. And as there is a kind of liberality which brings rich returns (St. Luke 6, 38), so also is there a withholding which tendeth to poverty. "He that hath pity upon the poor lendeth unto the Lord" (Prov. 19, 17). And God's bank pays the best interest. Jesus Himself says: "Make to yourselves friends of the mammon of unrighteousness" (St. Luke 16, 9). This means that we are to use the things so frequently employed for unrighteous purposes in such a way that our use of them will make us friends, on earth and in heaven. And this is one of the best investments against a day of want.

God has given us all these good gifts to serve us on our heavenward way. We have many needs, and God has abundantly provided for all our legitimate ones. We have need not only of food and clothing; we have intellectual, moral and spiritual needs. God's gifts are to help us in providing for all these. For the advancement, the betterment, the enrichment of life, all material things are to be used; and this not for our own individual life only, but for the lives of those whom God has given to us as objects of love and care; in fact, so far as possible, for the good of all our fellowmen. In other words, all the material things of this world have been given, and are to be used, for the furtherance of God's Kingdom; that means to the glory of God's holy name.

This address may seem to some to have a rather secular tone. It is so in seeming rather than in reality. It deals chiefly with material things, but it is a plea for the presence and operation of spiritual principles in our dealing with material things. It takes no small degree of spiritualmindedness to live and act on this lofty plane. One must have much of the mind of Christ, and be filled and ruled by His spirit.

Too many people make the mistake of trying to separate the religious from the secular life. They want to be religious on Sunday and festival occasions, and then they put their religion aside with their Sunday clothes while, during the week, they attend to their business affairs. The duties of everyday life, whether in the home, office, store or factory, require strenuous application. Men have not the time to always be talking religion; but they do always have the time to live it. We must learn to do our work, to handle our wages or our profits, as God's children. The principles of our religion are to be so completely a part of our lives that we daily in all things practice them. The Lord says: "Whether therefore ye eat, or drink, or whatsoever ye do, all to the glory of God" (1 Cor. 10, 31). This is the correct relation of the secular and religious life. If this could be fully realized in the lives of men we would no longer need the Seventh Commandment. May the truths here presented be of service to us in helping us to a better recognition of God's hand in every good thing we receive, lead us to appropriate thanksgiving, and to such use of God's gifts as will glorify the Giver.

THE LAW OF MINE AND THINE

"Thou shalt not steal." — EXODUS 20, 15.

"For this is the will of God, * * * that no man go beyond and defraud his brother in any matter; because that the Lord is the avenger of all such." — 1 THESS. 4, 3, 6.

MOST people speak with fluency, and often with a great degree of warmth, of the desirability of honesty. We are eager to maintain our standing as honest people. Nearly every one is ready strenuously to repudiate any insinuation that he is not strictly honest. If there is anything which is calculated to strengthen one in his love of honesty and in the determination to be uncompromisingly honest, it is to be found in such thoughts as we drew from the Word of God in the preceding address. If a man will not be prompted to love and practice honesty by the thought that, as a steward, he is handling God's gifts; by the thought that what his neighbor handles is not only the result of his labor, but that God has had a hand in bestowing it; by the thought that all of us will have to give a strict account of all the property we have handled, and for the way in which we have handled it,—if thoughts like these do not lead to honesty, then we know of no motives that will move men to it.

The honest man feels that all men ought to be naturally honest. But dishonesty is a very common thing in the world. Daily experience proves that many either do not know or do not feel bound by any such considerations as we have recounted. And the evidence is not wanting that many who assuredly know the teaching of God's Word on this subject live in violation of it. Yes, in spite of our boasted culture, and the advance of the spirit of altruism, there is still room in this old world and in every walk of life for the old commandment—"Thou shalt not steal."

In the light of what we have learned as to the nature of our right to property, let us consider to-day the subject of Honesty, or the Law of Mine and Thine.

Common Theft

Theft is one of the meanest and most despicable of crimes. Murder and some other sins are often committed under the influence of sudden passion that, for the time being, unbalances the judgment. Theft, on the contrary, is usually the result of cool calculation. Men plan for it in secret and then carry it out with cunning. Not infrequently the thief goes to his work of despoiling others, prepared and willing to take the life of any one who may discover him and resist his dastardly work. If a theft is committed as the result of an unexpected temptation, it is still largely the result of a chronic state of heart. The thief is one of the basest and most selfish of persons. He thinks only of himself. He has no conscience. There is no place in his mind for thoughts touching his neighbor's welfare. The law of equity is an unknown quantity to him. So far as other people are concerned, he recognizes no right of ownership which may not be violated by the one who has the power or the cunning. The thief has no regard for the feelings or the welfare of other people. That he may use that for which he has given no equivalent, he is willing that those who have laboured and sacrificed should be deprived of their hard-earned increment. Many people have willingly died rather than live by theft. The thief cares not if others die as a result of his deeds, just so he may live with as little exertion as possible.

The common thief, the ordinary pilferer, the sneaking purse-snatcher, the burglar, who, under cover of darkness, breaks into houses, the highwayman who waylays people in lonely places, or any one who in any kindred manner seeks to enrich himself at the expense of others—these, one and all, are looked upon with loathing by every decent citizen. When such fellows are caught and imprisoned, almost every one rejoices and says, It serves them right. This coarse and common sort of thievery is condemned, not only by Christians, but by all people who make any pretensions to decency. The laws of at least the better class of heathen condemn it. But even so we must be on our guard against the inclination. With respect to this sin also we need to watch and pray that we be not led into temptation. Christ was speaking of my heart and yours, as well as of that of others, when He said: "Out of the heart proceed evil thoughts, * * * thefts, false witness, blasphemies" (St. Matthew 15, 19). It takes supreme care to preserve God's gift of an unselfish heart, an honest purpose, and the determination to give to all men a square deal.

Luther felt that the disposition to dishonesty

and the practice of it was extremely prevalent in his day. He says: "God has commanded that no one damage or curtail the possessions of his neighbor. To steal signifies nothing else than to obtain another's property by unjust means. It briefly embraces every method, in all lines of business, by which advantage is taken of our neighbor. Stealing is a widespread, universal vice. But it is so little regarded and seriously dealt with that it exceeds all bounds. Should all be executed who are thieves, and yet resent being called so, there would soon be desolation, and there would not be executioners and gallows enough. * * * In short, thieving is a universal art, the largest guild on earth."

The old crude forms of theft are no longer in vogue in civilized countries. The pirates have been driven from the seas, though, as at the present time, professedly friendly nations may become pirates, and we allow them to take from our ships what they please, probably paying for it in the course of time, if they ever have the means and sufficient pressure is brought to bear upon them. The outlaw bands which existed in Biblical times, as we learn from the story of the Good Samaritan, and which flourished in our own land less than a half century ago, have been pretty well suppressed by the strong hand of the law, at least in countries like ours. The mailed fist is no longer the law which governs in the things which are mine and thine. Indeed, in no sphere of life have there been so many laws enacted respecting property. Property, rather than life or morals, is the chief consideration. But theft is by no means a thing of the past. New forms of taking advantage have been devised. New evasions of existing laws are constantly being brought to light. Our jails, reformatories and penitentiaries are constantly filled with those who have sinned against property. And there are unquestionably more outside these places who ought to be in them than there are in them. Taking everything into consideration, there is no occasion for taking offense in our day at the pointed, unsparing words of Luther. They may be applied with but little curtailment of their scope or force. And they furnish us food for serious thought and self-examination.

The Finer Forms of Theft

I have said that the large majority of people who have any sense of decency at all frown upon common thievery. But there is a multiplicity of methods by means of which men take advantage of their fellowmen. A strict morality, construed on the basis of God's Word, includes all these in the term theft. In many respects, in these days, theft has been reduced to a fine art. By many the questionable methods by which business competitors are put out of business and the purchasers of wares duped, are regarded as exhibitions of laudable business acumen. And, quite generally, the misrepresentation of the commodities one has to sell, and an unseemly decrying of the character and value of that which one wishes to buy, are considered as legitimate tricks of trade. To all such people, whether they operate in the penny market or measure their deals by the thousands of dollars, this Word of God applies: "This is the will of God, * * * that no man go beyond and defraud his brother in any matter; because that the Lord is the avenger of all such" (I Thess. 4, 3, 6). Men often apply to such conduct terms which extenuate, if they do not condone, the act, but in plain old Anglo-Saxon speech it is theft. This truth needs to be pressed home with all possible force in these days. The worth of people to-day is largely estimated, not by what they are in character, not by the good they have done, not by the influence they exert on the community; but by the size of their bank account or the number of farms they own. This helps along very decidedly man's natural disposition to greed and unscrupulousness.

This matter of taking advantage in business transactions is not by any means new. Men did not have to be very far advanced to see such opportunities. In those olden days men did not only steal, but they knew how to give light weight and short measure. In the distant days of Moses the law-giver, tradesmen were exhorted to honesty in these words: "Thou shalt not have in thy bag divers weights, a great and a small. Thou shalt not have in thine house divers measures, a great and a small. But thou shalt have a perfect and just weight, a perfect and just measure shalt thou have" (Deut. 25, 13-15). This form of taking advantage is so common in our day that the government, state and municipal, must keep constant watch over the matter of weights and measures. It was a subject of newspaper report only recently that in a certain city nearly all the market measures had been confiscated and destroyed, because they were below the regulation size.

Constantly we are learning, sometimes by sad experience, that materials of every character which were represented to be of a certain grade, and paid for on that basis, are of an inferior quality. Adulteration of goods is another form of misrepresentation, which comes under the same condemnation. In all such cases of misrepresentation as to the quantity or quality of material, the guilty fail to distinguish clearly between mine and thine. And in so far as they have failed to give to their neighbor what they should have given him, or have taken from him what they had no right to take, they are violators of the Seventh Commandment; they are thieves, for they have stolen.

In the sphere of labor and wages there is much violation of the Seventh Commandment. There is an exchange of commodities between the labourer and the employer of his service. The one sells his labour for a stipulated wage or barters it for a certain measure of the necessities of life. The fixed laws of trade apply to such cases of exchange as well as to any other. The one who takes advantage of conditions to grind the faces of the unfortunate, to keep wages down to a starvation point, and then refuses to pay or unnecessarily delays in paying what has been honestly earned, stands before God's tribunal branded as a wretched thief. "Woe unto him that useth his neighbor's service without wages, and giveth him not for his work" (Jer. 22, 13). "Behold, the hire of the labourers who have reaped down your fields, which is of you kept back by fraud, crieth; and the cries of them which have reaped are entered into the ears of the Lord of Sabaoth" (James 5, 4). On the other hand, the labourer may be, and often is, just as much of a thief as the unjust employer. When he stipulates to do a certain amount of work for a stipulated price or work a certain length of time for a given wage, and then loiters on the job; or, when unobserved, does shoddy work, he is a thief also: he steals both the time and reputation of his employer. Luther speaks some pertinent words to this class of people. He says: "It is stealing when a servant is unfaithful in duty, and does, or permits, any injury which could have been avoided; or when he or she is otherwise indifferent and careless through laziness, negligence, or wickedness. * * * I may say the same of mechanics, workmen, and day labourers, who act wantonly, knowing not how to cheat their employers enough. Besides, they are lazy and unfaithful in doing their work. All such are worse than secret thieves. Against the latter we can guard by locks and bolts, and, when they are caught, we can restrain them by punishment. But against the former no employer can be protected." Let us remember these things, whether we be employers of men or are employed by them. We owe something, the one to the other,—and the failure to pay this debt is theft.

Taking advantage of the necessities of men, simply because one has the power and the opportunity to do so, comes within the scope of the condemnation of this commandment. Monopolistic enterprises, manipulating the market by corners or other unscrupulous methods, and the like, may get one a name as a financial genius, and may even be within the sanction of human law; but it nevertheless brings down upon one's head the condemnation of God's law and the detestation of all right-thinking, right-feeling people. God speaks His denunciation of those greedy people who care only for themselves in these words: "Woe unto them that join house to house, that lay field to field, till there be no place, that they be placed alone in the midst of the earth" (Isa. 5, 8).

Even in the great crises of national and international life, such as war, pestilence, famine, and the like, experience proves that there are always plenty of men heartless enough to take advantage of the direst needs of their fellowmen to squeeze the last possible cent out of them. And this is not something new under the sun. It is the record of history from the days long before the time of Christ to the present time. This is a direct contravention of our text, which says that no one should defraud his neighbor. And Levitical law, of which we should have a finer conception than was possible to the ancients, says: "If thou sell aught unto thy neighbor, or buyest aught of thy neighbor, ye shall not oppress one another" (Lev. 25, 14). This passage, and many others of like tenor, places God's condemnation on much of the so-called big business of our generation.

Games of chance, betting and gambling of whatever nature, is a form of theft. And it makes little difference whether it is carried on in a joint in the slums, in a palace, or, as is sometimes the case, under the auspices of a congregation. It is sometimes urged, in extenuation of the sin, that it is an arrangement entered into by mutual agreement, with open eyes, and that men, therefore, have no right to complain if they lose. The latter contention may be granted, but that does not make the matter right. Gambling stands in about the same relation to stealing that dueling does to murder. Because a man is willing to risk losing his life in an encounter, does not make it right for him to take another man's life. Nor does the fact that a man is willing to risk his own property in a game of chance, make it right for him to take another man's property without the payment of an equivalent. There is nothing considerate or brotherly in a gambling transaction. Men gamble simply as a result of their feverish desire for quick and easy gain at any cost, even of their souls.

That the practice of gambling is wrong, is further shown by the fact that the gambling fever is one of the most fruitful causes of direct theft. Much petty thieving is prompted by the mania for gaming. Most of those who loot banks of the thousands which others have earned and saved, do it for the purpose of some kind of speculation. This lust to have without toil, to be able to spend without earning, lies at the root of all gambling. At every one who would put his hand to that which he has done nothing to produce or for which he is giving no equivalent, should be thundered the Seventh Commandment: "Thou shalt not steal." The gambler is a thief in the sight of God,—he should be esteemed as such in the sight of men.

So far I have enumerated but a few of the more general types of dishonesty. This commandment is directed against all plunderers of their neighbor's property. Every form of usury, cheating, and extortion is forbidden. It may be perpetrated under the forms of human law; that, however, does not excuse it. The laws of men cannot make void the laws of God. Against all those who refuse to consider the rights pertaining to that which is "thine" in order unlawfully to increase that which is called "mine," Christ closes the gate of heaven. "Ye do wrong, and defraud, and that your brethren. Know ye not that the unrighteous shall not inherit the Kingdom of God? Be not deceived; neither * * * thieves, nor covetous, nor drunkards, nor revilers, nor extortioners, shall inherit the Kingdom of God" (I Cor. 6, 8-10).

The Word of God makes no distinction in theft as to great or small. Now in the light of what this Word teaches on the subject let us hastily review our past life. Are we in this respect as entirely free from guilt as we, in thoughtless moments, may have considered ourselves? Have we never taken any advantage of a neighbor in a deal? Have we never misrepresented what we had to sell nor unduly decried what we wanted to buy? Have we always given good measure and full weight? Have we always tried to pay our honest debts? Have we always been frankly truthful when the assessor came around? Do we always pay our fare on the street cars, even when there is a chance to evade it? Riding, recently, on an interurban train I spoke to a little girl who, sitting on the next seat, made friendly overtures. In the course of the conversation I asked her how old she was. The question very much confused her. And the mother explained, rather as a matter of fact, that the child had been instructed to tell the conductor, if he asked her age, that she was five years old. She was evidently eight or nine. Was this honesty? Was it inculcating love for the truth?

There is still another form of dishonesty, of which we might not be led to think by this summarization of the Seventh Commandment. Men not only often cheat their fellowmen, but they often try to cheat God. "Will a man rob God?" asks the Lord through the mouth of the last of the prophets. And in answer to the question: "Wherein have we robbed Thee?" He says: "In tithes and offerings" (Mal. 3, 8). We owe God much; indeed, everything. We owe Him our means, our time, our worship. To the Israelites the Lord said: "When thou hast eaten and art full, then thou shalt bless the Lord thy God for the good land which He hath given thee. Beware that thou forget not the Lord thy God, in not keeping His commandments, and His judgments, and His statutes, which I command thee this day" (Deut. 8, 10, 11). How many are doing this constantly! It is robbing God.

Honesty

This commandment demands honesty. The Lord is not satisfied with the absence of dishonesty, least of all where the restraining force is no more than the fear of consequences. As in other relations, so here also God wants the heart; not merely the absence of vice, but the presence of virtue: a heart fervently devoted to honesty is what God requires. He wants a heart so in love with moral beauty and nobility of spirit, so imbued with fear and love of Himself, so filled with respect for the majesty inherent in the image of God he bears, that it spontaneously recoils from the thought of stooping to meanness. In this sense it is true that "an honest man is the noblest work of God."

Human conditions, despite our boasted culture and moral progress, are not favorable to the cultivation of such ideal honesty. The natural human heart is inclined to be selfish and greedy. Everywhere around us we behold dishonesty flourishing. Graft and bribery are common on the part of those in high position. The greatest extravagance is practiced by the majority of those engaged in doing work for the government, national, state, or municipal. This is because the people pay the bills. It is all a form of theft. We cannot expect much of the ordinary man when legislators set the example of plundering those whose interests they were elected to serve. It would be asking much to expect the common man to think very highly of human laws when many of them seem to have been drawn for the purpose of furnishing loopholes for the extrication of expert tricksters, and when they protect those whose gigantic so-called business operations are but schemes for swindling the unsuspecting.

No, the prevailing conditions are not favorable to the growth of a general spirit of honesty.

Another condition, which is itself both an expression of dishonesty and a means for its promotion, is the injustice prevalent in the punishment of offenders against the Seventh Commandment. The Constitution of our land contains the axiom that all men are equal, at least in the eyes of the law. This proposition has come to be more of a beautiful theory than a reality. At least this is the conclusion to which we should have to come if we looked only at the work of many of those who fill the very offices instituted for the purpose of expounding and enforcing this lofty principle of equality and justice. I refer to our judiciary and the whole process of law enforcement. The poor man who steals a bushel of potatoes or a few pounds of meat, usually gets short shrift at the hands of the officers of the law. He is generally railroaded to prison, and the full penalty of the law exacted. We do not mean to condone such a man's sin. Whoever the man, whatever the circumstance,—he who steals is a thief; for a man of high honour will die rather than steal. Under normal conditions he does not need to do either. There is usually something for the honest, efficient man to do whereby he may support himself. If not, there are always those who are both able and willing to help him. In contrast to the petty thief and the drastic punishment meted out to him stand the inaugurators of the schemes of frenzied finance. They gather in their thousands, or millions. The young and inexperienced who have inherited a few hundred dollars, the aged who have saved a small sum from their earnings against the time of need, the widow with the proceeds of a small insurance policy—these are their dupes. Or there is the respected and trusted officer of a bank who loots its strong box because he has speculated or desires to do so, with other people's savings, in order to grow rich quickly at the risk of other people. What happens to these fellows? If they suffer arrest they soon get out on bond and go about their business or seek their pleasure, while the petty offender lies in jail. The big fellow spends a tithe of his spoils in hiring the best obtainable legal talent. These hirelings, who prostitute their talents to the end that justice may be defeated, take advantage of every technicality. They wear out courts and juries. They prolong the case till the edge of the resentment against the criminal is dulled, and then he either goes free, or gets a nominal sentence, a large part of which is in the form of a money fine. This is the character of a large part of our American justice. It is not justice, but injustice. It is not in keeping with our Constitution. There is an aristocracy of wealth in this country as truly as there is one of lineage and position in other countries. And it is not productive of a high ideal of honesty on the part of the general public. It is calculated to beget the desire to get out of the class of little thieves, which does not pay, and into the class of big thieves, which does pay.

The condition just described is not by any means a modern development. It prevailed in ancient Greece and Rome. Luther tells of its existence in his day in the following words: "There are also men whom you may call gentlemen robbers, land-grabbers, and road-agents, quite above the safe-robber, or pilferer of petty cash. These occupy seats of honor, are styled great lords and honorable, pious citizens, and, under the cloak of honesty, they rob and steal.

"Yea, we might well let the lesser individual thieves alone if we could arrest the great powerful archthieves, with whom princes and rulers associate. They daily pillage not only a city or two, but all Germany. * * * Such is the way of the world that he who can publicly rob and steal runs at large in security and freedom, claiming honor from men, while the petty, sly thieves, guilty of only a small offense, must suffer, to contribute to the appearance of godliness and honor in the other class. Yet, these latter should know that before God they are the greater thieves, and that He will punish them as they merit." Change the word Germany to America, and it would be hard to get a better description of present conditions.

Christian people, of course, will not be ruled, or seriously affected, by such considerations as have just been condemned. They will be honest because it is God's will, insures His approval, and the approval of the inner monitor,—conscience. The Christian would rather suffer from guileless simplicity than profit by mean cleverness.

There are some things which we Christian people ought to do to cultivate a keener and more general sense of honesty. We should begin with our children, and by painstaking care inculcate in them a detestation of everything mean, everything savoring of unjust advantage in dealing with our fellowmen. We can help them in the clear distinction between mine and thine by giving them complete possession of certain things that pertain to their well-being and comfort, and then safeguard them in this possession against the encroachment of others, even brothers and sisters. Likewise we should insist that they respect the same rights in others. In all things and everywhere we must cultivate a love for honesty; and do this by practice as well as by precept.

We can avoid many of the temptations to dishonesty by avoiding extravagance, by living well within our means, and cultivating the virtues of simplicity and godly contentment, remembering that the life is more than meat, and the body than raiment.

God alone, however, can give the truly honest heart. Where His Spirit rules men, teaching them to love Him supremely and their fellowmen as themselves, there alone shall we have a truly honest people—a people honest, not simply because honesty is the best policy, but because they love honesty as the holy and beneficent requirement of the God they love and serve.

When men have become such children of God, recognizing, in all things, their stewardship; when the center of gravity in life has been shifted from greedy selfishness to love of God and man, from time to eternity, from earth to heaven; when the law of righteous dealing, of mine and thine, has become a law of the inner life—then men will not only refrain from robbing the neighbor of what is rightfully his, but they will be at pains to help him in the preservation of his own, and they will do this even when it requires a sacrifice on their own part to do it.

From the lack of faith in Christ and His teaching that lies at the root of all worldliness and greed; from the accompanying selfishness and lovelessness and lack of honour that despoils the neighbor to enrich the spoiler, may the good Lord deliver us!

Toward that state of heart in which men are truly rich, even with but little gold and silver, having treasures laid up where moth and rust do not corrupt and thieves cannot break through and steal; a state of heart with which the unhealthy desire to become hastily and unduly rich in the things that perish is absolutely incompatible; a state of heart prompting men to live and labour and and have possessions altogether for the one great end of furthering the true interests of life, for themselves and others; a state of heart which will mean the realization of a high ideal of God's Kingdom here on earth,—toward such a state of life may the enlightening and sanctifying Spirit of God lead us all more hastily.

GOD'S GIFT OF SPEECH

"Thou shalt not bear false witness against thy neighbor." — EXODUS 20, 16.

"I say unto you, that every idle word that men shall speak, they shall give account thereof in the day of judgment. For by thy words thou shalt be justified, and by thy words thou shalt be condemned." — ST MATT. 12, 36, 37.

I WILL praise thee; for I am fearfully and wonderfully made. Marvelous are thy works, and that my soul knoweth right well." Thus did the Psalmist speak when he had meditated on God's works, especially as he found it in his own nature.

We human beings are, indeed, wonderful creatures—wonderful as to our origin and nature; wonderful as to the constitution of our being, and the adaptation and use of the various members with which God has endowed us; wonderful as to the part we are to play in this great universe; wonderful as to our end. Do we think of these things as often and as seriously as we should? Would it not have a salutary influence on our conduct if we did think a great deal more of them?

These bodies of ours, of which the Psalmist says that they are fearfully made, are units. But each body is formed of a number of members of widely differing character and use. There are, besides many others, hands and feet, eyes and ears, nose and tongue. Each of the members of the body serves a different, often a widely different, purpose; but each one of these helps to form that wonderful unit—the body, the home of the soul, yea, the temple of God Himself.

The members of the body are all important. And if we were compelled to sacrifice any one of them we should probably hesitate long before we could decide which one it should be. However this may be, there is but little doubt as to which of these members is used most frequently, which gives us most of pleasure, which gets us into trouble oftenest. It is the tongue, the organ of speech. The tongue, though subject to abuse, as are all our other members, is a gift of God. There is much evil speech, but before ever sin came into existence there was speech in Heaven, and speech in Eden. Let us then have in mind, as the underlying thought of our discussion, this fact: Speech is God's Gift.

Thought, Language, Speech

Before we proceed to consider speech as to its practical usage in the affairs of life, I invite you to consider with me what we may call the philosophy of speech; that is, some of the deeper thoughts it suggests. It will help to impress the import and importance of the following more practical discussion. Three words present the matter which I ask you to consider with me and not only in this hour, but in many an hour to come. They are: thought, language, speech.

Man is a thinking creature. He is able to take hold of things with the inner man, with the hands of the spirit. With these hands he is capable of taking things apart, even the things which are immaterial, intangible. He analyzes them, looks at them first in one light, then in another. He is often able to combine the data thus secured into proper, legitimate conclusions. This faculty of thought is a wonderful one. It tells us that mere flesh and blood is not all of man, that there is something immaterial, spiritual in man's make-up and that this spiritual something is the real man. This power of thought tells us that man lives on a higher plane than anything else in this world.

We cannot think rationally, sanely, till we are able to resolve our ideas into language, words, and combinations of words. Have you ever thought of what a truly wonderful thing language is—this contrivance by which we are enabled to convey to others, through the medium of words, these incarnations of our thoughts, the impalpable possessions of our souls? We talk, we write, constantly; but I am afraid we seldom remember that this is one of the marvels of life. This is another one of the things which lifts man to a position high above everything merely material, yes, high above every other creature that God has put into this world.

Finally, there is speech, the power of articulating, of expressing, by means of words, through the medium of the voice, the far-reaching thoughts of the mind, the deep feelings of the soul. What a faculty! How godlike its possibilities! We have in human speech one of the marvels of the universe. If the earnest consideration of these things does not lead thoughtful people back to God, and to the conviction that we are the children of an all-wise

Father, then I do not know of anything in the realm of nature calculated to do so.

The Tongue

The tongue is the member whereby uttered speech is made possible. Back of the tongue is the man with his character. And the tongue is continually laying bare, like the scalpel in anatomical dissection, the soul of its owner. Every day we are revealing, through our words, the kind of men and women we are at heart. In all ages the part the tongue has played in the affairs of life, for good or ill, has been recognized. And most of the peoples of the earth have proverbs which express their conception of the power of the tongue to heal or hurt. Some of the most suggestive of these have been put into verse, as follows:

"The boneless tongue, so small and weak,
Can crush and kill," declared the Greek.
"The tongue destroys a greater horde,"
The Turk asserts, "than does the sword."
The Persian proverb wisely saith,
"A lengthy tongue,— an early death;"
Or sometimes takes this form instead:
"Don't let your tongue cut off your head."
"The tongue can speak a word whose speed,"
Says the Chinese, "Outstrips the steed."
While Arab sage doth this impart:
"The tongue's great store-house is the heart."
From Hebrew hath the maxim sprung —
"Though feet should slip, ne'er let the tongue."
The sacred writer crowns the whole:
"Who keeps his tongue doth keep his soul."

What power is recognized to be in the tongue! What power to hurt, to harm! What power to bless! Like all man's other members, the tongue needs to be converted so that its power will be used for good and not for ill.

Truth

The tongue should ever be enlisted in the service of truth. This is indicated by the commandment we are studying. It says, "Thou shalt not bear false witness." These words point, primarily, to some form of judicial procedure and require truthful dealing there; but the injunction is much more comprehensive. It implies that there is to be truthfulness in all things.

So many people are careless in the handling of truth. They do not seem to have any appreciation of its beauty and worth. They handle it as unknowing children might handle costly wares, with the result that it is often broken and outraged at their hands. When people thus handle truth it shows a coarse moral fibre, and that their ideas of life and living move on a very low plane.

Truth is a subject so large, so interwoven with every subject in the world, that it is practically inexhaustible. Truth is the foundation both of the moral and physical universe. All that God requires of the children of men as duty is but the expression of truth in terms of action. Failure to love and worship God aright, failure to love and serve our fellowmen aright, what is this but a species of falsehood? It is so because it is a failure to act in conformity with the constitution of our being.

Such failure takes us out of the sphere where life moves harmoniously and starts it in the direction of conflict, the end of which will be that it misses its true goal.

There can be no knowledge and no communication of knowledge without truth—the truth which is inherent in the nature of things, the truth which sets forth the relations of things. In all the phenomena of the universe God is revealing Himself—the great original, unchangeable, eternal truth. And only as we come to know God and the way in which He is giving expression to Himself in nature and the relation of things do we really come to know the truth. The true child of God, therefore, is best qualified to understand what truth is.

In the sphere of spiritual things God has given to the world, for its enlightenment and guidance, a special revelation of truth. His Word, the sacred Scriptures, is this body of truth. This volume contains and communicates to man the knowledge of God's person and the work He has done to make possible man's salvation. The world has no other body of truth given for this purpose. The Bible is not only a book of information, but a book of power; because in and through it the Spirit of God works effectually, where not opposed, to lead men into fellowship with God Himself who is the truth.

How inexpressibly precious, in its nature and purpose, is truth. Truth is related to the very heart of God and to all the deep mysteries of the universe. And he who violates truth, in any of its many forms, sins against himself, the universe and God. How we ought to love truth! How we ought, by God's gracious help, to teach our souls to recoil from all untruth!

When we speak of a man as truthful, our first thought usually is of his speech; that he is guarded and careful in what he says. As every person of character loathes lying, and has no use for the liar, the person who has no regard for truth; so every person, even the liar himself, appreciates the person who loves and speaks the truth. There is no truer criterion of inherent nobility of character than a native love of truth, and the care such a person exercises in his speech; guarding it scrupulously against the semblance of untruth, jealous of the truth.

These few observations on the general character of truth ought to enable us to appreciate, still better, God's gift of speech, and emphasize the care with which it should be guarded and the blessings of which it may be the means of bestowal.

Proper Speech

Let us now consider some of the blessings of which speech may be the fruitful parent. Speech is much used in Heaven. The angels, we are told, are ever busy sounding the praises of their great Creator. We know how, on that first Christmas night, they came down to earth to sing their glorias over the manger of the new-born Saviour. And when Jesus, grown to man's estate, walked the earth, words of healing, words of wisdom, words of peace, words of life, were constantly falling from His lips. Never man spake as He did.

And what blessed speech it was when the

Apostles went forth on their mission to the people sitting in the starless night of ignorance, and spoke forth to them the Gospel of light and life. What blessed speech it was when the missionaries of all ages went forth and found souls yearning for the true bread of life, and pointed them to Jesus, who is this bread of life.

All the greatest joys of this world are intimately associated with the proper employment of speech. How much speech means to the family circle. Through it the members give their recitals of conflicts and victories, renew their vows and make their avowals of continued affection. The delights of lovers, as they plight their troth, and form the plans whereby two lives pursue a common purpose, are enhanced as they put these dreams into words and utter them in speech. Friendship is a sacred word. It is speech which cements the tie, as friends in their association recount the experiences of the past, and seek to explore the untrodden path stretching into the future. Consider the fond mother as she presses her child to her breast; note the light from the far-away land which beams in her eye, as she listens to the imperfect prattle of her first-born, and answers with that depth of feeling which can have its birth only in a mother's soul. These, and many other innocent and ennobling delights, are inseparably connected with the employment of this God-given gift of speech.

There is a time when it is well to be silent—a time when silence is golden; a time when it shows a loving, considerate heart to keep the lips sealed. If to speak means harsh judgment; if it means bitter, cutting words; if it means to condemn, then, unless truth and justice absolutely demand speech, it is best to keep silent. When suspicious or unsavory rumors about a neighbor come floating around, it is generally best to keep silent or to counteract them by recounting some of the good things we can usually find to say of those same persons. Bringing the truth home to ourselves: when we are spoken against, when our good name is assailed, when our best-meant efforts are misunderstood or misrepresented, when our natural hearts would prompt a reply that would scorch and wither, through words that are veritable arrow-points covered with poison, then is a good time to be silent; then is the time to remember Him of whom it is said: "When He was reviled, He reviled not again." To do this, is not easy; indeed, for mere flesh and blood it is impossible. But for those in whom Christ largely lives and rules, it is possible. Let us remember the beatitude spoken especially for those who are called upon to endure such treatment: "Blessed are ye, when men shall revile you, and persecute you, and shall say all manner of evil against you falsely, for my sake." Let us give no cause for offense, have a good conscience, and then—keep silent.

Perhaps most of us ought to say less than we do, or at least change materially the character of much of our speech. The Apostolic injunction is: "Let every man be swift to hear, slow to speak" (Jas. 1, 19). We have the statement of inspiration that "in the multitude of words there wanteth not sin, but he that refraineth his lips is wise" (Prov. 10, 19). The thought that every word shall be weighed in the unerring balance of God's impartial judgment, and that the character of our speech, as the revelation of the condition of our souls, will have much to do with our acceptance or rejection at the hands of God, should tend to sober us and lead us to weigh well our words.

With all the exercise of due caution, there is still plenty of room for the use of proper speech. The largeness of the sphere where speech may be employed to brighten, cheer and help the world is indicated in the language itself. How many words there are in our vocabulary which are most intimately bound up with the noblest virtues and sweetest amenities of life. It takes speech to put into them the breath and bloom of life. Take the words love, kindness, courtesy, sympathy, good-will, gentleness, friendship, mercy, forgiveness, comfort, prayer, praise, and many others—when these words come from the lips of persons in whom the realities for which they stand have first been wrought into life, and then come forth pulsating with the warmth of loving hearts, accompanied by conduct that confirms the sincerity of their utterance, how much they add to the joy of living, both on the part of those who hear and those who speak them.

Let us, then, employ this blessed, God-given, gift of speech as it ought to be used: to God's glory, for the accomplishment of His purposes in the lives of our fellowmen. Let us use our tongues to make life better and brighter for others as well as ourselves. Let us not be afraid nor hesitate too much to speak the word of appreciation, of good will, of encouragement, which will make some one else feel better. As a result, we ourselves shall also feel better. Such words have a reflex ennobling effect. To this end we must cultivate our speech, not only or mainly as to form and fluency, though this also is well worth while; but especially as to quality. True culture of the heart will ever manifest itself in graciousness of speech. A good heart will give forth helpful speech, even though it may limp as to grammar and logic. A corrupt or embittered heart will give forth speech which wounds and kills, even though it may be faultless as to diction and utterance. "Out of the abundance of the heart the mouth speaketh," says Christ.

No other agency has ever done the good in the world which the tongue has done. The extent of its helpfulness is beyond all computation. It does not always take an oration to do a great deal of good. A few words often suffice. A brief word of advice has often changed the course of a life that was being misspent. A word of encouragement has put new life into a downcast, disheartened brother. A word of friendly goodwill has given to many a despairing person a new vision of human brotherhood. A word of love and appreciation has lifted the galling burden from the shoulder of a weary, despondent toiler, making life worth living and toil a benediction. Ponder the following lines, and then ask yourself whether it describes your conduct:

"A nameless man amid the crowd
That thronged the daily mart,
Let drop a word of hope and cheer
Unstudied from the heart.
A whisper on the tumult thrown —

A transitory breath, —
It raised a brother from the dust,
It saved a soul from death.
O word! O thought! O germ of love!
A thing at random cast,
Thou wert but little at the first,
But mighty at the last."

Was it you who spoke that little word which gave a downcast, despondent brother his new grip on life?

Especially ought all of us who are professing Christians to speak more frequently, more freely, to others on the all-important subject of their soul's welfare. I know that there is a seemingly natural reticence on this score which it is hard for most of us to overcome. I conceive that there are two chief reasons for this reticence. We are all conscious of our own frailty in living what we profess. I wonder, however, whether the chief reason is not this that it is a sly work of the devil bent on hindering God's work of rescuing souls? Whatever the cause, it can, in large measure, be overcome. History records that when Cyrus captured Sardis, a soldier who did not know King Croesus, was about to strike him on the head with a scimiter. Croesus had only one son, a youth who, all his life, had been dumb. But when he saw the danger threatening his father, so violent was his agitation and the effort to speak that the string of his tongue was loosed, and he was enabled to cry out: "Soldier, spare the life of Croesus!" So it will be with us. If Christ Himself has become dear enough to us, if the worth of perishing souls is adequately realized, we shall find the required speech to make known to men their need of Christ and His preciousness to them if they learn to know Him. We speak of the value of friendship. A precious theme! But have we reached the heights of friendship when we are interested in a person's physical and financial welfare, but fail in our efforts to interest that person in spiritual things, fail in our efforts to make him possessor of the greatest of all riches, the imperishable riches of God's Kingdom?

We should all come nearer doing our duty if we had the spirit of the Scotch mother whose bairn, a student in a theological seminary, was getting ready to deliver his first sermon. Her last word to him, as he was about ready to ascend the pulpit, was: "Spake a gude word for Jesus Christ." Yes, let us take or make the opportunity to speak a good word for Christ!

In the community, in the school, in the home, in the church, we need more people—men, women, and children, who will use their tongues for God and the good of their fellowmen; people who have the courage to speak a word for the absent when they are attacked, who will try to find something good to say of their neighbors when others are looking only for faults; people who have a pleasant word to say of and to the living, and not wait to send them flowers when they are dead; people whose presence, because of their cheerful, helpful words, radiates sunshine and dispels the clouds. Such words are "like apples of gold in pictures of silver." Such people are the salt of the earth. Men will rise up and call them blessed. And if their loving words proceed from faith, God will add His benediction.

There is only one place where this grace can be learned—in fellowship with Christ, in the school of the Spirit. But there must be an effort to practice what the Spirit prompts. Our children should be trained, from earliest years, to practice restraint in speech; restraining the evil word, constraining themselves to speak the helpful word at the opportune moment. But only as we open wide the door of the heart and let Christ come in richly, not to sojourn, but to abide, will any of us gain a reasonable mastery over this naturally unruly little member.

We should all try to learn so to speak, as we journey through this lower world, that our tongues will be trained to take part with the heavenly choir above in the song of Moses and the Lamb; where—

"Innumerable choirs before the shining throne
With harp and trumpet raise
Glad notes till Heav'n's vast halls vibrate the tone
Of their melodious praise;
And all its host rejoices,
And all its blessed throng
Unite their myriad voices
In one eternal song."

THE DEVIL'S PERVERSION OF SPEECH

"Thou shalt not bear false witness against thy neighbor." — EXODUS 20, 16.

"If a man offend not in word, the same is a perfect man, and able also to bridle the whole body. Behold, we put bits in the horses' mouths, that they may obey us; and we turn about their whole body. Behold also the ships, which though they be so great, and are driven of fierce winds, yet are they turned about with a very small helm, whithersoever the governor listeth. Even so the tongue is a little member, and boasteth great things. Behold, how great a matter a little fire kindleth! And the tongue is a fire, a world of iniquity: so is the tongue among our members, that it defileth the whole body, and setteth on fire the course of nature; and it is set on fire of hell. For every kind of beasts, and of birds, and of serpents, and of things in the sea, is tamed, and hath been tamed of mankind: but the tongue can no man tame; it is an unruly evil, full of deadly poison. Therewith bless we God, even the Father; and therewith curse we men, which are made after the similitude of God. Out of the same mouth proceedeth blessing and cursing. My brethren, these things ought not so to be." — JAMES 3, 2-10.

IN ORDER to appreciate properly the significance and force of our message to-day it will be necessary to recall the introduction to the preceding one. Everybody recognizes that the tongue is a mighty instrument for evil. But we get to see the real blackness of the many sins of which it is guilty only by contrasting them with the godlike service of which it may be the instrument. Recall, then, that the tongue is one of the members which God, in His infinite wisdom and goodness, gave to man. Its mission is one of the noblest and most beneficent, to minister unto the highest functions of the soul. Thought, the human counterpart of the working of the Mind Divine; language, the expression of thought, and the chief mode of its communication; these wonders of the universe the tongue utters in speech—speech which comes from the soul scintillating with the glow of the mind's activity, vibrating with the intensity of the heart's emotions.

Through the gift of speech audiences are electrified, as the trained master of speech pours out from the alembic of his mind and heart the garnered treasures gathered from the storehouses of knowledge and emotion. By the gift of speech the ties of friendship and love are cemented and new links welded to the chain. In the use of the same gift man approaches the very throne of God. True, at times, there are feelings in our hearts and anticipations of truths in our minds for which we have not yet been able to find an adequate expression in words, to which we can give vent, as the Apostle says, only in groanings which cannot be uttered. But this King of kings gives audience to his children when they come, as they most frequently do, to hold converse in speech, to own their allegiance, to adore His Majesty, to return their thanks, to plead their need, to renew their vows.

Unfortunately, this is but one side of the story of the tongue; the brighter, the blessed side. There is another, a darker side, dark with the hue of the raven's wing. Another history has been written, the pages whereof have been sullied by being dragged through the filth of the pit where no light or love has ever penetrated.

As God is the giver of the tongue, the author of thought, language, and speech, so the archenemy of God and man, the devil, is the author of every perversion of these heaven-born faculties. That dread fall, which wounded all nature to the heart, and whence issued all man's miseries, came from a misuse of the tongue, from a perversion of God's gift of speech. The devil came with seducing lies, the acceptance of which meant the entrance of the destroying poison into the stream of human life. To this point we trace all the ills to which flesh is heir. To-day we are going to confine ourselves to some of the chief of the ills which come from The Devil's Perversion of Speech.

The Unbridled Tongue

"Every kind of beasts, and of birds, and of serpents, and of things in the sea, is tamed, and hath been tamed of mankind; but the tongue can no man tame, it is an unruly evil, full of deadly poisons." These are strong words, and there is no compromise about them; but who will say they are overdrawn? Is it possible to put on the color too thickly in describing the depths of depravity to which this little member has often descended? It certainly would be impossible to measure the streams of tears which inconsiderate, cruel words have set flowing. Who would have the time to recount the murders, and bloody wars of which the deceitful, poisoned tongue has been the exciting cause? What a volume we should have if some one could adequately tell the story of the wounded feelings, the broken hearts, the ruined reputations, the blighted lives, the estrangements, the divided families, caused by this restless, ungovernable little member, the tongue. Hearts naturally tender and loving have been steeped in the gall of bitterness, community feuds have been started, governments have been overthrown, churches have been rent in twain, the most laudable projects in all spheres of human activity have been thwarted. How? By the tongue; by ill-advised, ungovernable tongues. And the same kind of history is still everywhere being made. There is no poison more prompt, potent, progressive, painful, and permanent than that which drops from the thrice-barbed tongue. It kills friendship; like a canker, it eats away love, and curses with quarrels and strife the homes alike of prince and peasant.

In order to get an idea of the magnitude and blackness of the service to which the tongue can be put, and often is put, let us recount but a partial list of the evils mentioned by inspired writers in which the tongue is the chief instrument: talebearing, slander, backbiting, lying, blaspheming, perjury, bearing false witness, deception, calumny, cursing, tattling, quarreling. The list might easily be much extended. Indeed, there are but few sins to which the tongue is not an accessory. But these are enough to cause one to stand aghast at the possibilities of the tongue for evil. No wonder St. James, speaking of the uncontrolled tongue, says: "The tongue is a fire, a world of iniquity, and it is set on fire of hell. The tongue is an unruly evil, full of deadly poison."

Even Christian people are not always so free from this evil as they ought to be. It is an insidious evil. There are so many excuses which apparently justify these dagger thrusts of the tongue. In our text St. James is speaking chiefly to and of Christian people, of such as had made at least a beginning in the Christian life. It is therefore, first of all, to church members, frequenters of the house of God, that these words of his apply: "With the tongue bless we God, even the Father, and therewith curse we men, which are made in the similitude of God. Out of the same mouth proceedeth blessing and cursing. My brethren, these things ought not so to be." We are all ready to grant the unseemliness of such conduct, but, in spite of our knowledge and better feeling, it still occurs.

The Gossip

We will now consider a little more in detail a few of the more common faults of speech condemned by this commandment. First of all there is gossiping. Very few of us, perhaps, have altogether escaped the attacks of these wagging tongues. May I not go further and say that, in all probability, there are few of us who have not, at some time, forgotten ourselves and used our tongues in the thoughtless, useless way which may be termed gossiping?

There are many new things in the world, but gossiping is not one of them. Virgil, led on by the flights of his vivid imagination, thus describes this disturber of the peace: "The gossip, than whom no pest on earth is more swift, by exerting her agility grows more active and acquires strength on the way; small at first through fear, soon she shoots up into the skies and stalks along the ground. A monster, hideous, immense, who, wonders to relate, for as many plumes as are in her body, numbers so many watchful eyes beneath, so many babbling mouths, pricks up so many listening ears. By night, through the mid-regions of the sky, and through the shades of earth, she flies buzzing, nor inclines her eyes to balmy rest. Watchful by day, she perches either on some high housetop or on some lofty turret, and fills cities with dismay." Long before this versatile Roman penned his scathing denunciation of the gossip, the Hebrew seers set upon him the stamp of God's strong disapproval. Moses, the great law-giver, gave the wandering tribes of Israel this command of God: "Thou shalt not go up and down as a talebearer among thy people" (Lev. 19, 16). And the great son of the greater David added these observations: "A froward man soweth strife, and a whisperer separateth chief friends" (Prov. 16, 28). And again: "The words of a talebearer are as wounds, they go down into the innermost parts" (18, 8).

The tendency to gossip in some people becomes a passion. Their tongues simply run away with them. It must wag, though it be without either rhyme or reason; and regardless of consequences. Sometimes there is no conscious desire to do any one an injury. But even where there is no evil intent harm is nevertheless often done. The idle talker usually loses the power of perspective so far as truth and untruth are concerned. While there may be a thread of truth in the fabric which comes from his loom, it often becomes lost or obscured in the elaborate design he fashions. He is apt to set forth facts in disjointed relations, to take no account of circumstances, to assume motives or disregard them, to suit the color scheme of the narrative, as his fancy or purpose may suggest. The result is that the hearer usually gets a distorted image of the matter reported.

Excuses are often made for the gossip on the ground that this is but a fault, a human frailty. True, it is but a human frailty; but so is theft, adultery, and murder. Sometimes the gossip deals with matters so inane, so inconsequential, that no evil could come from it, save to the dawdler who wastes his time in the recital. But when one becomes a confirmed gossip the matter with which he deals is not usually harmless in its nature. There is not enough of spice, of excitement, in that kind of gossip to suit him. Choice subjects for him are the character and conduct of his neighbors. And the more of harm he can find or thinks he finds, the better he likes it. He becomes full of innuendoes. "I have heard," "it is rumored," "it looks as if," are favorite formulas of the gossip. Here is where reputations are injured and hearts wounded beyond cure. This is the reason that in all our Scriptures this and kindred sins of the tongue are pursued with all the energy of multiplied and scathing denunciation. But in spite of all that God and men have said against gossip it is still rife. In social life there are circles where all interest would be lost if every exaggeration, every confidentially whispered rumor about neighbors, were taboo. This is evidence of a very low moral tone. And we, as Christians, by word and example, should set our faces against it.

The Slanderer

The slanderer is the gossip, grown to man's estate. The gossip may be a harmless nobody. The slanderer is one who gossips with intent to injure; he goes about with tongue or pen, or both, dipped in vitriol, murdering reputations. His work may be done by raising false reports, by magnifying a man's failures, or by spreading reports which have a basis in fact, but which, in charity, ought not to be made public. Slandering is the particular sin against which the Eighth Commandment is directed.

"Thou shalt not bear false witness against thy neighbor," is a law of God frequently broken in public life; and often by those who, in a special way, have obligated themselves to uphold truth and justice. When lawyers, for a fat fee, attempt to make the guilty appear innocent, or fasten guilt on innocent persons because, perchance, they may not be able to defend themselves, or even besmirch the names of the dead, they are bearers of false witness. When judges prostitute their sacred office, as the result of the influence of the rich or great, to defeat justice, setting the guilty free or condemning the guiltless, they break this law of God. When witnesses, for similar or other reasons, suppress or distort facts, or fabricate statements, to the end that their friends may be cleared or their enemies punished, they break this holy law of God and man.

In other spheres of public life also this command is broken. It is a matter of constant experience that when a man of good reputation comes into public notice, as a candidate for public office, for instance, a thousand people begin to dissect his life's history. All his foibles, which nobody ever heard of before, are exploited. A score of skeletons are supposed to lie hidden in the closets of his private life, and everybody feels called upon to try and expose them. All kinds of base motives are attributed to him. In political life, especially, is this supposed to be an excusable, if not an honourable, expedient for ruining the prospects of a rival. In most instances it is nothing less than defamation of character. It is a violation not only of the law of love, but, most frequently, of truth as well. And those guilty of it prove themselves unworthy of confidence.

This disease is found even among ministers of the Gospel. Professional jealousy often gets hold of them. Not only do they, at times, become affected with a species of theological madness, which leads them to rail with the greatest rancour and ill-will against the views and the honesty of those in other religious communions, but the brethren of the same household of faith are often made to feel the keen edge of the same weapons.

In private life also this sin is frequently committed. How often do people become envious of the possessions or gifts of their neighbors, or for some other reason come to dislike them; then the process of detraction begins. All kinds of insinuations as to the secret of their success are set in motion. Veiled hints are thrown out as to the revelations which could be made if the person speaking was only minded to do so. In this way the reputation, which is the ripe fruit of a lifetime of duty honestly performed, of service willingly rendered, of lofty ideals tenaciously held and progressively realized, is often irreparably injured. What deed can we think of more dastardly than the injury to a good person's reputation by the malicious thrusts of a vile detractor. And yet there are many who take a fiendish delight in this kind of work.

There is something in the natural human heart which makes us loth to give due credit for worth of character or achievement to any one save ourselves, or our own particular circle of intimates. How often we have all been in circles where the characters or work of excellent persons was under discussion. And nearly always there is some one who is ready to get out his little hammer, or his bucket of cold water. It is hard for us to praise people, to speak well of them. And even when nothing positively derogatory can be said, how often, in the words of Pope, people will:

> "Damn with faint praise, assent with civil leer,
> And, without sneering, teach the rest to sneer;
> Willing to wound and yet afraid to strike,
> Just hint a fault and hesitate dislike."

Why is it that we cannot be more generous, rejoice more in other people's honest and deserved success, and speak the word of praise and encouragement rather than of detraction? Why, even when there is not so much to praise, do we not have the happy faculty of looking for the good qualities of people rather than the faulty ones? Let us change our glasses, friends, and the miracle will be wrought! When we look through green glasses the world looks green. The reason we look so largely for faults and see so many faults, is accounted for by the medium through which we look. If we had the right kind of heart — the heart Christ would fain give us — we should see more beauty and goodness in the world. And where we could not but see the evil we should not proclaim it from the housetops; but, if we had to speak of it, we should go to the source and in the spirit of Christ, seek to correct it.

A man's good name is one of his most priceless possessions. To preserve this to him is one of the chief objects of this Eighth Commandment. To know that we deserve a good name is essential to our own self-respect and peace of mind. To have a good name in the eyes of others is necessary to the full enjoyment of what we deserve and essential to our social well-being. The value of a good name has always and everywhere been recognized. The sacred writer says: "A good name is rather to be chosen than great riches" (Prov. 22, 1). You all remember the lines of the bard of Avon:

"Who steals my purse, steals trash; 'tis something, nothing;
'Twas mine, 'tis his, and has been slave to thousands;
But he that filches from me my good name,
Robs me of that which not enriches him,
And makes me poor indeed."

These sayings of the inspired writer and of the keenest observer of human conditions express the feelings of all honourable men. Probably just because a good name is such a precious and unpurchasable possession, so many people are trying to rob others of that which they themselves do not possess, and are too indolent and evil-minded to obtain. Some will even stoop to the basest trickery, and the baldest kind of lying in order to blacken fair names and cast upon reputations which have required for their establishment long years of the most painstaking care a life-long and intolerable burden, and all because some one out of spite and resentment broke the Eighth Commandment.

To speak of a person as an ordinary, every-day liar is considered to express very nearly the limit of human depravity, but the wilful slanderer is one who aims the envenomed darts of his lying tongue at that which is most vital to the wellbeing and peace of his fellowman — his reputation, his character. This vice often so completely obsesses a person that no tie, no relationship, is sufficiently strong to safeguard one from these attacks. "Thou sittest and speakest against thy brother; thou slanderest thine own mother's son" (Ps. 50, 10).

One of the names of the devil is slanderer, and human slanderers are, in a special sense, his offspring. They are also likened to that most universally detested of earth's creatures — the serpent. Men of God have given to this brood the following description: "There is no faithfulness in their mouth; their inward part is very wickedness; their throat is an open sepulchre, with their tongues have they used deceit; their mouth is full of cursing and bitterness. The poison of asps is under their lips. Destruction and misery are in their ways" (Ps. 5, 9; Rom. 3, 13ff.).

If people have not a sufficient measure of Christian faith and love to restrain their tongues; if they have not enough humanity to be held in check by the mental suffering caused by the slanderer's tongue, they ought to be held in restraint by the thought of God's anger and punishment. "Thou shalt not bear false witness against thy neighbor." "Lying lips are abomination to the Lord" (Prov. 12, 22). "The false witness shall not go unpunished, and he that speaketh lies shall not escape" (Prov. 19, 5).

If bearing false witness against a neighbor or misinterpreting his character or deeds, is such a crying sin, what must be said of those who break this commandment in their treatment of God Himself? And this is the sin of which men are guilty when they pervert God's Word. God has given us His Word as an outline of His own character and the working plan of His dealings with man. To deny, or misrepresent, this Word is a species of slander against God Himself. It leads men to have a false understanding of God Himself, and of His dealings with men. The consequences are much farther reaching than the slander directed against man. To slander a man injures his standing among men, it stands in the way of advancement in life and often injures his body by destroying his peace of mind. This is bad enough. But to lead a man to believe the slanders directed against God, the disbelief of His Word, the misrepresentations of either the person or the work of God, endangers, if it does not completely destroy, his soul. It is in a special sense this sin of which St. James is speaking.

The Positive Requirement

The Eighth Commandment is, in form, prohibitive: it forbids false and evil speaking; but it includes a positive requirement. As we have seen from Luther's explanation, it does not only mean that we are not to "deceitfully belie, betray, slander, or defame our neighbor; but excuse him, speak well of him, and put the best construction on everything."

The requirement of this command is absolute truthfulness in all things. God abhors lying. So do truthful people. But one need not go a whit beyond the truth and still violate the spirit of this commandment. We are never, under any circumstances, to excuse, or make light of, sin. But we should not publish our neighbor's faults to the world. In the best regulated families there are occasional slips of conduct. Some one says or does something which should not have been said or done. But if the other members of the household have the right spirit these errors are not blazoned abroad. Efforts are made to correct them; but the erring member is not humiliated or made obdurate, by making his weakness public property. The neighbor should receive the same treatment. He is a brother, only a short step farther removed in relationship.

The poet spoke the truth when he said of unregenerate human nature:

> "There is a lust in man no charm can tame,
> Of loudly publishing his neighbor's shame."

But this ought not be true of a child of God; and it is not true if he is a faithful, considerate child of God. The true Christian considers other people's feelings, and other people's welfare as well as his own. If no harm is done thereby, he would much rather cover a neighbor's fault than reveal it. Every fault of man spread abroad adds only that much more to the shame and burden of the common humanity.

The spirit of brotherly conduct requires that we should mention and emphasize rather the good points of our neighbor than his weaknesses. There is a proverb which requires that we speak only good of the dead. It is of much more consequence that we speak only good of the living. The exceptions to this rule being the occasional cases where truth and justice, in the hands of the proper authorities, demand that facts be made known, however much they may hurt. Where good can not be said charity demands, in most instances, that we put a bridle on the tongue and be silent.

The Christian does not cultivate the spirit of suspicion with respect to either the motives or conduct of others. He does not suspect faults. He does not impute evil motives. And when others exhibit such disposition in dealing with neighbors, a faithful brother will defend the one thus suspected and assailed. He will put the best construction on his words and deeds. Suspicious people, if they will not be held in check by the evil they are doing to others, ought to remember that in their suspicion they are only revealing their own conception of the working of the human heart, a judgment based on their own inner experience. Thinking to portray another, they portray themselves.

Father Luther has this to say of this commandment: "Slanderers are they who, not content with knowledge of sin, presume to judge; and, becoming aware of a trivial offense of another, spread the intelligence everywhere, having such satisfaction in his wrongdoing as have swine in their wallowing and rooting in the mire.

"The sum and substance of this commandment, then, is: none shall do injury with the tongue to his neighbor, be he friend or foe; he shall not speak evil of him, true or false, unless by command, or to effect his reformation. We are to use our tongues to speak only good of every one, to cover the sins and infirmities of our neighbor, to overlook them, and adorn him with due honor. And our chief cause for so doing shall be to fulfill Christ's command, in which are comprehended all commandments concerning our neighbor: 'All things therefore whatsoever ye would that men should do unto you, even so do ye also unto them' " (St. Matt. 7, 12).

Controlling the Tongue

Scientists tell us that the words we utter, as all sounds, set into motion waves of air which keep on undulating to the farthest confines of boundless, limitless space. Their moral effect is somewhat analagous. An evil word spoken of a person or whispered into the ear of another, may ruin a life. That ruined life will, in all probability, ruin other lives. And so the evil keeps on moving, spreading.

When a person begins to realize how many and great are the evils wrought by an unguarded, envenomed tongue, he is almost inclined to feel that the ancient ascetics were right when they retired from the haunts of men and took their vows of perpetual silence. But sober reflection shows us that such a course is not necessary. The abuse of the tongue is no argument against its proper use. Indeed, there may be a guilty silence as well as a guilty speech. What we need is to learn to control it, to use it for the purposes for which God gave it. The tongue is not to be the master but a servant. And the one of whom this can be said the Apostle declares to be the most perfect of men. "If any man offend not in word, the same is a perfect man, and able to bridle the whole body." Who, then, is the strong man? Not the Samson with knotted muscles, and the strength of a team of oxen; the strong man is the one who can hold his tongue. Who is the wise man? Not the one who has all history, and all the sciences at his fingers' ends; the wise man is the one who knows when to be silent, when and what to speak.

Let us remember, then, that just as powerful, just as far-reaching, as is the influence of an evil word, so powerful and far-reaching, and still more powerful and far-reaching, is the influence of the good word. On the far off shores of heaven those waves are breaking which have been set in motion by good words, the words of truth leavened with love.

Who is equal to the task of thus governing his tongue, of restraining his tongue from speaking the evil word an angry, or excited, soul may suggest; or of speaking the appropriate word, the needed word, of loving helpfulness? No mere man, not unaided flesh and blood. So the Apostle tells us: "Every kind of beasts, and of birds, and of serpents, and of things in the sea, is tamed, and hath been tamed of man; but the tongue can no man tame." These words are spoken of the unregenerate man, and experience demonstrates their truth. But with God all things are possible; and the child of God, if he will, may claim the same help, and make the same declaration as did St. Paul: "I can do all things through Christ, who strengtheneth me."

The tongue, while removed from control of physical forces, is amenable to the influence of the Holy Spirit. Where He has entered the soul and rules the spirit of man, there the tongue becomes His instrument, an organ of grace and truth and love.

"So let our lips and lives express
The holy gospel we profess;
So let our works and virtues shine,
To prove the doctrine all divine."

GOD'S WARNING AGAINST COVETOUSNESS

"Thou shalt not covet." — EXODUS 20, 17.

"I had not known sin, but by the law; for I had not known lust, except the law had said * * * Thou shalt not covet." — ROMANS 7, 7.

THE Ninth and Tenth Commandments treat, so far as specified objects are concerned, with things already prohibited. The Ninth reminds us of the Seventh; and the Tenth is, in part at least, touched upon in the Fourth and Sixth. But the thought contained in the Ninth and Tenth is by no means exhausted in the former commandments. Indeed, they take a decided step in advance of anything contained in the Second Table of the Law. There is a sense in which these last two commandments present but the negative side of which the first is the positive. The first says God is to be supreme in our thought and affections. These two say that not even in thought or affection is anything to be enshrined in place of God.

These last commandments deal with the root and source of all sin; namely, the evil desires of the heart. It is true that, in the explanation of all the commandments, we bring out the fact that they are broken first of all in the heart, and that they are kept aright only when kept in and from the heart, and that in their scope they are all-inclusive. The Fifth Commandment, for instance, does not only forbid murder, but also anger, malice, and every kind of malevolent affection. This is Scriptural, though it is not expressed in so many words in the commandments themselves. Luther correctly introduces this in his explanations, but he gets it from other Scripture teaching and from the central thought of the Ninth and Tenth Commandments.

The primary object of these commandments is to emphasize a right state of heart, the absence of which is sin. God's laws must be kept in thought and desire as well as in word and deed. No one keeps them unless he is free from the desire to break them. This is the very point man is prone to overlook. When he has been a good son and citizen, a good husband and father, an upright business man in his outward dealings, and a friendly, helpful neighbor, he is inclined to life up his head and say: "I have met all the requirements of God and man, and lack nothing." But here is where God steps in with His searching heart-test. Have you never entertained wrong thoughts or unlawful desires? To enforce His view of sin God, once and again gives the command: "Thou shalt not covet."

The sin denounced in both these commandments is the same so far as its nature is concerned. It differs only in the object toward which it is directed. And so far as the grosser sins are concerned, which result from the coveting, they have been considered under previous commandments, especially the Sixth and Seventh. As a result, I will combine the Ninth and Tenth in this treatment, and consider only the fundamental thought they are designed to emphasize — the sin of covetousness, the warning against it.

There are three leading thoughts I shall seek to keep in the fore-front: the nature of covetousness, the sin of covetousness, and the gain of godly contentment.

The Nature of Covetousness

Let us study briefly the nature of covetousness. "Thou shalt not covet." This commandment, this interpretation of the true inwardness of the other commandments, puts a distinguishing mark on the whole Moral Law of God. Many of the other commandments, in some form or other, are found in the literature of other ancient people besides the Hebrews. They probably derived them, directly or indirectly, from the Hebrew Scriptures; in any event, it is clear that they were capable, in a measure, of appreciating them, of discerning their practical value. But in no code of laws besides that given by God to the Hebrews do we find anything resembling the fundamental, heart-searching prohibition of the Ninth and Tenth Commandments: "Thou shalt not covet."

We have here, then, one of the fundamental differences between the religion, the morality, which God sets forth in His Word and demands of his children and that which natural religion recognizes and demands. God looks at the inner life and not merely at external conduct. He wants an outward virtue; but it must not be assumed: it must be the outward expression of inner holiness.

What is covetousness? To covet means to have an inordinate, irregular, unlawful desire for that which we do not possess, and cannot lawfully, innocently, possess. The original meaning of the word covet was to take delight in some object, and, because one delighted in the object, to set his heart upon it. This explains the use the Scriptures, in a few places, make of the word, applying it to the desire for laudable objects. "Covet earnestly the best gifts" (1 Cor. 12, 31). But it is now used almost exclusively of the desire for the possessions, more particularly, of the wealth, of others. Covetousness is a passion to grow rich, usually at any price. This passion becomes the great aim of life. And with the growth of this passion the heart becomes corroded; inconsiderateness, mercilessness, and injustice characterize the covetous man's treatment of his neighbor.

Avarice is a term sometimes used as a synonym of covetousness, but it is not wholly synonymous. Avarice is specifically a passion for money; a love of money for its own sake, not for the good one may do with it or get out of it for one's self. The avaricious person loves the glitter of coin, the touch of currency. He delights to hoard it, rejoices to feast his eyes upon it. He loves money as some people love their children, as the saint loves God. The avaricious person never wants to part with his money. This spirit is well represented by the message the Spanish adventurer, Cortez, sent to Montezuma: "Send us gold, for we Spaniards have a disease which can only be cured by gold." This disease is highly contagious. Many in all ages, and every clime, have caught it. It feeds upon itself, and yields but slowly to treatment.

Dante, in his description of his travels, represents the dangers to the inner life under the form of various beasts. He likened the pleasures of life to a leopard, sly and cunning; but he was able to make his way past it in safety. Ambition is compared to a lion, fierce and combative. The poet acknowledged himself afraid of it, but was not conquered by it. Avarice he depicts as a wolf, gaunt and hungry; and he confesses that he was forced back by it, step by step, into the darkness. This has been the experience of many a person in his conflict with this enemy.

One of the particular dangers of avarice is that it is frequently found in people who are, otherwise, exemplary in their lives. A man may detest uncleanness in word and deed, he may be a man of his word, and discharge the duties of life he assumes with fidelity, and still set this undue, exaggerated value on the perishing things of this life, with the result, however, that his finer perceptions gradually become bleared and his nobler feelings blunted.

Covetousness, while it has, in general, the same significance as avarice, is to be distinguished from it. The covetous person, as we have seen, has an inordinate desire for gain; but covetousness is wider in its application, going out toward all kinds of possessions. It includes the desire to get them by unlawful means if necessary; by craftiness, as Luther expresses it, or a show of right. Furthermore, the covetous person may not desire to get and to have in order to keep, but to squander. The covetous man may be a veritable spendthrift. Indeed, he often covets only that he may have that wherewith to gratify his whims or his lusts.

A man may be covetous also of other things than wealth. David and Herod each coveted another man's wife. Ahab coveted Naboth's vineyard, not because he needed it, but because it would complete his pleasure grounds. And many a man covets another's good name, his friends, his social position, or his station in life. Envy, therefore, is first cousin to covetousness, for it is a feeling of dissatisfaction at beholding the good fortune of another.

Covetousness is often given other and less repulsive names. We often say of a man that he drives a close bargain, that he knows how to take care of number one. We sometimes designate him as a thrifty or far-sighted man, when, in reality, he is actuated by covetousness. But however we may modify the term, God does not look on real covetousness as a little thing. The Bible tells us that God abhors the covetous man (Ps. 10, 3).

The Sin of Covetousness

That covetousness, the desire for things, perishing things of the earth, is a sin will not come as news to any one acquainted with Bible teaching in only a general way. There are not many sins which receive more frequent or more scathing treatment at the hands of those who spoke for the Lord. One reason for this is the fundamental, far-reaching character of the sin. Another is its frequency and the many other ills to which it is related as cause or effect.

Covetousness is a sin against the neighbor. The covetous man soon becomes, if he does not start out with being, a loveless man. He is afflicted with a concentrated form of selfishness. In a moral sense, he is the victim of hardening of the heart, and a consequent atrophy of the feelings. Not caring for other people, he soon comes to look down upon them, especially if they are less fortunate than himself. He begins to feel that the man whose hand lacks skill, whose mind is less sagacious than his own, whose plans are marked by feebleness, was made to be trampled upon, and plucked at every opportunity. As the spirit of covetousness grows in a man he will begin to justify this conduct. He pretends to see in man's poverty or helplessness an evidence that God does not care for him; and, he argues, if the unfortunate man is not considered by God in heaven, he need not be considered by man on earth. As a result we have such designs conceived and executed on other men's property as are described by the prophet: "They devise iniquity, and wish evil upon their beds! When the morning is light, they practice it, because it is in the power of their hand. And they covet fields, and take them by violence; and houses, and take them away; so they oppose a man and his house, even a man and his heritage" (Micah 2, 1, 2). This same spirit of covetousness, in another direction, is back of the story of David's fall. It led him not only to take another man's wife, but to cause that man's death.

A large part of the sins of the world owe their

parentage to covetousness. The class distinctions and rivalries, the labor wars, the capitalistic combines and other methods of oppression, are all largely fathered by it. The lust for land, for commerce, for prestige sets nations to cutting each other's throats. It is the same greed, in a smaller way, which leads some men to theft and forgery and business deception, and others to gambling. Still others it leads to engage in trades and manufactures which are the curse and destruction of mankind. It leads them to sell the honor of their sons and the virtue of their daughters. No wonder a loving God, who desires the welfare of men, for time and eternity, thunders His command from Sinai: "Thou shalt not covet!" No wonder that the gentle Jesus adds His warning: "Beware of covetousness."

Covetousness is in a special way a sin against oneself. It stands as a barrier in the way of the realization of the ideal or goal for the attainment of which man was created. It is closely akin to the materialism which regards this life as the all of existence, and, therefore, present gain as the only possible gain. Jesus was warning against this danger to oneself when He said: "Take heed, and beware of covetousness; for a man's life consisteth not in the abundance of the things which he possesseth. * * * The life is more than meat, and the body is more than raiment" (St. Luke 12, 15, 23). The development, the unfolding of life itself in beauty and power, the bringing of life into harmony with its original natural environment — into fellowship with God, and into the love of truth and righteousness; the setting of life's forces into the movement toward the realization of its Divinely appointed goal; and then to help others to come to the same glorious heritage — these are the purposes for which men are to live, and in the pursuit of which alone they can attain to peace and happiness here and bliss hereafter. The covetous man defeats these ends in his own life. Covetousness leads man to put his body above his soul, pleasure above duty, time above eternity, the creature above the Creator.

The covetous man, in thus perverting God's law, does not only greatly endanger his prospect of attaining eternal life, but he largely defeats his own present purpose. He is covetous and employs the means of the covetous man, because he thinks thereby to increase his pleasure, but instead of augmenting it he progressively destroys it. The covetous man has ceased to be a satisfied man. And his dissatisfaction increases. The more he gets the more he wants. The desire to get comes to gnaw like a ravenous beast at his vitals. He becomes suspicious of everyone, even his nearest kindred. He scents everywhere plots against him and what he has. And the sight of even little things which he does not possess and cannot find ways of possessing, makes him miserable. Ahab is a good example of this. He was a ruler. He had a high station in life. He had riches. But he wanted Naboth's little vineyard. Naboth, because it was an inheritance, and was not to be alienated from the family, would not part with it. As a result, we are told that Ahab "laid him down on his bed, and turned away his face and would eat no bread" (1 Kings 21, 4). A very foolish piece of business, we are inclined to say; but covetousness makes people foolish.

Zophar, counsellor to Job, gives us a striking picture of the pass to which the covetous man finally comes: "He hath swallowed down riches, and he shall vomit them up again. * * * He shall suck the poison of asps, the viper's tongue shall slay him. He shall not see the rivers, the floods, the brooks of honey and butter. That which he laboured for shall he restore, and shall not swallow it down. According to his substance that he hath gotten he shall not rejoice. Because he hath oppressed and forsaken the poor, he hath violently taken away an house which he builded not; surely he shall not feel quietness within, he shall not save aught of that wherein he delighteth" (Job 20).

Covetousness, being a sin against the neighbor and oneself, must, necessarily, be a sin against God. All sin is, directly or indirectly, against him. But much more than many another fault is covetousness a sin directly against the person and majesty of God. It is not only a violation of His expressed will, it is the dethronement of God from His place of primacy in the heart. It is a putting of the creature in the place of the Creator. This is the reason it is called idolatry (Col. 3, 5), a sin so heinous that God declares that no covetous person shall inherit His Kingdom (1 Cor. 6, 10; Eph. 5, 5).

Let us not think that the wealthier people are the only covetous people. This is a great mistake many are liable to make. A man of great wealth may not be covetous. A very poor man may be. A poor person may hoard pennies with as much lust for money as the man of thousands does his banknotes. A young woman may have a heart as full of covetousness for finery as the rich person has for a summer home at Newport and a private yacht. It is not so much the amount or nature of the things coveted — it is the coveting itself which is sin.

Not till man has been enlightened by the grace of God to understand the nature of covetousness, to recognize that the impulses of his corrupted nature are sin — the root, the fountainhead of all sin; that covetousness is really sin, and condemns, — not till he has learned this, is he in a condition to know himself as he is — a helplessly lost, unworthy, condemned creature. This is what St. Paul tells us in Romans seven. He was a Jew, who knew the Jewish law. But it did not alarm him. He had kept its requirements outwardly and justified himself on that ground. But when he came, by the grace of God, to know that lust, the evil desire within that breaks out in a thousand directions, was condemning sin, then he recognized himself as a lost, undone creature, and was led to cry out: "O wretched man that I am!"

Before we close this part of the discussion let us hear, and take with us, a few words of Christ on this important subject, and remember that they are the words of the Son of God: "Take heed, and beware of covetousness" (Luke 12, 15). "Lay not up for yourselves treasures upon earth, where moth and rust doth corrupt, and where thieves break through and steal. * * * No man can serve two masters, for either he will hate the one, and love the other; or else he will hold to the one and despise the other. Ye cannot serve God and Mammon" (St. Matt. 6, 19, 24).

The Gain of Godly Contentment

Covetousness never brings lasting gain. It never brings what the covetous person fondly hopes. The covetous person loses not only heaven, if his covetousness is pronounced, but also the best things of earth which he had hoped to gain. Covetousness has ruined nations. It has brought the cup of bitterness to countless thousands. It loses a man his friends. It destroys his peace of mind. It often leads to a state of mind, and to efforts, which destroy his health. But godliness brings gain. We have the Word of God for it that it is profitable, "having promise of the life that now is, and of that which is to come" (1 Tim. 4, 8).

By godliness is not here meant that which is such only in form, but that which is essentially so. It is the godliness which really knows God as a Father, loving, merciful, careful of his children; which really knows Jesus Christ as a personal Redeemer, as the one through whom, by faith in His name, we richly and daily receive the full and free forgiveness of all sins; which possesses the indwelling Spirit of God bearing witness to our spirits that we are the children of God, and the assured heirs of eternal life; and disposes men to kindly feelings for one's fellowmen, and willingness to help them in every need. Such godliness as this takes the sting of carking care out of our souls. It assures us that, as God is in heaven, all must be well with his children.

To be truly godly does not mean, as some of the ancient ascetics taught, that we must abjure all property. Jesus never disparaged wealth. He never spoke slightingly of the powers by which men are enabled to make it. He never indicated that it was a sin to earn money, or to take pleasure in acquiring it. Contentment does not mean that one must be careless and indifferent with respect to the good things of this world. Laziness and carelessness are not indicative of precocious piety. But contentment does mean that when we have formed our plans with care and prayer, and have put our best powers into their execution, that we take the result as God's answer to the prayer which works, and the work which is a prayer. To this man God says: "Be content with such things as ye have, for * * * I will never leave thee, nor forsake thee" (Heb. 13, 5). If we can honestly accumulate something beyond the daily need, and not set our hearts upon it, but be ready to use it as our good or the good of others may demand, neither God nor his saints will say nay. But if our plans do not succeed as we had hoped, the godly man does not become sour, fretful, and unbelieving; he knows God does all things for the best, and he is able to say with St. Paul: "I have learned, in whatever state I am, therewith to be content" (Phil. 4, 11).

This state of mind and heart is found only in those who have been renewed in their nature; only in those who are rich toward God, rich in their trust in God, and in their love for Him. This love casts out all fear. "Why dost thou fear?" cried Caesar to the terrified boatman, "thou carriest Caesar!" The true Christian does not fear, for he has God with him — always, everywhere. It is not in such a man to make gods of the things of this world, and thus sell his soul for a mess of pottage. He would not, if he could, accumulate a fortune by dishonest or hurtful methods; for he knows that it would profit him nothing if he should gain the whole world, and lose his soul when he came to the end of the little span of life. Nor would he sacrifice the respect, love and friendship of men for the wealth of the Indies. Alexander the Great, the conqueror of the then known world, gave orders that when he was buried his hands should be left exposed from the coffin as a reminder to others that though he was the acknowledged master of the world he could take nothing with him when he left it. Shrouds, they say, have no pockets. "We brought nothing into this world, and it is certain we can carry nothing out" (1 Tim. 6, 7). The godly man knows, and is satisfied with, the unfailing riches. He lives so that he can say with the prophet: "Although the figtree shall not blossom, neither shall fruit be in the vines; the labour of the olive shall fail, and the fields shall yield no meat; the flock shall be cut off from the fold, and there shall be no herd in the stalls; yet I will rejoice in the Lord. I will joy in the God of my salvation. The Lord God is my strength, and He will make my feet like hind's feet, and he will make me to walk upon mine high places" (Heb. 3, 17-19).

THE SUPREME DUTY OF MAN TO MAN

"Thou shalt love thy neighbor as thyself." — St. Mark 12, 31.

YOU doubtless recall that at the close of the First Table of the Law we considered Christ's synopsis of those three commandments. He put it into positive form. He did not say, Thou shalt not; but, Thou shalt. The throbbing heart of all the Law was given in those old, but still new, words: "Thou shalt love the Lord thy God with all thy heart, and with all thy soul, and with all thy mind, and with all thy strength."

God would not be satisfied, could not be satisfied if the human heart were purged of every trace of idolatry, if man's lips never uttered a blasphemous sound, did not a higher obedience follow. If man's soul were simply like a piece of white paper, with never an ugly mark or blotch on it, that could not satisfy God. He does not want a colorless, inactive, unresponsive life. God wants man's life to be blood-red with human affection and energy; He wants to be enshrined in that man's heart as the object of his highest affection. He does not want man's lips to be dumb, but vocal with praise and thanksgiving, and Himself the primary object of it. God wants man to love Him, reverence and serve Him with that rapture of delight which pure, strong love alone can give. In this desire of God there is not a vestige of what we, in the language of mortals, call selfishness. The very nature of God and of His universe demands this; and the highest good of his creature, man, demands it. This is the first commandment. It is the law of the supreme duty of man.

There is a second commandment like unto the first. It is also a summary of the Second Table. As in the first, so here, Jesus is not satisfied with prohibitions. It is not enough that we do not kill, or steal, or bear false witness against the neighbor. He wants something living and positive. "Thou shalt love thy neighbor as thyself." If the first commandment were fully realized in our lives, this second would follow from it as naturally as the stream follows the channel which nature has provided as its outlet.

As the first commandment, without any qualifications, sets forth the supreme duty of man — that toward God, so this second commandment sets forth the supreme duty of man to man. This is the subject to which, in this hour, we will give our attention. There are two leading thoughts which I shall elaborate: What it means to love one's neighbor; and the conduct implied.

The Obligation — to Love

The requirement of this second great commandment is very simple of statement; but exceedingly deep and difficult of comprehension, and still more difficult of realization in life. The simple, easily understood injunction is, "Thou shalt love thy neighbor as thyself;" but it penetrates to every nook and corner of human life and conduct, where we are to follow it with our obedience.

In our generation there has been more discussion of problems of social welfare than ever before. Almost every phase of human need and human progress has received attention from some body, or class, of people. Laws are being rapidly proposed and not infrequently enacted that look to the improvement of the living or working conditions of this or that class. And the end is not yet. Diverse are the motives prompting this activity. Some of it is political and looks to party prestige. Some of it is done by hired agitators, whose only interest is monetary. Some of it is the result of dawning class consciousness and pride. Some of it results from refined selfishness, having as its object the betterment of man as an efficient productive factor in the world's activities. Some of it directly, much of it indirectly, is the result of the growth of a nobler spirit of human brotherhood, a result of the church's existence and teaching. But, as conditions at home and abroad abundantly teach, the world as such, the civilized, the so-called Christian world, has still very far to go before it will begin, even approximately, to understand and appreciate the second great commandment, "Thou shalt love thy neighbor as thyself." Indeed, anyone who has spent any number of years in fellowship with a Christian congregation, in business dealings with fellow-Christians, or as a co-worker in religious enterprises, knows, from his own experience, that, in spite of our nineteen hundred years of blessing and growth, we are all, laymen and preachers, far from perfectly obeying this commandment.

What is it we owe our fellowman? We owe it

to him to let him make a decent living, to let him have the opportunity for cultivating his mind and inner life, the enjoyment of his rights. We owe him the financial help necessary to bridge over a season of enforced inactivity. But this is not all, it is the least that is required of us. The Divine requirement is, "Thou shalt love thy neighbor." The fundamental requirement in the religious and ethical system of Jesus Christ is love. And love is more than money or a dole of bread. Human life originated and originates in love. Love holds together the basal human institution, the family. It recreates, gives new visions and new impulses to, the individual human life. It is the principle which leavens and transforms all human relations. It is the active principle of all heavenly conduct on the part of God and the holy angels.

What is the standard by which we are to gauge our love for the neighbor? We are not asked to love him supremely,—that would be idolatry. In some instances, especially in the case of parents and children, husbands and wives, this is done. Some one is idolized, all the wealth of love is showered on that person; and when misfortune, sickness, or death comes to this one, complaint is made against God's dealings. He is charged with inconsiderateness or injustice. This is idolatry. There are persons whom we probably love better than ourselves, for whom we would be willing to sacrifice our own life. But even above this love must be the love of God. "He that loveth father or mother more than me is not worthy of me, and he that loveth son or daughter more than me is not worthy of me" (St. Matt. 10, 37). But for every one there must be this measure of love — as we love ourselves.

As we love ourselves! Let us calm ourselves for a few moments' serious reflection, and see what this means. Why and how do we love ourselves? That most people have great love for themselves, needs no special demonstration. But why do we love ourselves? Is it because we are so great or so good? Because we are worth so much to our fellowman? If we honestly threw the searchlight of our own better consciousness, not to say, of God's holy law, upon the recesses of our inner life, and weighed our credits as they are estimated in the impartial balances of truth, should we have very much of which to be proud? Is our self-esteem based on superior knowledge? Most of us have none to spare: it is not above the average, and with the best it is very fragmentary. The truth is that, if we were severely candid, we should have difficulty in making out a strong bill of justification for our self-love on the ground of any extraordinary conduct or achievement. What, then, is the ground of our self-love? The real ground of this self-appreciation, often debased to self-gratification, is the possibilities inherent in our nature. We may be only partly conscious of them, they may operate sub-consciously or unconsciously; but they are the real ground, nevertheless. We were created by God, who gave us His own image. He gave us an imperishable life. We have fallen far, and have sustained great injury; but great possibilities are ours still. This nature, so greatly marred, so sadly perverted and abused, accounts for the esteem in which man holds himself. It is often, to be sure, a perverted form of the respect and esteem in which man should hold himself, and of the law of self-preservation which he should exercise — but the fact remains. Our fellowman, however, has the same Father, the same nature, is affected only by the same infirmities, and has the same wonderful possibilities before him; consequently he is entitled to the same esteem and consideration in which we hold ourselves. This is one of the reasons why we should love him as we do ourselves.

And we dare not, by any subterfuges, try to get away from the obligations of the second great commandment. It is God who says, "Thou shalt love thy neighbor," — love him as we do ourselves. We have no more right to say that we will not love our neighbors than we have to say that we will not love God. Jesus Himself says this second commandment is like unto the first. It comes from the same high source of authority. It requires the same thing. Its binding force is just as irrevocable. Its violation comes from the same fundamental source, offends the same supreme authority, and leads to the same consequences. It is vain for us to claim to be children and worshippers of God while we entertain feelings which lead us to look down upon or hate our brethren of mankind. The Word of God tells us that "if a man say, I love God, and hateth his brother, he is a liar; for he that loveth not his brother whom he hath seen, how can he love God whom he hath not seen" (1 John 4, 20). The love of God and man are but two sides of one great emotion. The love which goes out to God supremely is, as far as part of its rays are concerned, simply deflected toward man, the child of God.

But we often hear people say, "I simply cannot love everybody; especially can I not love such and such a person." They argue that love does not come at one's bidding, that it is a sphere of life over which men exercise no absolute control, that love is elicited by the nature or characteristics of the person who awakes it. We mean by this that we can love only those who please us, whose traits or qualities we admire. And, so far as mere human love is concerned, this is undoubtedly true. But here stands the law of God, "Thou shalt love thy neighbor," — all thy neighbors, everybody; and love them as you do yourself. True, this love, also, does not come of itself. It does not come from mere likable qualities, for often these are absent. In a Christian sense of love, wishing people well and being willing to serve them — in this sense we can love even those whom we cannot like. This love is God-given. It comes only to those who have learned to love God supremely, and, enlightened by His Spirit, begin to see humanity as He sees it. The child of God loves humanity because God loves it, and gave His life for it, and is continually giving His life to it. The Christian loves men not so much because of what most of them are, but because of what they may become. It becomes possible for the true child of God reasonably to fulfill that apparent paradox Jesus propounds when he says: "I say unto you, love your enemies, bless them that curse you, do good to them that hate you, and pray for them which despitefully use you, and persecute you" (St. Matt. 5, 44).

Let us not say that this is a Utopian dream about which we need not much concern ourselves, because it is something beyond our power in this world. That would be to deny God's power and to give the lie to His Word. Unfortunately it is true that this commandment has not been realized as it could have been. And we know very well that it is not going to be perfectly realized on this side of the Golden Gates. But it has been realized by some people in such measure that if it were generally so realized this old earth would become so transformed as to become a portal of Paradise, a heaven on earth.

In view of what has been done in the way of living up to this commandment, of bringing men to love one another — all of which is but an earnest of the still greater things which might have been achieved, what an indictment this commandment brings against the conditions which still prevail in the world; yea, which still, in far too large a degree, prevail in the Church. The people in whom the spirit of the world prevails, and their name is legion, look on every one else and everything else as a lemon to be squeezed whenever, and to whatever extent, it may suit their purposes. And too often even among professing Christians it happens that they "bite and devour one another," with the result that they are "consumed one of another" (Gal. 5, 15). My brethren, these things ought not so to be. And where people have truly experienced the love of God in Christ, and have thus had their hearts enkindled by contact with the heart of God, it will not be so.

"Thou shalt love thy neighbor as thyself." This is the divine ideal for human society. It is the goal to which humanity must come before it can be crowned. To what has been achieved in this direction we owe all that is really worth while in this life. An entirely loveless world would soon become a hell, a seething cauldron of hate. Love is the crowning delight of the intercourse in heaven. But what do we still find among men? On the part of, oh, so many! a colossal selfishness and heartlessness. A disposition to turn, with iron heel, on the very hearts of others; to grind them down into the dust, to take advantage of their direst necessities; like Shylock, to exact to the last ounce the pound of flesh, to be steeled against the needs and the tears of widows and orphans. The world has caught some of the reflections from the Kingdom, and practices occasionally some of her amenities; but at heart it is the same old loveless world, and as world it will always be so. But the sad part of it all is that those in the Kingdom, many of them, have learned so little of this commandment. They forget that Jesus said: "By this shall all men know that ye are my disciples, if ye have love one to another."

Brethren, this commandment is not a problem of merely academic interest; it is not a problem only for discussion, it is a principle to be put into practice in our living. This commandment does not deal with ancient history or present-day theories.

It is a matter as vital to our physical, moral, and spiritual well-being, individually and collectively, for time and eternity, as is the heart-beat to the welfare of our physical organism.

This second commandment condemns every one of us; for no one, by nature, loves his neighbor as he loves himself. And those of us who are under the influence of God's grace are fully conscious that our love for our brethren, as our desire for our own highest good, is wavering and fragmentary. But if we are truly converted, regenerated, people, then this commandment has begun to be realized in our lives; we have begun to love men, even all men. Let us to-day give ourselves a candid self-examination in the light of this God-given, Christ-enforced commandment, "Thou shalt love thy neighbor as thyself."

The Implication as to Conduct

The things implied in the second commandment, so far as the practical application of it to life is concerned, are manifold, if we would set them forth in detail; but they may all be set forth in one comprehensive rule of conduct, prescribed by Jesus Christ Himself: "Therefore all things whatsoever ye would that men should do to you, do ye even so to them, for this is the law and the prophet" (St. Matt. 7, 12).

The love of which the second great commandment speaks is not a cloistered virtue. Men do not shut this love up in their hearts, brood over it by day, dream of it by night, but never put it into action. The specific nature of this love is that it is active. It was an active love when first it dwelt in the bosom of the eternal Father; for it is written, "God so loved the world that He gave,"—gave His only begotten Son to save. The love of Jesus was ever an active love. Having loved his own, He loved them unto the end. This love led Him not only to His exhaustive campaigns, but to the cross and the grave. And so it is when in human hearts love has been enkindled at the Divine altar.

Mere human love is chiefly, in all its forms, a passion to possess; the love of a child of God, in its human outgoing, is chiefly a passion to bless. It starts with a passion for God and the righteousness and blessedness which it is His to give. Having found these it begins to reach out. It becomes a passion for humanity, for the righting of their wrongs, for the upbuilding of their ruined estate — for their salvation. While this love takes many forms, it is always a desire to serve man out of love for Christ.

Human love often proves a powerful passion. By it the sorrows of the mother are changed into ministries of joy; by it the wearing toil of husband and father ceases to be a burden and becomes a pleasure. All the arts of literature have been exhausted to exalt this love. Yet, the hearts which beat with this passion become stilled and their activity ceases. But the love which Christ inspires never ceases. Age does not wither its ineffaceable charm, nor the flight of years exhaust its energies. Nineteen centuries have passed since they took Jesus and laid Him in the tomb. But the love He had begotten they did not bury, for it did not die. And every day since then it has proved itself alive by the victories it has won. This is the one love which abides while the lovers die, for it is possessed of perpetual youth, and the inexhaustible energies which are born of God. It is passed on as man's priceless heritage from age to age.

What has not this heaven-born love done for the world? Let us think of the innumerable men and women who have caught the vision this commandment sets before us as the ideal, and whom the Spirit of God has helped on toward its realization, making them patient, sympathetic, and helpful in all their relationships. Let us think of the forbearance, longsuffering, and forgiveness it has taught them to practice. Let us think of the unbroken line of faithful workers in every sphere of life this love has inspired, from John and Paul down to the many unheralded men and women labouring in obscure places, led on because their hearts have been taught to yearn for the bodies and souls of men, and not only for the fortunate and well-favoured, but even, and in a sense we might say especially, for the physically, morally, and spiritually unfit and defective. Let us think of the labors, deprivations, and sufferings many of these people have endured in the service of those for whose good they gave their lives. Let us think especially of the missionaries to heathen lands; the men and women who have gone into the wild and waste places of the earth, to be brought into association with the most ignorant, debased, and vicious of human beings, not for name or fame, but because the love of Christ constrained them. Let us think of how these people, when for long years their best efforts seemed not only unavailing, but were actually requited with the most cruel persecutions, continued to love their unlovely tormentors, refused to forsake them, and worked on faithfully for and with them. In this connection we must not fail to think of the tens of thousands of those at home who supported this advance guard with their gifts and their prayers.

When we think of these things, and others less notable, which the partial realization of this commandment has wrought in this world, we take heart and thank God. We thank Him for the power of His great grace whereby these wonders were wrought in man. We thank Him for these people through whom they were wrought. They have helped to redeem humanity. They have helped to give us renewed confidence that man is a creature that can be saved and restored. They have done more than any others to bless this world and make life worth living.

How much better off this world would be if there were only more of this love of Christ which becomes the love of man. Natural love needs to be sanctified and ennobled by it. And when this is done it is also heightened. How different many homes would be, even many professedly Christian homes, if there was enough of the love of Christ in the hearts of the inmates to lead them to begin to love the other members of the family as they love themselves. The cloud which hangs over many a home, keeping out the sunlight and cheer which means so much to life, is exaggerated self-love, which destroys love for others. If these people would open their hearts more to the love of God, which is the indispensable requisite, and then cultivate more love for others, a surprising transformation would be wrought. The old home itself would seem like a different place. The people in it would not only seem to be—they would really be, different. They would not always want to be served, but would find pleasure in serving. They would not constantly be seeking to get the best of everything for themselves, but they would want to share it with others. And, if people are seeking for happiness, this is the best recipe for it in the world. The truest happiness the world knows does not come to the selfish seeker, but to the unselfish server.

The ancient Rabbis tell us of two brothers who owned and tilled a little farm as partners. One of them was childless, the other had children. The man with children felt sorry that his brother was deprived of this blessing. The heart of the one without children went out to his brother because of his added responsibilities. So one night after wheat harvest the childless brother found it in his heart to help his brother's situation by carrying part of his sheaves over to his brother's portion. But the same night the father, rejoicing in the little ones God had given him to rear for heaven, and sorry for his solitary brother, sought to add to his pleasure, and carried a similar number of his sheaves to his brother's side. How many brothers and sisters have this loving interest in one another's welfare? There are some, there ought to be many more. And life, all around, would be much happier if it were so.

Nothing can so regulate human relations as

Christian love. It makes us not only kindly affectioned towards others, but also patient and forbearing when others exhibit their weaknesses toward us; it keeps down pride and envy in self; it seeks to keep self and those we love from everything unseemly; it seeks for self and all those we love everything good.

The same principle applies to congregational life. Selfishness and hatred are divisive and destructive; love is a unifying, constructive force. In every congregation there is need of all the tenderness, patience, and forbearance the grace of God can give his children. Love in a church member does not look for honors and preferments, however great the service may be. Love does not look for slights, nor rashly resent them if they should come. Love does not become impatient, nor frown down upon those who, from lack of training, or temperamental infelicity, have difficulty in keeping up with the procession. Love helps to bear the weak brother's burdens. And it does not do this with airs of superiority, but with meekness. Love knows better than to seek to drive men to good things. Jesus says, "No man can come to me, except the Father which hath sent me draw him" (John 6, 44). He draws us with the cords of love, and it is by the subtle magnetism and sweet compulsion of heavenly love that the Father's children must go forth to make their conquests.

Oh, that there were everywhere among Christians, pastors as well as people, more of the practice of this love which the Apostle calls "the bond of perfectness" (Col. 3, 14). Not a word of depreciation have I to say of the desire for a wider intelligence on the part of churchmen or for a more refined culture. The love of music, beautiful church buildings, an imposing form of worship is permissible. They are things much to be desired. I love all of them. But what the church needs more than all else is a love which not only keeps pace with, but leads the advance in all other directions. We have, doubtless, enough ceremonies, confessions, and churchly privileges. What we do need is the faith-born love which puts the real soul into these things.

Are we speaking of something which is the result of mere caprice? Is this love the only thing in God's universe not governed by law? It is not so, my brethren. There are laws governing the begetting and the growth of Christian love just as there are laws governing all other things. "God is love" (I John 4, 16). And only by so truly knowing God in Christ that we come to love Him above all things, and trust Him completely, is love for man begotten. And just as surely as we have the first, shall we have the second. But even this love must be exercised in order to grow. The arm which is not used soon loses its strength. The memory which is not developed by the effort to retain soon loses its power to retain. And love which is not put to the test soon ceases to be love. Do we entertain some grudge? Let us determine by the grace of God to root it out. Has some one offended us? By the same grace let us determine to forgive and to forget. Is there someone who seems to exercise a specially repellent influence on us? Let us summon our powers and determine that we will overcome it all by special graciousness. Such conduct will gather momentum by its own weight, and we shall grow in love, the crown of Christian virtues. "And now abideth faith, hope, love; but the greatest of these is love."

GOD'S THREAT FROM SINAI

"I the Lord thy God am a jealous God, visiting the iniquity of the fathers upon the children unto the third and fourth generation of them that hate me." — EXODUS 20, 5.

OUR text you doubtless recognize as part of the Conclusion of the Ten Commandments. In our Catechism it is introduced by this question, "What does God say of all these commandments?" The implication of this question is correct. These words do apply to all the commandments. But I hope that most of you are well enough acquainted with your Bibles to know that these words, which we call the Conclusion, are found in connection with the First Commandment. Indeed, a considerable portion of the Protestant church uses this Scripture passage, together with those other words about graven images, as the second commandment. I shall have something to say at another time about the divisions and numbering of the commandments. At this time I shall confine myself to showing why we use these words as a conclusion.

First of all, the words themselves tell us that they refer to all the commandments. In the next verse, which contains the promise, the Lord says, "To them that love me, and keep my commandments,"—not one, or part of them, but my commandments, all of them. The probable reason why the Lord attached this threat and promise to the

First Commandment is because of its supreme importance and comprehensive character. The First Commandment includes all the others. And if we could comprehend the First aright we should need no others. It is only as an accommodation to our weakness that the others were drawn from the First for our instruction.

It would, of course, not be wrong to treat of the words of our Conclusion in connection with the commandment with which they are associated, but we should have to be at pains to explain that it refers to all of them. Luther prepared this catechism, first of all, for children and simple folk; so he gave it that position which in itself would show its purpose and scope. It is indeed a conclusion. It tells us how God feels toward those who do not keep His commandments, and how He feels toward those who do keep them. And this is the point which I want now to emphasize. But, as my text indicates, I am going to confine myself this morning to the first part of the Conclusion, that which sets forth God's threat against the violators of His commandments. I shall take as my subject—God's Threat from Sinai. It is the threat of a jealous God, a threat against sin, a threat to punish sin.

The Threat of a Jealous God

The natural man cannot but conclude that there is a God, but his conception of His nature is never a very exalted one. Even during Old Testament times, and not infrequently during the New Covenant, the ideas of God's own children, with respect to His nature and disposition, were often rather dark and forbidding; they regarded Him as a stern, ruthless, relentless taskmaster. Jesus' revelation of God was far other than this. He showed God to be a Father, approachable, merciful, loving, forgiving iniquities and sins. We can never afford to lose this conception of God. But, as is so frequently the case with weak, vacillating human nature, many have gone to the other extreme. They conceive God to be a being whose love excludes all other attributes, one whose love has so weakened His character that, though He may feebly demand righteousness, He will not punish even where His requirements are disregarded.

The commandments are all of a nature to disabuse man's mind on this score. Especially is this Conclusion of such a nature. Here God comes before each one, and addresses each one personally. The same God who says, "I am the Lord thy God, thou shalt have no other gods before me," says, Here are your tables of duties. My nature, your nature, and the constitution of the universe, demand their fulfillment. Violation of them cannot go unpunished. It will bring its own punishment. But I, the personal God, the author of your being, this law, and all things, shall be personally outraged. The violator will incur my displeasure and such punishment as the demands of justice and righteousness require.

Let those who incline to the theory that God may make threats to scare men into being good, but that He cannot bring Himself to be really severe even with the obstinately disobedient—let them ponder carefully, prayerfully, these words of our text: "I the Lord thy God am a jealous God, visiting the iniquity of the fathers upon the children unto the third and fourth generation of them that hate me." These are God's words. They have never been recalled, or modified.

"I * * * am a jealous God." These words rather startle us, and incline us to draw back. The word jealousy has, with us, a rather unsavory meaning. We are inclined to think of a jealous person as one who is unreasonably touchy, easily estranged, full of exaggerated demands and feelings of resentment. We speak of jealousy as the green-eyed monster. And yet we are taught by God Himself to look upon Him as a jealous God. There must be a jealousy, therefore, which is perfectly proper. The person who is not capable of jealousy is not capable of love. Jealousy is the pain of neglected, wronged love. Jealousy is the shadow which falls when the sunshine of love has been intercepted. Jealousy is the heart's counterpart of the mind's sense of justice. Justice has a right to expect a recompense where service has been rendered. Jealousy asks for love in return where affection has been bestowed and has a right to expect reciprocation.

Now to understand somewhat at least of what God means when He says, I am a jealous God, all we need to do is to apply this principle. We owe God everything. He is our Creator, the author of our every good. He loves us, condescending to love us in our lovelessness, to seek our good in everything, to win us back to His image. God's exalted nature calls for our reverence and adoration. His goodness obligates us to gratitude. His holy laws, the expression of the perfection of His attributes, and the most perfect instrument for achieving man's welfare, demand obedience. And when man fails to give God what is His due, and gives to imperfect creatures like ourselves, or even to merely material objects, the affection which belongs to Him, then He is rightly offended. He would not be God, the perfect, the holy, the just, if He were not so. And this is what He means by being a jealous God.

Let us remember, then, O children of men, that God is watching us with sleepless, never diverted, eyes. Nothing escapes Him which relates to His Moral Law, even though it be but a secret thought or a desire hidden in the depths of the soul. As Luther says: "These precepts are not human trifles, but commandments of the most high God, who earnestly enjoins them, and who, in anger, sternly punishes those who despise them; but abundantly rewards those who keep them."

The devil constantly tries to whisper into our ears that it can make but little difference to the great God even if we, as individuals, are somewhat unbelieving, careless, loveless, disobedient. We are a great nation of many millions of people, but does not our government take note of the violations of individuals? Honest citizens are righteously indignant when criminals succeed in creeping through the meshes of our law; shall God not see that His laws are vindicated? We have a national honor, and we are inclined to become very much wrought up when the rights, sometimes the questionable rights, of a few of our people are infringed; shall God not insist upon His honor?

It will have a salutary influence on our lives, of the old as well as the young, if we will follow the advice of Luther with respect to this Conclusion. "It should be kept before the young and impressed upon them, that they may learn and remember it; that they may observe what those circumstances are that make obedience to the commandments imperative. They are to regard it as a seal to each commandment, and as the soul which pervades them all."

God's Threat Against Sin

If there is one thing which we should have learned from our study of God's Law, besides the loftiness of the ideal He sets before us, it is this—the universal failure of mankind to realize this ideal. In other words, the unpalatable, but stern fact that we have not kept this holy Law, that we are sinners.

We all know, the vilest and most ignorant of heathen know, that a terrible blight has fallen upon the race—a blight which has enfeebled and put chains on man's powers, and filled him with love for evil and hurtful things. But as to the explanation for the presence of this blight, there is no general agreement. Some think that it is only a lack of knowledge and power which man is to outgrow as he follows the law of development. God's Word gives us another, and by far the most satisfactory, explanation. It tells us of man's original state of perfection, that he was made in the image of God; and that it was disobedience, rebellion against God, which marked the birth of sin in man's nature.

Human history, from its earliest dawn down to the present moment, is largely a history of sin.

The first man and the first woman broke God's clear commandment, and brought "death into the world, and all our woe, with loss of Eden." The first son born into the world became a branded murderer, the second, his victim. When the conduct of men rose as a stench to heaven and so displeased God that He resolved to destroy the race, the father of the one family he saved, almost as soon as the Ark found a resting place, became the first victim of the intoxicating cup. The Scriptures declare that "There is none righteous, no, not one. There is none that understandeth, there is none that seek after God. They are all gone out of the way, they are together become unprofitable; there is none that doeth good, no, not one. Their throat is an open sepulchre; with their tongues they use deceit; the poison of asps is under their lips; their mouth is full of cursing and bitterness; their feet are swift to shed blood; destruction and misery are in their ways; and the ways of peace have they not known; there is no fear of God before their eyes" (Rom. 3). The reeking pages of secular history confirm this statement. They are ill-smelling with the stories of lust and rapine; they are dark hued with flowing streams of blood; they tell of innocence debased, of justice outraged, of fortunes wrung from the tears of widows and orphans, of empires built on the bleaching bones of the ignorant or helpless who were enslaved and exploited by the powerful and selfish.

What is the burden of the message of our great newspapers? Is it not largely made up of the stories of lust and intrigue? It is the recital of devastations, themselves the expression of the condition of a nature itself which, because of sin, travails in pain during this present age; of thefts, murders, adulteries, warfare, and the tricks of scheming politicians.

And this is not, by far, the whole story. Much of the fruit of sin is unwritten history. It does not reach the ears of men, though it never fails to reach the ears of the Lord God of Sabaoth. Many of those whose names never appear in print as transgressors, have compromised with Mammon, have entered into league with death, and have covenanted with hell. But even if all were known to men, no pen could ever do justice to the universal, never ceasing ravages of sin. The tragedy of creation's wound is felt, but felt too deeply to be described. Every tear, every heartache, every pricking of pain, every wail of a lost soul, is part of the history of sin.

Many refuse to be included in the class of gross sinners. No excesses can be attributed to them. They are fathers and mothers, sons and daughters, of respectable families. They observe the commonly accepted code of morals in business and professional life. They are good citizens. They practice the amenities of life. Shall we be classed with sinners? they sometimes rather indignantly inquire. Yes, we have all failed. There is not a clean record among us. The fact that we are not criminals does not free us from being sinners. We have all done things we should not have done. And we have, perhaps more frequently, failed to do the things we should have done. "If we say," even Christian people, "that we have no sin, we deceive ourselves and the truth is not in us" (I John 1, 8).

The universal prevalence of sin in action has led many to inquire about its origin. Even many heathen moralists were forced to the conclusion, confirmed by the Word of God, that sin dwells in the very nature of man. Indeed, as to the nature, extent, and consequences of this birth-sin the Word of God is our only source of trustworthy information. We usually call it original sin, because it comes with us into the world. As David said, so all must say, "I was shapen in iniquity, and in sin did my mother conceive me" (Ps. 51, 5).

When sin came into human life, it destroyed the image of God in man, and so alienated man's affections from God and things holy that "the carnal [that is, the natural] mind is enmity against God; for it is not subject to the law of God, neither indeed can be" (Rom. 8, 7). Our nature being enfeebled, and more, turned against God Himself, we lack the power of appreciating the things of God. "The natural man receiveth not the things of the Spirit of God, for they are foolishness unto him; neither can he know them, because they are spiritually discerned" (I Cor. 2, 14). This spiritual deadness, so often and so strongly affirmed in God's Word, and so constantly experienced in human life, Jesus has in mind when He says: "Verily, verily, I say unto thee, except a man be born again he cannot see the Kingdom of God" (John 3, 3).

The idea of original sin is objectionable to a great many people. And many others who recognize and are willing to admit that life must have sustained a great loss, are not ready to admit that God can be seriously offended at it or hold men responsible for it. But God's Word, as in all things, settles this question for us. "As by one man sin entered into the world, and death by sin; and so death passed upon all men, for that all have sinned" (Rom. 5, 12). "That which is born of the flesh is flesh" (John 3, 6). And that which is of the flesh is by its very nature a child of wrath (Eph. 2, 3). Common experience bears out these statements of God's Word. The first great curse of sin spares none, death comes even to the infant. And the workings of all the dreadful passions, which soon begin to bring forth their bitter fruit, show themselves in the earliest life of the child. But only that which inheres in the nature of a thing can regularly and persistently show itself in its development.

We must learn to get away from the idea that sin inheres only in action. The very essence of all sin is not action but perverted relationship. The heart, the life, alienated from God, failing to recognize His fatherhood and authority, rebelling against Him and entertaining feelings of enmity toward Him because of His claims—this is the heart of all sin and the germinating source of all sinful action. In this Conclusion God comprises all sin in the term "hate." Hatred may and generally does show itself in some form or forms of action; but not necessarily so. It is primarily and essentially a state of the heart.

The reason men want to hear nothing of original sin, a sin which has robbed human nature of its beauty and power, set it against God, and filled it with all kinds of ugly, deforming passions, is that it hurts their pride. For its rectification a renewal of the whole inner life is needed—a cleansing and a power which God alone can provide, and which He has provided in His dear Son, who became man's Saviour. For its reception there must needs be repentance and confession of emptiness and need. This hurts the natural man's self-esteem and he tries to justify himself by denying the too evident corruption of his nature.

Only the enlightened child of God can begin rightly to apprize the true character of sin, because he alone has the spiritual faculty which enables him to see the contrast between sin and righteousness. A man immured for years in a dungeon would be blinded on being brought suddenly into the brightness of the noon-day sun. In this condition he would not be a good judge of the relation, or appearance, of things. Sin has blinded man to the glory of God and the beauty of holiness, hence the sinner can have no true standard of valuation in the sphere of spiritual and holy things.

God Threatens to Punish Sin

The one thing which God, in the first part of the Conclusion, aims to set forth and emphasize is the fact that He punishes sin. And this is a truth of which this generation needs especially to be reminded. A false optimistic hope has blinded many eyes to this truth of God. If men did but open their eyes, they could not help seeing that all history, secular as well as sacred, teaches that sin is punished. It is a universal law that no man can escape. When a man sins, he is entering into a conflict with Almighty God, whom no man can fight and expect to win.

We meet people occasionally who affect to think that it does not become a being such as God is to punish sin. Much more does it appear that God could not be a perfect being if He did not punish secession and rebellion against Him and His perfect government. With all our imperfections, our fractional vision of things, does not the best that is in us feel outraged when truth is perverted, justice trampled under foot, innocence outraged, purity defiled, and all principles of honor violated? Would it not indicate a lower, a more calloused, rather than a higher standard of moral perfection not to feel thus? We can rest assured that God feels these things a thousandfold more than we do; and that, having the right and the power, He is going to punish them. "I the Lord thy God am a jealous God, visiting the iniquity of the fathers upon the children unto the third and fourth generation of them that hate me."

The punishment of sin takes many forms. There are present punishments. There is a punishment known to none but the offender. It comes through the conscience. Many a person moves among friends and appears joyous when, in reality, the heart is full of pain within. In the still watches of the night the haunting spectres of ill deeds torment. At the feast, where joyousness reigns, in the very hour of some signal triumph, there is a tugging at the heart and a paling of the cheek; from out the abyss of years long past capricious memory has brought, like a half-forgotten dream, the recollection of some deed which put a stain on the soul, and, mayhap, wronged, or put fetters on, another soul.

Many sins are punished in the bodies of the transgressors. Every sin, whatever its nature, injures the sinner. "He that sinneth against me wrongeth himself" (Prov. 8, 36). There are many sins which are in a special way sins against the body. These sins have a tendency to bestialize the very features of the sinner, and they sow in the body the seeds of early decay and dissolution. I know a Lutheran minister who said that one of the most solemn and effectual lessons he ever heard on the operation of God's laws was from the lips of a hospital physician whom he was permitted to accompany on one of his rounds. When the doctor came to treat a young man, whose dying body was full of pollution and chancred sores, he repeated these words: "Whatsoever a man soweth, that shall he also reap." The young man had been determined to have his fling, to sow his wild oats, and now he was reaping—reaping the whirlwind.

"Thou makest me to possess the iniquities of my youth" (Job 13, 26). Sin does not always bring men to such a pass as this, but the penalty always comes. No power can stay it. "Be sure your sin will find you out" (Num. 32, 23). The gluttonous man, the drunkard, the licentious person may not have to pay at once; but the bond comes due, and payment has to be made. "'My Lord Cardinal," said the unhappy Queen of France to Richelieu, "God does not pay at the end of every week, but at the last He pays." Truer words were never spoken.

The ancients said that Nemesis, the goddess of vengeance, was slow of movement, being lame of her feet; but that she never failed to catch her victim, for, while the victim slept, she was still relentlessly pursuing. The sinner may congratulate himself that he is succeeding in his career of evil doing; but, with movement surer and swifter than that of the stars in their courses, the day of reckoning comes. Pull and graft do a great deal in this world; but all the power that hell can muster cannot shield one sinner any more than, in the eyes of God, it can blacken one saint. "Though hand join in hand, the wicked shall not be unpunished" (Prov. 11, 21).

In communal, in national, as well as in individual life, sins are punished. That sin is punished by sin is the constant record of history. When men cultivate the spirit of lovelessness and selfishness, when they practice fraud and oppression, they often reap rebellion and bloodshed. When men generally shut their eyes to any of God's laws it leads to blindness in other directions, and this is often followed by widespread suffering. The mind of man is incapable of following all the intricate workings of God's sovereign providence, on account of which we should be very careful in our judgment; but the Word of God tells us that the whole creation feels the curse of sin and that the calamities brought by the forces of nature are judgments setting forth the nature and consequences of sin. The same is true of all the evils which affect human life. What is the meaning of our physical ills, what gives us the explanation of the graves over which love weeps, what the interpretation of all our losses? It is sin. They are the results of sin, the penalties of sin.

Perhaps the most perplexing phase of the great

problem of sin and punishment is that presented by by our text in the words, "Visiting the iniquity of the fathers upon the children unto the third and fourth generation of them that hate me."

One thing is very clear: no one ever has to bear the moral consequences of another's sin. God never punishes one person for the sins of another. "The soul that sinneth, it shall die. The son shall not bear the iniquity of the father, neither shall the father bear the iniquity of the son; the righteousness of the righteous shall be upon him and the wickedness of the wicked shall be upon him" (Ezek. 18, 20). However, the present physical consequences of sin very frequently are transmitted. No human life exists in isolation. All our interests are intertwined. There is a solidarity of the human family. We are not only individuals. There is a humanity, a something which pervades and unites us all, so that if one member suffer, all the members suffer with it.

Some of the most terrible afflictions come to innocent offspring as a heritage of parental sins. Physicians learn more of this than anyone else, and the things revealed to them are often of a nature to incline one's blood to boil. And if those guilty of saddling a lifelong legacy of suffering, of mind and body, on their own flesh and blood, do not themselves suffer a hundredfold more than their innocent offspring, then their hearts have ceased to be hearts of flesh and have become hearts of stone. I know of nothing better calculated to lead such a guilty person to join in the cry, "Whichever way I turn is hell; I am hell itself."

To a certain stage in life, the sufferings which come from sin, are chastisements meant to remind men of the presence and operation of sin, to the end that they may serve as calls to repentance. "Blessed is the man whom Thou chasteneth, O Lord, and teachest him out of Thy law, that Thou mayest give him rest from the days of adversity" (Ps. 94, 12, 13). They help to keep us mindful of our tendency to evil, and its final consequences, and thus keep us close to the Lord's side. There is a stage, however, beyond which punishment comes as an evidence of God's wrath, as was the case with Jerusalem, and doubtless with many visitations since then. But whatever the nature or extent of the punishment for sin, truth would compel every one to say: "God has punished us less than our iniquities deserve" (Ezra 9, 13).

Terrible are the consequences of sin as we experience them here and now, in our own lives, and in the lives of all those around us. But it does not by any means end the dark chapter. The Son of God, our gentle brother, pictures the last earthly scene which has to do with sin. It is the last day of earthly human history. The countless multitudes are assembled before Him to hear pronouncement of sentence on their lives. After the children of the Kingdom have heard the sentence which shall confirm them in their goodness, the eternal Judge shall say to the godless: "Depart from me, ye cursed, into everlasting fire, prepared for the devil and his angels" (Matt. 25, 41). In another place the same great Teacher lifts the veil, gives us a glimpse into that unexplored region where none of us hope to come, and shows us, whether in parable or history makes no difference as to the teaching, a condition of life separated by an impassable barrier from the realm of real life, and light, and blessedness. I refer to the rich man and poor Lazarus, and the heaven and hell that holds them—a prophecy of humanity's eternal night or eternal glory.

When we come to realize our condition and the limitations imposed because we are carnal, sold under sin; having some vision of better things, indeed, but lacking the power to stimulate our laggard faculties to realize the better things for which we yearn; having a certain hatred of evil—resolving and reresolving to overcome it and to keep it in subjection, but failing again and again; and, added to all this, the consciousness that we have deserved God's displeasure and His sentence of eternal banishment, we feel as did St. Paul, himself a faithful child of God and a veteran in His service: "O wretched man that I am! who shall deliver me from the body of this death?" (Rom. 7, 24).

There is only one hope of deliverance. It is through Christ Jesus; "there is therefore now no condemnation to them which are in Christ Jesus" (Rom. 8, 1).

GOD'S PROMISE FROM SINAI

"I the Lord thy God am a jealous God, * * * showing mercy unto thousands of them that love me, and keep my commandments." — EXODUS 20, 5, 6.

SO terrible were the manifestations of God's power at the time the Law was given that Moses, when he beheld them, did exceedingly fear and quake (Hebrews 12, 21). Those circumstances, so awe-inspiring, were unquestionably designed by God Himself to give expression to the character of the covenant He was establishing. In the covenant of the Law God stands before mankind in the majesty of His holiness and justice, and says, as it were: Here are my decrees; such are the rewards of obedience, and such the penalties of disobedience. This do, and thou shalt live; failure means death.

One does not need to stand before a literal Sinai, with its thunderings and lightnings and earthquake, to share to a considerable degree the feelings of Moses. Any person with a fair consciousness of the demands God's inexorable Law makes on human life, of the degree of human failure to meet them, and of the nature of this transgression, will be torn with fear. But the second part of the Conclusion introduces an entirely new element into the consideration of God's Law. This is contained in the word—mercy. "I the Lord thy God am a jealous God, * * * showing mercy unto thousands of them that love me, and keep my commandments." In keeping with the line of thought pursued in considering the first part of the Conclusion, I shall today take as my subject —

God's Promise From Sinai

It is God's promise; it is a promise of mercy; it is a promise made to those who love and serve.

I. It is just as essential to remember that it is God who makes this promise of mercy as that it is God who threatens to visit penalties upon the head of the transgressor. The latter is frequently overlooked. Men judge God too much by the standard of human frailty, and conclude that He says a great deal which He does not mean seriously or forgets. But let us not forget that He says: "I am God, and there is none else; I am God, and there is none like me; * * * my counsel shall stand, and I will do all my pleasure; * * * I have spoken it, I will also bring it to pass; I have purposed it, I will also do it" (Isa. 46, 9-11). For our peace and comfort it it just as necessary for us to remember that this truth applies as truly to God's promises of mercy as it does to His threat of punishment.

God is a God of truth. He keeps His Word. Heaven and earth shall pass away, but not so much as the dot of an *i* or the cross of a *t* of God's Word, shall fail of fulfillment. This applies with just as much force to His words of love, of mercy, of forgiveness, of fatherly kindness, as to His legal enactments.

Let us likewise remember that God's words

about being a jealous God apply as well to His promise as to His threat. To be a jealous God, so far as those are concerned who neither fear nor love and serve Him, means that He has a character to maintain, rights which inherently belong to Him, and that He must insistently demand that His rights be recognized, that the obligations due Him be discharged, and all failures be punished. Now this same energy expends itself where the obligations imposed are met. It is expended in shielding the loved one against all hurtful influences, and in bestowing on him all possible benefits. Jealousy does not exist with respect to persons or things concerning which people are indifferent. God would not be jealous of us human beings if He was not concerned about us, if He did not love us. If we have begun to meet God's requirements, if we have begun to reciprocate His love, then all the wealth of His wisdom and power are taken up into the service of His love, and put to working for our good. Let us not be afraid of the words, "a jealous God," if we are His children; for every time we hear the sentence we should feel the Father's strong, protecting arm tightening around us in love.

II. The promise which the eternal truth-speaking God holds out, even from the fire-flaming mount, is one of mercy.

The words, "Thou shalt" and "Thou shalt not," spoken by holy God, together with His threats against all violations, are anything but reassuring to man. The inexorableness of God's Law has brought the proudest of men into the dust; it has reduced mighty empires to ash-heaps. The Law binds men with iron fetters. Instead of setting man free, it shows him justice—like a Juggernaut, crushing all that comes in its way. Law, or justice, is represented by the goddess with blindfolded eyes. She does not take into consideration beauty nor relationships nor anything of the kind. She is absolutely impartial. She knows no passion. She cannot be bribed. She is cold, passionless; but, oh, how resolute! how relentless! But what Law could not do, mercy found a way to do.

How like balm upon wounds which bleed and ache, must have fallen this one note of mercy upon the ears of those who witnessed the scenes and heard the words of Sinai. Since that far-off day in Eden the only religion which can help, which can be true, must have Gospel in it—a note of music, a heart-balm. The Gospel note was sounded already in Eden. It is contained in the promise that the seed of the woman should bruise the serpent's head and cure its deadly bite. And here we find it as the counterbalance to the terrors of Sinai.

Mercy, fairest of God's attributes, fair as the sunlight! Mercy is kindness exercised toward the undeserving, those who, because of their lack of desert, are miserable. Mercy includes pity, compassion, forbearance, gentleness, and helpfulness. In men we sometimes associate mercy with weakness of disposition. In the case of true mercy it is not so with men, least of all is it so with God. It was when He stood before Israel in the awe-inspiring sights and sounds of Sinai, saying: I am thy God; here are the requirements I make, and have the right to enforce, and, in the case of failure, here are the penalties my justice demands, and which I have the power to exact. In the hour of this most signal exhibition of power on God's part, and of fear and submissiveness on man's part, He breathes His plans of mercy. And this love of a holy God, showing itself in mercy to men deserving only of death, temporal and eternal, is one of the most mysterious attributes of the Divine nature.

What would have become of the world if God had not been merciful? Not a soul would have been saved. There is not a door of refuge open for the sorely afflicted children of men, save the door of mercy. Thank God! the door of mercy stands open. Our refuge is the very heart of God. And no mother's breast was ever so secure, so peaceful, a refuge as is the Divine mercy for those who seek safety there.

Consider what wealth of meaning is added to God's assurance of mercy by contrasting it with His threat. His threat was to visit the iniquity of the fathers upon the children, who followed in the wicked ways of their fathers hating God, and doing despite to his laws, unto the third and fourth generation; but His promise of mercy is unto the thousandth generation of those that love Him, and keep His commandments.

We see, then, that Sinai itself is linked with Calvary;—it prepares the way for it. Indeed, from the very beginning, love necessitated the cross. There could be no stopping place in the logic of mercy, when we remember that it is full sister to justice, till it consummated itself in the cross of

Jesus Christ. Only thus could forgiveness be provided for the sins of which the Law finds all men guilty.

This little phrase, "shewing mercy," would seem to an unenlightened reader, commonplace and inconsequential. But the whole plan of salvation is embraced in it. God was here looking forward to Bethlehem and Calvary. It was only thus that it could be said, "Mercy and truth are met together; righteousness and peace have kissed each other" (Ps. 85, 10).

Let us thank God that it is written, even in the very heart of the Law, that He is a God of mercy; the crown of all His other works is His work of mercy. Mercy encircles the very throne of Heaven, it spans the earth like a rainbow. Inclined to flee from the awe-inspiring attributes of Divine sovereignty and impartial justice, we flee to the outstretched arms of a loving Father, who speaks of mercy, and has shown what it means, in its height and depth, as it was wrought out by Jesus our Savior in the manger and upon the cross. But only those are really capable of appreciating this mercy who have truly learned the lesson which it is the great mission of the Law to teach; namely, the exceeding sinfulness of sin, and the justice of the sentence of condemnation which the Law pronounces on all men, because all have sinned.

III. God's offer of mercy is as broad as human need, but its application is conditioned—not by God's inability, but man's willingness. "I * * * am a jealous God, shewing mercy;" that is, making mercy effective in the lives of "thousands of them that love Me."

God is mercifully inclined toward all men. Not to believe this, is to give the lie to all of God's plainest statements. He would like to make all men the recipients of the whole scope of the blessings His thoughts of love have devised for them and His labor of love provided. To forgetful Israel He said: "As I live, saith the Lord God, I have no pleasure in the death of the wicked; but that the wicked turn from his way and live: turn ye, turn ye from your evil ways; for why will ye die, O house of Israel" (Ezek. 33, 11). And Jesus, who gave the clearest revelation of the Father's heart, wept over the Jerusalem, which was persecuting Him unto death, and said: "O Jerusalem, Jerusalem, thou that killest the prophets, and stonest them which are sent unto thee, how often would I have gathered thy children together, even as a hen gathereth her chickens under her wings, and ye would not" (St. Matt. 23, 37). And St. Paul tells us that "God commendeth His love toward us, in that, while we were yet sinners, Christ died for us" (Rom. 5, 8). This is God's side of the matter; there is another which man represents. And as long as men are loveless, with hearts full of enmity toward God, and breathe the spirit of rebellion; refusing to acknowledge God's love, and rejecting His offers of mercy—so long even God Himself cannot make His mercy effective in human lives. Such people have closed every avenue through which God can bestow His gifts.

In view of the fact that God deals with men as rational, responsible creatures, whom He is anxious to bless but will not force to accept His blessings, this dealing has always had as a primary object to prove to man that God is a loving God, seeking his good, willing to pardon his faults if he would let Him do so. Throughout the whole history of God's dealings with man He has been seeking to convince him of His true fatherhood, His willingness to enfold him in His arms of love, to guide him and provide for him as only infinite wisdom, power and love is capable of doing. This is shown in the covenants He made with Israel, the guidance and defense He vouchsafed them, the services He instituted for their observance, the sacrifices He required at their hands. They were reminded of this by the offer of mercy in the body of the Law, which, as a whole, presents the sterner aspect of God's nature. The cumulative evidence of God's love has increased a thousandfold, reaching its climax in the New Testament, with its Gospel of Jesus Christ.

When the bright rays of God's love begin to break down the icy barrier of man's lovelessness and hate; when man begins, somewhat reluctantly at first, to accept God's statement concerning Himself that He is good, that He wants to bring only good to man, that He has provided means whereby he may be relieved of his difficulties and ample supply made for all his necessities, faith comes to birth in the human heart. This is the coming back of the prodigal, not only with the confession: Father, I have sinned against thee, but with the further confession: Father, I have learned that there is no place like home, no place like my heavenly Father's house; because no one in all the world loves me as

Thou dost; no one is so capable and willing to heal my wounds and supply my needs. And the birth of faith, the establishment of confidence in God, all of which rests on the assurance of His goodness, means the begetting of love for Him also. From this point on, under favorable conditions, love grows apace. Love begets love. God's undying love begets this love in man. And the constant, and ever increasing, experience of God's love nurtures the flame of love in our hearts. Here is fatherhood and childhood: God is the Father, man the child. Here we have the conditions where mercy and forgiveness are shown and accepted.

This part of the Conclusion, requiring love on man's part as the condition of receiving mercy, contains the germ of Christ's summary of the whole First Table of the Law; "Thou shalt love the Lord thy God with all thy heart, and with all thy soul, and with all thy mind, and with all thy strength" (St. Mark 12, 30). And it helps to emphasize anew that religion is not merely a matter of formal relationship, much less of deeds performed under stress of fear; it is a matter of heart, of life, of right relationship.

If there were abundant reason why the people of Israel at Sinai, fresh from centuries of bondage, just starting on the way to the land of promise, should recognize so much that was worthy in God's person and so much good in His dealings with men as to recommend Him to their love and lead them to surrender their lives to Him, something increasingly true of each succeeding generation—how much greater are our obligations to love Him! We know not a promised Redeemer, but a Savior given. We know a real Deliverer from sin, not merely prefigured in the bood of sacrificial beasts. Oh, let us contemplate more frequently, more reverently, with more consciousness of our own unworthiness, God's great love, that our love for Him may grow stronger! We should love Him in the highest degree. He is worthy of it. And it would have its reflex action on us. Love is a force that unites and transfroms. If we truly love God and Divine things, we shall become more and more divine. The love of God is the delight of serious minds. It furnishes a paradise for devout souls. And where love for God dwells in human hearts, there can be no question that His mercy has been received.

"When thy heart, love-filled, grows graver,
And eternal bliss looks nearer,
Ask thy heart, nor show it favor,
Is the gift or giver dearer?

Love, love on; love higher, deeper;
Let love's ocean close above her;
Only, love thou more love's keeper,
More the love-creating lover."

IV. The proof of love is service, which is love in action. It is the proof of God's love for man. It is also the proof of man's love for man as well as of man's love of God. Therefore we find the bestowal of Divine mercy further conditioned by the possession on man's part of a right relationship. God says He will show mercy to those who love Him—"and keep my commandments."

This brings us to the consideration of the question of good works, their place in the Christian life, their relation to our salvation. From the outset it must be understood that we attribute no merit, no saving efficacy, to any work of ours, however extensive in quantity or excellent in quality we may think it to be. We owe our salvation wholly to God's mercy which provided for us Christ's atoning sacrifice, appropriated by faith. "By grace are ye saved, through faith; and that not of yourselves, it is the gift of God; not of works lest any man should boast" (Eph. 2, 8). Not only is salvation God's free gift, but the faith by which it is received is Divinely wrought. "No man can say [believingly, effectively], "that Jesus is the Lord, but by the Holy Ghost" (1 Cor. 12, 3). But the moment faith is begotten in us, though it be like a grain of mustard seed, God accepts us as his dear children, and applies to us all the merit of Christ. This act of acceptance we call, in the language of Scripture, justification. It is wholly God's work, a work performed without any merit or worthiness on our part. "After that the kindness and love of God our Saviour toward man appeared, not by works of righteousness which we have done, but according to His mercy He saved us, by the washing of regeneration and renewing of the Holy Ghost; which He shed on us abundantly through Jesus Christ our Saviour, that being justified by His grace, we should be made heirs according to the hope of eternal life" (Tit. 3, 4-7).

Even after we have become God's children, being richly provided with all good spiritual blessings, our good works are, in reality, the result of the Divine indwelling. The great St. Paul, speaking of his spiritual life, says, "I live, yet not I, but Christ liveth in me; and the life which I now live in the flesh I live by the faith of the Son of God, who loved me, and gave Himself for me" (Gal. 2, 20). And what St. Paul says of himself, Jesus lays down as a principle applicable to all—"I am the vine and ye are the branches. He that abideth in me, and I in him, the same bringeth forth much fruit, for without me ye can do nothing" (St. John 15, 5). The true child of God gives Him the full credit for every good work he is enabled to do.

Discarding, then, wholly the idea of making payment to God for anything we have received from Him and, just as completely, putting aside all thought of ever being able by anything we can do to earn His favour in the future; discarding forever all this, it would be difficult to over-emphasize the importance of a life of loving service. If we are the children of God it is because He has made us so, because His Spirit recreated us, because His Son is the animating spirit of our new life. If this is true, it will, it must, show itself in our lives. Some of us have been a little too much afraid of that passage in St. James which says: "Faith, if it hath not works, is dead, being alone" (2 17). We do not need to surrender one iota of the comforting doctrine of justification by faith to give this passage its proper emphasis. It is simply this way: If we have real faith it has made new creatures of us, for it has brought us into living fellowship with Christ. And if we are living in Christ, and Christ is living in us, we will hate the things He hates and love and seek the things He loves. It cannot be otherwise. A living man must breathe. If he has never developed his lung capacity or if his lungs have been injured by disease, he may find no special delight in breathing or he may even breathe with difficulty and pain,—but as long as he lives he breathes. So it is with the child of God. He is not a child of God by virtue of the recital of creeds or having his name on a church record. A man is a Christian by virtue of a living relationship to God in and through Christ Jesus. And just as surely as that relationship exists there will be some evidence of it in life.

We just used the passage in which Jesus illustrates the relationship between Himself and his disciples by the vine and the branches. Now if a branch of a vine or tree has been twisted, or partly broken, the leaves will be somewhat yellow, and the fruit scarce and knotty. But as long as the point of contact between the parent stem and the branch is of a nature that the latter appropriates the life of the former, the branch continues to perform, in some measure, its accustomed functions. And as long as the branch is in full connection with the parent stem it partakes of its full nature and does its work. Are we really branches of the vine which is Christ? Then He says, we must bear good fruit —loving, upright service prompted by a holy, loving heart. It is our new nature to do so. It would be denying, going contrary to, our new nature not to do so.

God has a right to expect, and does expect, this

kind of service. To this end we were created and recreated. "We are His workmanship, created in Christ Jesus unto good works, which God hath before ordained that we should walk in them" (Eph. 2, 10). It is idle to talk of loving God if we do not try to do His will. "This is love, that we walk after His commandments" (II John 6).

God wants us to exercise ourselves unto the godliness which exhibits itself in righteousness for our own sakes. As in all other spheres, so here also, we profit by practice. The athlete, if he ceases to practice, will soon lose his power. With the fullest, richest measure of God's gracious power at our disposal, if we do not use it, we shall soon cease to possess it and have increasing difficulty in obtaining it. It is impossible to keep a correct theory of Divine things if we do not apply the knowledge we have, and the power it brings, to the betterment of our practical lives, and the upbuilding of the Kingdom of God about us. Because of this we have such exhortations as the following: "Giving all diligence, add to your faith virtue, and to virtue knowledge, and to knowledge temperance, and to temperance patience, and to patience godliness, and to godliness brotherly kindness, and to brotherly kindness charity. For if these things be in you, and abound, they make you that ye shall neither be barren nor unfruitful in the knowledge of our Lord Jesus Christ. But he that lacketh these things is blind, and cannot see afar off, and hath forgotten that he was purged of his old sins. Wherefore the rather, brethren, give diligence to make your calling and election sure; for if ye do these things ye shall never fail; for so an entrance shall be ministered unto you abundantly into the everlasting kingdom of our Lord Jesus Christ" (2 Peter 1, 5-11).

Showing our love to God in the keeping of His commandments, even under the most adverse circumstances, should be the earnest aim of every child of God, also out of consideration for his fellowmen. Everywhere there are plenty of people ready to point the finger of scorn at the professing children of God, and to say: See, Christianity does not mean anything; Christians are just as weak, just as selfish, as we are. For this reason it is incumbent on us to walk "Blameless and harmless, the sons of God, without rebuke, in the midst of a crooked and perverse nation, among whom ye shine as lights in the world" (Phil. 2, 15). And we should live in the same way for the sake of the weak brother.

Especially ought we to be lovingly in earnest in keeping God's commandments that thereby His holy name may be glorified. The chief end of man is to glorify God and to enjoy Him forever. In all things, the small as well as the great, there should be present, if not in the conscious form of active thought, still as the deep, settled purpose of life, the glorification of God. And, thank God, this may be done in the very common things of life, the eating and drinking, the resting and sleeping, and the daily toil, as well as in the greater things such as church-going, Bible-reading, and the giving of alms. "Ye are the light of the world. A city that is set on a hill cannot be hid. Neither do men light a candle, and put it under a bushel, but on a candlestick; and it giveth light unto all that are in the house. Let your light so shine before men, that they may see your good works, and glorify your Father which is in heaven" (St. Matt. 5, 14-16). If we so live we shall have the assurance not only of God's promise of mercy, but of its possession, with the joy and peace it brings.

SOME MINOR QUESTIONS OF THE LAW

"My son, forget not my Law; but let thine heart keep my commandments; for length of days, and long life, and peace, shall they add to thee. Let not mercy and truth forsake thee; bind them about thy neck, write them upon the tablet of thine heart; so shalt thou find favour and good understanding in the sight of God and man." — PROV. 3, 1-4.

"The Lord said unto Moses, write thou these words; * * * for after the tenor of these words I have made a covenant with thee and with Israel. And he wrote upon the tables the words of the covenant, the ten commandments." — EXODUS 34, 27, 28.

WE have given the commandments a rather extended treatment, not exhaustive by any means; for, as some one has well said, the whole Bible is, in a sense, but an elaboration of the First Commandment. But we have covered fairly well the points of the Law which are applicable to the every-day problems of life. There are, however, a few questions which, while they have little to do with either the interpretation or the application of the commandments proper, often trouble our people. One is the question which has to do with the number and proper order of the commandments. Our people often, in reading, or discussing the commandments, meet with these difficulties. They find that the order we follow differs from that followed by others. If they read or hear some one speak of the Fifth Commandment, for instance, they find that an entirely different subject is presented from that of which we think when the Fifth Commandment is mentioned. And the same difficulty arises if others hear us or read after us. When we come to understand the facts in the case we find that it is not such a serious matter, but until that time the trouble exists.

Let me explain at once that the difference is not to any great extent the result of a difference in interpretation. It has arisen from the fact that God's Word has not settled the question of the number and order of the commandments. It does not say, This is the second, the fifth, the eighth, or the tenth commandment. It tells us explicitly that there are ten words, or precepts, in the Law of God; but that is as far as the Word of God goes with respect to the question of order or number.

Another somewhat analagous question does not give the same amount of perplexity, owing to the smaller number occupying themselves with the question. It is that which has to do with the division of the Law into tables. The Bible tells us there are two tables, but it does not tell us how they were originally divided or how they are now to be divided.

As with most of the questions that men have to settle for themselves, so, with respect to both the foregoing questions, we find a difference of opinion. As in a good many other things, men probably began to look for grounds of difference because they did not want to agree. And now, finding themselves differing, men are eager to justify their points of difference. I shall attempt to give especially the history of the origin of the different systems of dividing and enumerating the commandments, with the reasons for so doing. But first of all a word with respect to —

The Two Tables of the Law

In Exodus thirty-two and Deuteronomy ten, it is expressly mentioned that there were two tables of stone on which the commandments were originally written. The writer of the Epistle to the Hebrews corroborates the statement. In Exodus thirty-two, we are told that the tables of stone were written on both sides. But in no place in the Scriptures are we told how many commandments were on either table. From the days of Philo or, probably, before, a good deal of arguing has been done on this subject; all of which is practically useless. It is all mere speculation, which, however ingenuous or probable, can never lead to any positive conclusion. As for the question itself, that affects no vital issue. There are too many people who get lost in the pursuit of these minor problems and eventually lose sight of the main subject. It is well enough for us to have our preferences in these matters, and now, that the difference exists, it is necessary to our peace of mind to know the grounds on which they rest; but it is much more important that we know the Ten Commandments and earnestly seek to heed them than it is to know and be able to quote all the arguments for maintaining that there were three or four or five commandments on the one table and seven or six or five on the other. Whatever we may believe about this subject, let us be sure that all the commandments are written on the one table of our hearts.

When we speak of the Two Tables of the Law we are not thinking of the original tables of stone; but of the content, the subject matter, of the commandments. And if it could be shown that there were, for instance, five on the one table and five on the other, it would not seriously affect our view, which is decided by the nature of the commandments themselves. Of course, a Lutheran artist, in making a pictorial representation of the commandments, would reproduce our view: he would have three on the one table and seven on the other.

That the commandments fall into two groups, Jesus Himself shows in His discussion of the nature of the Law, as recorded in St. Matthew twenty-two. These groups are determined by the character of the commandments forming them: the first group setting forth our relationship to God and the duties involved therein, and the second group setting forth our relation to man and the duties it involves.

This twofold grouping is universally recognized, but there is no general agreement as to just where the line between the two groups is to be drawn. The usual view of our Church is that to the First Table belong only the first three commandments, because these alone treat of our direct duties toward God. A good many theologians, however, and among them some Lutherans, include in this table the commandment which treats of the duties of children to parents. The ground for this division is that parents, in a very special sense, are God's representatives on earth, and because this, our Fourth Commandment, sets forth, as do the first three, a filial relationship and filial duties. Personally I am of the opinion that the ground for including the Fourth Commandment in the First Table is not sufficiently strong. The object of the First Table is to teach us the importance of loving and serving God supremely. And Jesus Himself teaches us that it is possible so to love one's parents as to become idolaters and unfitted for the reception of God's love and grace. High and holy as is the Fourth Commandment, it yet stands so far removed from the First Table and is capable of such perversion that it seems clear to me that it ought not to be included in the First Table.

The Second Table sets forth our fraternal duties, the duties the children of men owe one to another. And, excepting the discussion concerning the proper place of the Fourth Commandment, there is with respect to it practical unanimity.

The division of the commandments as to tables stands then as follows: The older division, followed by our church, embraces only the first three commandments in the First Table, the other seven in the Second. We are guided in this division only by the content, or nature, of the commandments themselves; but the numbers of each, three and seven, are the two most sacred numbers of Scripture. Those who accept our method of dividing and numbering the commandments proper, but add the Fourth Commandment to the First Table, have four to their first and six to their second table. Those who follow the later method of dividing the commandments, that adopted by the Greek church, in which a separate commandment is made of the explanation concerning images, have two pentabs — two tables of five commandments each.

The Division and Number of the Commandments

The great practical difficulty of the people is not about the Two Tables but the division and number of the commandments themselves. The former is not a popular question. But the question as to why our church calls one commandment the second, while another denomination calls the same commandment the third, is always with us. Before proceeding, let us recall that this is not a question to be settled by Biblical statement, for there is nothing in the Bible by which it can be settled. It is a question of tradition, of church history, and of inferences from accepted theological principles.

There are three general methods of dividing and numbering the commandments, though there are, by actual count, fourteen different ways of arranging them. The commandments were first delivered to the Jews. And from earliest times this is the way they divided and numbered them: The words of Exodus 20, 2, "I am the Lord thy God, which brought thee out of the land of Egypt, out of the house of bondage," they considered the first commandment. That which the universal Christian Church considers to be the real substance of the first commandment, the words, "Thou shalt have no other gods before me," they counted as the second commandment. To this, their second commandment, they added the words prohibiting the making of graven images for purposes of worship. It may be well to note here that this, from earliest times, was the understanding of those to whom the commandments were given. They considered these words concerning images an explanation or amplification of the commandment prohibiting idolatry. Making the preface to the commandments a commandment itself, the Jews were compelled to combine the two statements concerning covetousness, in order not to exceed the number ten.

The Christian Church of the West at first followed the Jewish method of separating the commandments. But under the leadership of St. Augustine, the introductory words, "I am the Lord thy God," were no longer counted as a separate commandment, but regarded, as is now done by the whole Christian church, as a preface to all the commandments, though having special relationship, not only by position but also in thought, to the First. Augustine agreed with the Jewish method in not counting the words concerning graven images as a separate commandment, but as an explanation of that prohibiting idolatry. But, having omitted the Jewish first commandment, as a commandment, and agreeing with them in not counting the words concerning graven images as a separate commandment, Augustine was compelled to divide the two prohibitions against coveting. And he justified it on the ground of the difference between coveting merely material possessions and the coveting which is largely of the nature of concupiscence.

This view of the Western Church, which adopted that of the ancient Jewish Church, is fundamentally the one Luther accepted. He did not refuse to accept a position simply because those from whom he was compelled to differ on other points accepted it.

Early in the Christian era, under the leadership of Josephus, certain of the Jews departed from their older method of dividing and numbering the commandments. They ceased to regard the preface as a distinct command, but considered the explanation concerning images as such. Thus, to include all the commandments and not exceed the number ten, they likewise had to combine the two prohibitions of covetousness. This view, adopted and defended by Philo in his Explanation of the Commandments, was accepted by Origen, and became the system of the Eastern, or Greek Catholic Church. And when certain of the reformers could not agree with Luther on certain other points, though they were lineal descendents of the Western Church, they introduced the view of the Eastern church on this point.

It is to be admitted that the arguments used in favor of either division, possess elements both of strength and weakness. The chief argument on the side of those who make a separate commandment out of the words concerning images is that the First Commandment prohibits idolatry— the having of a false god or false gods; while the second, as they number them, prohibits the use of images, or representations, of God or Divine things in the worship of God. It must be granted that intellectually this distinction can be made. The question is whether people of very limited culture, as the Jewish people unquestionably were at the time of the giving of the Law, could make this distinction or appreciate it if made?

The chief ground urged by those who take our position is that the words about images are but an explanation. The First Commandment, in a few brief words, prohibits idolatry. The succeeding verses proceed from the general statement to the specification of instances of idolatry as often practiced then and now. In setting up these words as a distinct commandment, the adherents of this system violate one of the universally accepted principles of the interpretation of the Law. I will give it as it is given in the Westminster Larger Catechism, page 249: "Under one sin or duty, all of the same kind are forbidden or commanded; together with all the causes, means, occasions, and appearance thereof, and provocations thereunto." Now if that kind of idolatry which uses images as objects of worship is not of the same kind as any other idolatry, if it is not a means of expressing it, then we should like to find some one who will tell us what the relationship is between the two. And you will find that every theologian who adheres to this system of dividing the commandments, labours under this difficulty. It is extremely difficult to explain the First Commandment without introducing the thought of the representations of God set up for worship. And it is just as difficult to treat of the second commandment of the exponents in question at any length, unless one accepts the extreme position that it is wrong to use any kind of representation of heavenly beings or things in the worship of God. Some do this, but it is contrary to the Word of God. These words themselves expressly prohibit, not the making, but the worship, of these representations. "Thou shalt not bow down thyself to them, nor serve them." It was not very long after the giving of these words that God Himself directed these people to make certain images and representations for the adornment of the house of God and for use in His service.

It is urged that the introduction "Thou shalt not," or its equivalent, marks this prohibition of image worship as a separate commandment. But if this be true, we shall have to admit eleven commandments, for it is on all sides acknowledged that the two prohibitions, "Thou shalt not covet thy neighbor's house" and "Thou shalt not covet thy neighbor's wife," are so introduced.

The charge that Luther kept the old method of the Western Church because he was in love with their imagery and pictorial representation is as baseless as would be the charge that the other side opposed this system only because of their fanatical iconoclasm. No one was more unalterably opposed to anything which approached idolatry, in form as in essence, than Luther. No one more strongly insisted on a direct spiritual worship than he. The Lutheran Church is just as far removed as any church can be from any approach to the idolatrous use of images or pictures. But we do believe that there is a place for pictorial representation and the splendid service rendered by it.

On the other hand, I am willing to admit that we find difficulty in maintaining the division of our Ninth and Tenth Commandments. And almost every one of our men who has attempted an extended treatment of the commandments shows this difficulty, just as the other side does in dividing the First Commandment. We can make a distinction, but it is, in my humble judgment, a distinction without much of a difference.

Brethren, we need not perplex ourselves about this difference. It is well for us to know that our position is not a novel one, lacking the dignity of historic worth. We may be thankful to God that both sides have the same matter and recognize it as an authoritative Word of God. We do not deny or question a thing that is in their second commandment. And they have our Tenth, though they conjoin it to the Ninth. Therefore I do not see that there is much to fight about in either the one position or the other.

The Bible writers themselves help to emphasize the fact that order and number have very little to do with the subject matter of the commandments or the spirit in which they are to be kept. If you will turn to the two books of the Old Testament, where the commandments were originally recorded, you will find that the order followed in Exodus 20, is reversed in Deuteronomy 5, so far as the Ninth and Tenth Commandments are concerned. And Jesus Himself, when repeating a portion of the commandments, did not follow the original order (St. Matt. 19, 18ff.). The same is true of the greatest Biblical expounder of the Law, St. Paul (Rom. 13, 9)

Brethren, the first thing to remember is that there is a Law, that it is the Law of a holy God, that He has given it to us as the rule for our lives.

This Law is not merely to be committed to memory, but it is to be written on the tablet of the heart, as our text says. This means that it is to be a living principle of conduct, so that we, out of love to God, keep the commandments from the heart. Having served as a schoolmaster to lead us to Christ, where we have found forgiveness and new life, the commandments have now become to us the regulative principle of our new life, the rule according to which we seek to live. "My son, forget not My Law, but let thine heart keep my commandments; for length of days, and long life, and peace, shall they add to thee. * * * Bind them about thy neck, write them upon the tablet of thine heart, so shalt thou find favor and good understanding in the sight of God and man."